Prais

"A second story bookshop leads to a second chance at love in this tenderly told tale of old wounds, forgiveness, and redemption. Book lovers, book clubs, and anyone who's ever dreamed of owning a bookstore will adore this cleverly interwoven story in which the business of books steers the business of life toward a beautiful new beginning."

—LISA WINGATE, #1 *NEW YORK TIMES* BESTSELLING AUTHOR OF *SHELTERWOOD*, ON *THE SECOND STORY BOOKSHOP*

"Hunter's latest is a healing and empowering journey of love. Told in Hunter's classic style, *The Summer of You and Me* will stay with readers long after the end."

—RACHEL HAUCK, *NEW YORK TIMES* BESTSELLING AUTHOR

"Yummy romance with a dash of mystery, this friends-to-lovers novel, *The Summer of You and Me*, is wonderful! Hunter's deft hand mixes grief with new beginnings to make a delicious read!"

—COLLEEN COBLE, *USA TODAY* AND *PUBLISHERS WEEKLY* BESTSELLING AUTHOR

"Poignant and powerful, *The Summer of You and Me* is an exquisite 'out-of-the-box' romance that will rack your mind and ratchet your pulse! The amazing Denise Hunter has done it again with a truly riveting read that's short on sleep but long on hope."

—JULIE LESSMAN, AWARD-WINNING AUTHOR OF *THE DAUGHTERS OF BOSTON*, *WINDS OF CHANGE*, AND *THE ISLE OF HOPE* SERIES

"This story pulled at my heartstrings from the first chapter right through to the last. I longed for Maggie and Josh to find their happily-ever-after, despite the emotional roller coaster they were on. Denise Hunter has written a beautiful story filled with the complexities that come with loving others, especially members of our own families."

—ROBIN LEE HATCHER, CHRISTY AWARD–WINNING AUTHOR OF *WISHING FOR MISTLETOE* AND *TO CAPTURE A MOUNTAIN MAN*, FOR *THE SUMMER OF YOU AND ME*

"Denise Hunter made me cry again. Wow—what a breathtaking, heart-tugging story! *The Summer of You and Me* has so many great surprises, twists, and turns that my head is reeling, and I could not stop reading. You will not be sorry you read this book."

—HANNAH ALEXANDER, AUTHOR OF *A WOMAN WORTH KNOWING* AND *ONE STRONG MAN*

"*Love, Unscripted* has it all—the funniest meet-cute ever, unique characters, and a charming beach town setting. If you love sweet romance with a lot of heart, this one has 'Hallmark movie' written all over it. Highly recommended!"

—COLLEEN COBLE, *USA TODAY* AND *PUBLISHERS WEEKLY* BESTSELLING AUTHOR

"Hunter (*Bookshop by the Sea*) opens this heartwarming romance with Queens, N.Y., western writer Sadie Goodwin learning that her publisher wants her to switch genres to romance . . . Hunter's charismatic and complex characters effortlessly propel the story. Readers won't want to put this down."

—*PUBLISHERS WEEKLY* FOR *A NOVEL PROPOSAL*

"A heartwarming tale written by an undisputed queen of the genre, *A Novel Proposal* is a love letter to readers, to writers, and, above all, to romance. As Sadie and Sam were forced out of their comfort zones, I sank deeper and deeper into my reading happy place. This cozy, clever, captivating love story is the perfect beach read and an absolute must for fans of happily ever afters. Denise Hunter charmed my socks right off with this one!"

—BETHANY TURNER, AUTHOR OF *PLOT TWIST* AND *THE DO-OVER*

"A tragic accident gives a divorced couple a second chance at love in the warmhearted third installment of Hunter's Riverbend Romance series (after *Mulberry Hollow*) . . . Readers looking for an uplifting Christian romance will appreciate how Laurel and Gavin's faith helps dispel their deep-rooted fears so they can find a way to love again. Inspirational fans will find this hard to resist."

—*PUBLISHERS WEEKLY* FOR *HARVEST MOON*

"Denise Hunter has a way of bringing depth and an aching beauty into her stories, and *Harvest Moon* is no different. *Harvest Moon* is a beautiful tale of second chances, self-sacrifice, and renewed romance that addresses hard topics such as child death and dissolved marriages. In a beautiful turn of events, Hunter brings unexpected healing out of a devastating situation, subtly reminding the reader that God can create beauty out of the most painful of circumstances and love from the most broken stories."

—PEPPER BASHAM, AUTHOR OF *THE HEART OF THE MOUNTAINS* AND *AUTHENTICALLY, IZZY*

"A poignant romance that's perfect for fans of emotional love stories that capture your heart from the very first page. With her signature style, Denise Hunter whisks readers into a world where broken hearts are mended, lives are changed, and love really does conquer all!"

—COURTNEY WALSH, *NEW YORK TIMES* BESTSELLING AUTHOR, FOR *MULBERRY HOLLOW*

"Hunter delivers a touching story of how family dynamics and personal priorities shift when love takes precedence. Hunter's fans will love this."

—*PUBLISHERS WEEKLY* FOR *RIVERBEND GAP*

"Denise Hunter has never failed to pen a novel that whispers messages of hope and brings a smile to my face. *Bookshop by the Sea* is no different! With a warm-hearted community, a small beachside town, a second-chance romance worth rooting for, and cozy bookshop vibes, this is a story you'll want to snuggle into like a warm blanket."

—MELISSA FERGUSON, AUTHOR OF *MEET ME IN THE MARGINS*

"Sophie and Aiden had me hooked from page one, and I was holding my breath until the very end. Denise nails second-chance romance in *Bookshop by the Sea*. I adored this story! Five giant stars!"

—JENNY HALE, *USA TODAY* BESTSELLING AUTHOR

"*Autumn Skies* is the perfect roundup to the Bluebell Inn series. The tension and attraction between Grace and Wyatt is done so well, and the mystery kept me wondering what was going to happen next. Prepare to be swept away to the beautiful Blue Ridge Mountains in a flurry of turning pages."

—NANCY NAIGLE, *USA TODAY* BESTSELLING AUTHOR OF *CHRISTMAS ANGELS*

"*Carolina Breeze* is filled with surprises, enchantment, and a wonderful depth of romance. Denise Hunter gets better with every novel she writes, and that trend has hit a high point with this wonderful story."

—HANNAH ALEXANDER, AUTHOR OF *THE WEDDING KISS*

"*Summer by the Tides* is a perfect blend of romance and women's fiction."

—SHERRYL WOODS, #1 *NEW YORK TIMES* BESTSELLING AUTHOR

"Denise Hunter once again proves she's the queen of romantic drama. *Summer by the Tides* is both a perfect beach romance and a dramatic story of second chances. If you like Robyn Carr, you'll love Denise Hunter."

—COLLEEN COBLE, *PUBLISHERS WEEKLY* AND *USA TODAY* BESTSELLING AUTHOR

"I have never read a romance by Denise Hunter that didn't sweep me away into a happily ever after. Treat yourself!"

—ROBIN LEE HATCHER, BESTSELLING AUTHOR OF *CROSS MY HEART*, FOR *ON MAGNOLIA LANE*

"*Sweetbriar Cottage* is a story to fall in love with. True-to-life characters, high stakes, and powerful chemistry blend to tell an emotional story of reconciliation."

—BRENDA NOVAK, *NEW YORK TIMES* BESTSELLING AUTHOR

"*Sweetbriar Cottage* is a wonderful story, full of emotional tension and evocative prose. You'll feel involved in these characters' lives and carried along by their story as tension ratchets up to a climactic and satisfying conclusion. Terrific read. I thoroughly enjoyed it."

—FRANCINE RIVERS, *NEW YORK TIMES* BESTSELLING AUTHOR

"*Falling Like Snowflakes* is charming and fun with a twist of mystery and intrigue. A story that's sure to endure as a classic reader favorite."

—RACHEL HAUCK, *NEW YORK TIMES* BESTSELLING AUTHOR OF *THE FIFTH AVENUE STORY SOCIETY*

"*Barefoot Summer* is a satisfying tale of hope, healing, and a love that's meant to be."

—LISA WINGATE, NATIONAL BESTSELLING AUTHOR OF *BEFORE WE WERE YOURS*

the Second Story Bookshop

Also by Denise Hunter

RIVERBEND ROMANCES
Riverbend Gap
Mulberry Hollow
Harvest Moon
Wildflower Falls

BLUEBELL INN ROMANCES
Lake Season
Carolina Breeze
Autumn Skies

BLUE RIDGE ROMANCES
Blue Ridge Sunrise
Honeysuckle Dreams
On Magnolia Lane

SUMMER HARBOR NOVELS
Falling Like Snowflakes
The Goodbye Bride
Just a Kiss

CHAPEL SPRINGS ROMANCES
Barefoot Summer
A December Bride (novella)
Dancing with Fireflies
The Wishing Season
Married 'til Monday

BIG SKY ROMANCES
A Cowboy's Touch
The Accidental Bride
The Trouble with Cowboys

NANTUCKET LOVE STORIES
Surrender Bay
The Convenient Groom
Seaside Letters
Driftwood Lane

STAND-ALONE NOVELS
Sweetwater Gap
Sweetbriar Cottage
Summer by the Tides
Bookshop by the Sea
A Novel Proposal
Love, Unscripted
Before We Were Us
The Summer of You and Me

NOVELLAS INCLUDED IN
This Time Around, *Smitten*,
Secretly Smitten, and
Smitten Book Club

the Second Story Bookshop

DENISE HUNTER

Thomas Nelson
Since 1798

The Second Story Bookshop

Copyright © 2025 by Denise Hunter

All rights reserved. No portion of this book may be reproduced, stored in a retrieval system, or transmitted in any form or by any means—electronic, mechanical, photocopy, recording, scanning, or other—except for brief quotations in critical reviews or articles, without the prior written permission of the publisher.

Published in Nashville, Tennessee, by Thomas Nelson. Thomas Nelson is a registered trademark of HarperCollins Christian Publishing, Inc.

Thomas Nelson titles may be purchased in bulk for educational, business, fundraising, or sales promotional use. For information, please email SpecialMarkets@ThomasNelson.com.

Publisher's Note: This novel is a work of fiction. Names, characters, places, and incidents are either products of the author's imagination or used fictitiously. All characters are fictional, and any similarity to people living or dead is purely coincidental.

Any internet addresses (websites, blogs, etc.) in this book are offered as a resource. They are not intended in any way to be or imply an endorsement by Thomas Nelson, nor does Thomas Nelson vouch for the content of these sites for the life of this book.

Library of Congress Cataloging-in-Publication Data

Names: Hunter, Denise, 1968- author
Title: The second story bookshop / Denise Hunter.
Description: Nashville, Tennessee : Thomas Nelson, 2025. | Summary: "She inherits the bookshop of her dreams . . . But she has to run it with the ex she vowed never to speak with again"—Provided by publisher.
Identifiers: LCCN 2025013094 (print) | LCCN 2025013095 (ebook) | ISBN 9781400348701 hardcover | ISBN 9781400348695 paperback | ISBN 9781400348725 | ISBN 9781400348718 epub
Subjects: LCGFT: Fiction | Romance fiction | Christian fiction | Novels
Classification: LCC PS3608.U5925 S45 2025 (print) | LCC PS3608.U5925 (ebook) | DDC 813/.6—dc23/eng/20250528
LC record available at https://lccn.loc.gov/2025013094
LC ebook record available at https://lccn.loc.gov/2025013095

Printed in the United States of America

25 26 27 28 29 LBC 5 4 3 2 1

In memory of my agent and dear friend Karen Solem. She was a tremendous booklover and a tenacious advocate for her authors. Her legacy in publishing lives on in well-loved novels and in the grateful hearts of authors and readers worldwide.

Chapter 1

Nobody thought Viola Thatcher would ever expire, if for no other reason than sheer stubbornness. She'd made it to eighty-seven, after all, without a single daily medication or chronic health condition. She was as spry as her cat Chaucer, bustled around her beloved bookshop like a woman half her age, and was known to ascend shelf ladders when no one was around to stop her.

But alas, no one was immortal. Not even Gram.

Shelby Thatcher dabbed her eyes with a tissue that now bore the remnants of her foundation, eyeliner, and mascara—none of which had kept their waterproof promise. She tried to block the canned music flowing into the restroom of Fancy's Funeral Home and the cloying lavender scent emanating from a potpourri dish on the vanity.

She'd nearly made it through the two-hour visitation with her dignity intact. She'd smiled and nodded her way through platitudes and comforting hugs. She'd even held up through quiet exchanges with Dad, whose bloodshot eyes belied his unwavering assurances and stoic posture. But then Miss Dahlia struck the strident chords of "Amazing Grace" on the organ, and Gram's favorite song twisted a key, unlocking Shelby's pent-up grief.

That and the arrival of Grayson Briggs, who'd strutted through the door just in time for the service. It all went downhill from there.

Could there be a worse time or place to encounter one's long-lost love? The daunting emotions of loss and grief seemed to compound the bittersweet—heavy on bitter—memory of heartbreak.

She blew her pinkened nose, losing more foundation and the last of her ruby-red lipstick. Vanity was a cruel teacher.

She was supposed to be in a breezy sundress when he saw her again, wearing just-fine-without-you makeup, her salon-styled light brown hair bouncing around her shoulders in slow motion. Not wilting in a matronly black dress she'd borrowed from Liddy, her best friend and sister-in-law, because she didn't own anything as dark and gloomy as this wretched day deserved.

The hollow restroom door opened and Liddy entered, a wan smile warming her features. She'd pulled back her beautiful red hair in a loose updo, leaving a few tendrils to frame her peaches-and-cream face. Her blue eyes softened on Shelby. "How you holding up, honey?"

"About as well as my makeup, I'm afraid."

"You're beautiful without it. What I'd give for that olive complexion of yours."

"Your freckles are adorable. If my brother hasn't convinced you of that yet, he's not doing his job." Shelby tossed her tattered tissue, then eyed the door. "Is he still out there?" They both knew she wasn't referring to Caleb.

"He is. And can I just say, *holy cannoli*!"

"Stop it. You've seen pictures of him."

"From a decade ago. Don't get me wrong—he was hot back then, but he's since reached holy cannoli status."

"Don't let Caleb catch you saying that."

"He's been glowering at Gray since he walked in. I left the baby with Caleb—hopefully that'll keep him in line."

"What's he hanging around for anyway? There's no graveside service."

"Maybe he wants to catch up with folks?"

Shelby huffed. Gray's one and only fan had just passed. And since when had he wanted to stick around Grandville a moment longer than necessary? He'd shot off like a rocket two seconds after graduation. And four years ago when he'd returned to North Carolina for his own grandma's service, he was gone before the funeral lilies could bloom.

"Maybe he wants to talk to you."

"He skipped the receiving line. And last time he was in town he didn't so much as glance my way."

Liddy arched an auburn brow. "Maybe he finally realizes what a putz he was."

Shelby could always count on Liddy to come to her defense. "Doubtful. I should get back to Dad. Folks will be coming by the house soon." Plus Logan was probably wondering where she'd disappeared to. She tugged at the dress, which was shorter on her five-seven frame than on Liddy's five-three, and resisted the urge to check her reflection one last time.

Liddy held the door, then took Shelby's arm in solidarity as they walked down the hall and into the flower-perfumed funeral parlor. A quick visual sweep of the room revealed most of the lingering guests had departed—including the man she'd been avoiding for the past hour. It wasn't too hard to convince herself that the funny fluttering in her stomach was relief.

Cars lined the street of Shelby's childhood home, and friends and neighbors swarmed the ranch-style house. Sounds of chatter and laughter dominated the living spaces, and the aroma of Miss Martha's peach cobbler filled the air.

As Shelby milled about the room, snatches of conversation reached her.

"She was quite the looker in her day, you know. Paul wooed her for weeks before she'd even go out with him . . ."

"They only had the one son, though Viola always said she'd have at least half a dozen . . ."

"She sure would've loved this beautiful October day . . ."

"What'll happen to the bookshop? I do hope Shelby keeps it open. What would Grandville be without it?"

Shelby's eyes caught on Caleb near the entry and she made a beeline for him. Her big brother was handsome in a trendy navy suit. He wore his wavy dark blond hair longer these days, and paired with artsy glasses and a casual scarf, he looked every inch the creative.

Currently, though, he was doing daddy duty with his fussy infant. Oliver was the most beautiful two-month-old on the planet. He had fine dark hair, a button nose, and wide brown eyes just like Caleb's.

She reached for the baby. "Give me that precious thing."

"He's fighting his nap."

"Aunt Shelby will get him right to sleep." She snuggled the baby in her arms, bouncing him gently, savoring the sweetness of new life. Just what she needed right now. Plus, she sensed her brother was struggling.

A couple from church arrived, and Caleb and Shelby accepted their condolences before they moved toward the kitchen.

"Where's your wife?" Shelby asked her brother.

"In the kitchen with the food. Where's Logan?"

"Something came up at work." He'd wanted to stay but she encouraged him to go. She needed to support her family today and run interference between Caleb and Dad. Logan's good intentions sometimes rendered him clingy.

"Have you talked to Dad yet?" she asked.

"Of course."

Shelby gave him a pointed look. "I mean really talked."

"Real talks between the two of us don't go very well, as you might remember."

"He misses you."

"Yeah, I could tell by his warm greeting yesterday."

"Well, you haven't been home in almost a year, Caleb. And you're not exactly the best about staying in touch."

"I've been busy with my work." No more had the words left his mouth than sadness crept into his eyes. His Adam's apple dipped. He took a long drink from a water bottle, then his gaze locked on Shelby. "Gram wrote me last month. I never wrote back. I meant to—I just hadn't gotten around to it."

Shelby's heart softened at the rough texture of his voice. "Aw, Caleb. She knew you were busy. And she knew you loved her. She was so proud of all your success. She hung that painting you sent for her birthday in the bookshop. It's right behind the register where everyone can see it."

He blinked away tears. "I know she was proud of me. I just wish I'd appreciated her more when she was here. I'm a little envious of all the time you had with her."

Shelby was grateful for all that time with Gram, but it hadn't been without its frustrations. Her grandmother hadn't exactly been open to new ideas. She had her own way of doing things, and they didn't always jibe with Shelby's. But it was Gram's bookshop.

Had been.

The thought caught in her throat. "Dad's on the porch. You should go talk to him. He needs his family right now."

"I doubt that includes me."

Shelby rolled her eyes. "Of course it does."

"I never realized how much of a buffer Gram was for Dad and me. She had a way of bringing us together and keeping things calm. I sure do feel her absence."

Seven years ago Caleb had dropped out of college and run off to New York to become an artist. The news didn't sit well with Dad, who thought Caleb would be following in his footsteps into academia—Dad was an English professor at Grandville University. The sudden shift in plans had caught them all off guard. And the switch to the competitive world of art . . . ? Let's just say Shelby had her own doubts. Her brother was very talented, but how many artists actually managed to eke out a living with their paintings?

To his credit, Caleb managed to make something of himself. He wasn't selling million-dollar projects, but he was regularly featured in galleries and selling well enough to support himself and Liddy, who now stayed home with Oliver.

His success had done nothing to soften their dad's heart, however.

Shelby glanced down at Oliver, whose eyes had closed. His dark lashes feathered the tops of his petal-soft cheeks, curling ever so gently. Her heart rolled over. She hadn't seen him since she and Dad went to New York for his birth. He'd already grown so much. By the time she saw him again, he might well be crawling. "How long can you guys stay?"

"A week or so—if Dad and I don't kill each other first. My next showing isn't until December, but I have a lot of work to do before then."

"You don't mind if I just keep Oliver here with me for a few months, do you?"

"You might change your mind when you've gotten up with him twice a night for a week straight."

She gazed at the baby's precious face. "Oh, I don't know. I think I could forgo lots of sleep for some sweet cuddles with this little guy."

"I think you'll have your hands full enough with the bookshop."

Shelby's mood plummeted. Gram had made it clear over the years that Shelby would always have a place at the bookstore. But the thought of working there, much less running the place, without Gram opened a hollow spot inside. It would never be the same again. "You're right about that. There's a lot I don't know." Gram had done the accounting and handled the inventory. She was a whiz with the computer program. Shelby had been happy handling the customers and managing the other booksellers. "She never really got around to teaching me her end of things." Mainly because Shelby had put it off.

"You're smart. You'll figure it out."

Maybe so, but Shelby would probably just hire someone to fill her grandma's role. They'd need an extra person now anyway, and Shelby would rather work the floor than be stuck in the office all day.

She didn't want to fret about the store right now though. She gazed down at her sleeping nephew and could practically feel the oxytocin flooding her system.

"I saw Gray skulk into the visitation at the last minute." His lips twisted on the name.

The feel-good hormone dried up like steaming pavement after an August rain. "I saw him."

"Did he say anything to you?" His tone implied that he'd better not have.

"Nope."

"Good. He doesn't deserve your time or attention. You're better off without him."

"I'm sure he's already halfway back to Riverbend Gap by now." Because, yes, that was where he lived these days. Only three hours away. She knew this because Gram had kept in contact with him. As Gray's grandma's lifelong friend, Gram had felt she owed it to Dorothy to look out for him after Dorothy passed. Shelby could respect her grandmother's loyalty, though she had long ago asked Gram to keep news of him to herself. She'd mostly complied, though sometimes things "slipped out."

Caleb glanced through the window to the porch where their dad was saying good-bye to someone. "Guess I'll go talk to Dad. Want me to take Ollie?"

Shelby edged the baby away from him. "I'm not finished collecting cuddles."

He ran a hand though his hair, which fell artfully into place. "All right."

"Want me to go with you? Be your buffer?"

"I probably need to stop depending on other people to fill that gap."

"Just ask him how he's doing. If there's anything you can do."

"He'll say I could move back home where I belong, and then we'll be well on our way to World War III."

"Good point. Well, just go be with him. Talk about something benign—the great start to Duke's season." The football team was about the only thing they had in common these days.

"Good thought. Thanks." He headed toward the front door like a man headed toward death row.

And Shelby headed to her old room. She wanted just a few minutes to enjoy little Ollie before she had to resume her role as grieving granddaughter. Her feet felt heavy as she made her way down the hall. *Oh, Gram, you're supposed to be here. You weren't supposed to die. What will we all do without you?*

Chapter 2

A rush of cool air washed over Shelby as she entered the offices of Barclay and Greenwood set on the edge of town just past Dottie's Donuts (which she might or might not have visited on the way). She'd passed the office a million times but had never had reason to enter. The lobby smelled like lemon Pledge and fresh reams of paper.

From behind her desk Becky Field's brown eyes softened on Shelby, her laugh lines visible even though she wasn't smiling. She was at least sixty, but her hair had been a coiffed platinum blonde for as long as Shelby could remember. They attended the same church, but Becky wasn't a reader and only ever came into the bookstore to shoot the breeze.

"Hi, honey. How are you doing? It was such a lovely service yesterday. Your gram would've loved it."

"Thank you, Becky. It's been a rough week."

"Of course it has. If there's anything I can do, you just let me know."

"Thank you. We're just trying to take one day at a time." Everyone had been so helpful. Dad already had over a dozen meals tucked away in the freezer, and Shelby had at least that many. The whole town had shown up to honor Gram yesterday. Shelby stopped at the desk, hitching her purse on her shoulder.

"I understand completely. Listen, this is terrible timing, but a few of my friends from church are heading up a fundraiser for the humane society, and we're collecting donations from area stores to give away in a silent auction. I meant to ask weeks ago . . . Would the bookstore be able to donate a book or two for that?"

"We'd be glad to." Though there was really no more *we*. Shelby's heart squeezed tight but she smiled through the sensation. "When do you need the donation?"

"Would tomorrow be too soon? I can swing by and pick it up."

"Sounds good." Shelby glanced past the desk. "Is anyone else here yet?" She hadn't seen her dad's or brother's cars, but she'd parked on the street.

Becky glanced over her shoulder. Then she stood, leaned over the desk, and lowered her voice. "Listen, honey, I thought you might like to know—"

"Becky, can you bring back some coffee, please?" Javon Greenwood appeared in the doorway, tall and handsome in white shirtsleeves and khakis. "Oh, hi, Shelby. I didn't hear you come in. Come on back. We'll be in the second room on the left. Make yourself comfortable."

"Thank you, Mr. Greenwood." Javon (legal suspense and true crime) was a fiftysomething newcomer to Grandville, which only meant he hadn't been born here. In truth he'd been in town for at least ten years.

Shelby shot Becky a parting smile before heading down the short hallway. The reading of Gram's will was just one more thing they needed to get through. But after yesterday this should be a piece of cake. Shelby had, however, forgone makeup altogether today. If there was one thing she wasn't, it was a slow learner.

They'd been surprised by the invitation to Mr. Greenwood's office. But apparently Gram had appointed him as executor and given him explicit instructions about how she wanted everything to play out.

Shelby was happy to comply with Gram's wishes. She just wanted to get past this difficult week so she could get back to the bookstore, which she'd mostly left to the other booksellers this week. Janet and the others had been so good about stepping up to the plate.

Shelby arrived in the doorway and blinked at the dark-haired man sitting at the conference table.

Grayson Briggs.

Her feet slammed to a halt. She gaped at him. Snapped her lips shut.

Gray eased to his feet, gaze locked on her like a laser. He had the nerve to look well rested and handsome, even under the harsh fluorescent lights.

He was supposed to be gone by now, not hanging around Grandville making her nerves twitch. And certainly not here at what would be the reading of her grandmother's will. "What are you doing here?"

"Mr. Greenwood asked me to come," he said in that slow drawl she used to find utterly sexy.

"What for?"

He lifted his shoulders, drawing her attention to them. They were broader than they'd been back then. His whole build seemed . . . thicker. Sturdier. She hadn't seen him this close-up for years. Time and maturity had sculpted his face. The boy had become a man. And the man was far too appealing for his own good. She frowned at the thought.

A shuffling sounded down the hall. Caleb approached, seeming somber even as he offered a wan smile. He lugged the baby carrier, Liddy on his heels.

Thoughts still roiling, Shelby greeted them and stepped inside to make room for the couple.

Once through the doorway, Caleb stopped so suddenly Liddy nearly crashed into him. "What are *you* doing here?"

Gray's blue eyes toggled between Caleb and Shelby.

Caleb moved forward and set the carrier down. "You have no business being here."

"Mr. Greenwood invited him."

"Why would he do that?"

Shelby could practically see the wheels turning in her brother's head. "I don't know."

Caleb scowled at Gray. "Why would you need to be here? What have you done?"

Gray put his hands up, palms out. "I didn't do anything. I don't know why he invited me."

"Alrighty then!" Mr. Greenwood swept into the office, seemingly oblivious to the thick fog of tension. "Your dad's on his way in so we'll get on with the reading in just a moment. Have a seat. Make yourselves comfortable."

They all settled as Becky brought in coffee service and set it on a buffet table behind Gray. "Can I pour y'all a cup?"

Since Liddy was taking Ollie from the carrier and her brother was busy glaring at Gray, Shelby answered. "We'll just help ourselves. Thank you, Becky."

Becky offered a parting smile that toppled when she glanced Gray's way, then she vanished through the doorway.

Mr. Greenwood pulled documents from a file while Shelby's mind spun. Gram must've left Gray something. She couldn't think what. Gram didn't have anything that— *Oh*. The necklace and china. Gray's grandma had left Gram a pearl necklace and her wedding china. Gram would now pass those items to Dorothy's grandson. Of course. It all made sense now. Shelby's shoulders slumped on an exhale.

Dad entered the room, seeming a little harried. "Sorry I'm a little late. There was—" His gaze stopped on Gray, his prominent brows pinching together over soft blue eyes. He'd combed his salt-and-pepper hair back, showing off a hairline that hadn't receded so much as a centimeter. He'd dressed casually in jeans and a button-down.

"You're right on time," Mr. Greenwood said. "Come on in and take a seat. Can I get you a cup of coffee?"

"No, thank you." Dad pulled his gaze from Gray and took a seat on Shelby's other side.

As he settled, Shelby dared a glance at her ex-boyfriend. He burned a hole through the conference table as he spun a to-go cup from Latte Da with his left hand.

"Alrighty then. Thank you for coming down today. You're all here as beneficiaries of Miss Viola's will. And as I conveyed on the phone, we usually don't hold formal will readings, but this is what Miss Viola requested."

He continued talking, but Shelby made a connection while he did so. Gram had always rooted for Gray and Shelby. She'd been so convinced they were meant for each other. Shoot, at one time Shelby had been just as convinced.

Gram had pushed her on it for a while. For years, really, until Shelby finally put her foot down.

"It's over between us, Gram. I know you don't like change, but sometimes it's for the best. Sometimes change is necessary for growth. Let it go."

But Gram had been stubborn and convinced she was right. She'd probably set up this reading to force them together in the same room. Ridiculous, since she couldn't have known when she was going to pass. For heaven's sake, Shelby could've been married by now. Not to mention Gray.

Her gaze flitted toward the hand still fiddling with the coffee cup. To the fourth finger. Bare.

"Did you just check out his ring finger, Sweet Girl?" Gram's voice held that familiar note of humor.

I'm just curious. It's completely natural.

"Whatever you say."

"Is that okay with everyone?" Mr. Greenwood said.

"Of course," Dad said.

Caleb folded his arms. "Fine by me."

Gray offered a nod.

All eyes were on her. What was the question again? Shelby squirmed in her seat. "Uh, yes. Sure."

"Overview it is then," Mr. Greenwood said. "I'll go ahead and pass these out so you each have a copy for your records." He proceeded to do just that.

Shelby took the stapled document and set it on the table, her eyes pinned on the heading: *Last Will and Testament of Viola Elaine Thatcher*.

Gram was dead.

No matter how many times Shelby told herself that, it still didn't seem real. Just last week she had entered the bookshop to find her grandma on a ladder, shelving a new first edition of *The Exiles*. After Shelby had shooed her off the ladder, they'd debated whether or not they needed a website—they did. Then they chatted about a few new releases, then *Normal People*, which led them as always to that dream trip to Ireland they'd always wanted to take.

And never would now.

Shelby tried to take comfort in the fact that Gram had had a good, long life and had passed peacefully in her sleep. Who could ask for more? But that wouldn't stop them all from missing her terribly. It wouldn't fix the gutted feeling that left her chest hollow and aching.

Mr. Greenwood interrupted her thoughts. "So I'll run through the list of assets in the order Miss Viola requested. Feel free to stop me if you have any questions."

Ollie let out a little squeak as Liddy shifted him in her arms.

Dad's face was stoic, his eyes tight at the corners.

Shelby took his hand under the table and gave it a squeeze.

He squeezed back.

"The first asset is Miss Viola's house." Mr. Greenwood made eye contact with her brother. "Caleb, she wanted you to have her home to do with as you and Liddy wish. Though she loved the home and cherished the memories made there, she wanted to make sure you felt no obligation to keep it. The contents are yours also, except for the items she designated for others. Though she asked that you allow your father and sister to take whatever they might wish to keep."

Caleb nodded. "Of course."

"She also wanted you to have your grandfather's wedding band and watch. She had fond memories of you playing with that watch when you were a child."

Caleb blinked back tears, gave a nod.

Liddy rubbed his arm.

Mr. Greenwood's glance shifted to Dad. "Stanley, your mother wanted you to have any monetary assets once outstanding debts are paid." He glanced down at the papers. "She also wanted you to have the letters she and your father wrote to each other when he was away at war, the grandfather clock he bought her for their twenty-fifth anniversary, and any gifts you gave her over the years that you might like to have, including the hummingbird feeder you made her, which provided hours of enjoyment, the diamond birthstone necklace you gave her for her sixtieth birthday, and the antique desk residing in her home office."

Dad swallowed hard. His jaw flexed.

"Grayson . . ."

All eyes swung his way.

"Your grandmother was a wonderful, lifelong friend to Miss Viola. She felt Miss Dorothy would've wanted you to receive the things she left to Miss Viola in her will—her pearl necklace and your grandparents' wedding china will go to you."

Gray offered a nod. Let go of his cup and slid both hands under the table.

Shelby's shoulder muscles loosened a notch. She'd been right about the bequeathments. But Gram had been wrong about getting them into a room together. There was no crucible powerful enough to make her open her heart to Gray again.

"Shelby, you know how much your grandmother valued her wedding rings."

"She never took them off." Even though Pop had died almost twenty years ago. "Pop was her first and only love."

"Exactly so. She wanted you to have those to remember them both by. Also, all of her first-edition copies in her home library and all the books from her personal library. She wanted you to have the antique settee in her living room. She had many fond memories of late-night chats dating back to your childhood. She wanted you to have her tea service, the diamond earrings your grandfather gave her for their twentieth anniversary, and the antique lamp that belonged to her mother. She also asked that you would care for Chaucer. Lastly, in regard to The Second Story Bookshop, which includes the business and the building's contents, she bequeathed you 51 percent."

Shelby blinked at Mr. Greenwood. "Did you say 51 percent?"

"That doesn't make sense," Dad said. "Shelby and Mom have run that place together for years. She always intended for Shelby to have it after she was gone."

"Who'd even get the other half?" Caleb said. "Not me. I have no interest."

"I understand your confusion. But I'd like you to recognize that Miss Viola was very clear in her wishes. Shelby, running the bookshop with you was one of your grandmother's biggest joys. She wanted me to express how thankful she was for the time she had with you over the years. Those memories were very dear to her. She realized you might not understand her wishes, but nonetheless"—his gaze shifted across the table and locked on Gray—"she bequeathed the other 49 percent of the bookstore to Grayson Briggs."

Chapter 3

"*What?*" Gray had heard the words. They just didn't quite compute. Miss Viola had left him half of the bookstore? His gaze shot to Shelby, who stared at him as if he'd just killed her cat.

Caleb shot to his feet, eyes hot and aimed straight at him. "You manipulated her. I know you stayed in touch with her, and there's no way she would've done this on her own."

Gray frowned. "I didn't know anything about this."

"I don't believe you."

Liddy took Caleb's arm. "*Honey.*"

"I refuse to accept this," Shelby's father said to Mr. Greenwood. "Mom always planned to leave Shelby the shop. She mentioned it many times."

"She did express that she wants the shop to continue under Shelby's direction."

Caleb glared at Gray. "She wouldn't have done this without some kind of coercion."

Mr. Greenwood cleared his throat. "I know this must be upsetting and you may not understand her reasons. But I assure you, Miss Viola was adamant about this decision."

"We must have some legal recourse," Stanley said.

"There's always that option. But your mother was of sound mind—

there's not a soul alive who would dispute that. Frankly, I don't think you'd have a legal leg to stand on."

As Mr. Greenwood rambled on about legalities, Gray's gaze slid to Shelby. Her long dark lashes swept downward, hiding her brown eyes. She clamped her lush lips together the way she'd always done when she was angry or about to cry. Which was the case right now?

Either way he couldn't blame her. He had no right to that bookshop. Maybe he'd helped Viola a bit from afar, but he hadn't even stepped foot inside the store since he'd left town eleven years ago. And the last thing he wanted was to hurt Shelby.

Time and distance had shown him what an idiot he'd been. Long before his tour in the Army was up, he'd realized he'd made a terrible mistake. But it was far too late. He'd already lost her.

Maybe he could somehow use this opportunity to finally make things right. He so regretted the way he'd hurt her. And the weight he'd carried for years seemed to get heavier by the day.

And seeing Shelby yesterday had stirred more than a desire for closure. At the first sight of her doe eyes, all those old feelings resurfaced. And seeing her with her boyfriend at the funeral home, his arm draped around her chair, sent jealousy roiling through him. He had no claim on Shelby. No right to these feelings. But they were there anyway.

Shelby lifted her eyes and narrowed them, pinning him with a flinty look.

Anger it is.

More anger. He would forfeit his share of the store. It was the least he could do. Maybe then she'd finally forgive him for being such an idiot when he was a kid.

He opened his mouth to say so . . . just as Mr. Greenwood's last words rang out. "Whatever her intentions, your grandmother had your best interests at heart, Shelby. I can promise you that."

The Second Story Bookshop

She lowered her gaze to the table. Her fist closed around a tattered tissue.

Gray shut his mouth. No doubt he had a fair share of business acumen, but that wasn't what this was about. Miss Viola had made no secret of her wish for Shelby to forgive him. The woman had arranged this stunt to accomplish just that.

Maybe he could carry out Miss Viola's wishes while still making an honorable decision regarding the bookstore.

He cleared his throat as he stood, and all eyes darted his way. "I'd like to talk to Shelby alone."

"I'll bet you would," Caleb said.

Mr. Greenwood gathered his papers. "I'm finished conveying Miss Viola's wishes, so I'll excuse myself. Feel free to read through the will and contact me with any questions you might have. You're welcome to use the conference room as long as you like."

Stanley stood and shook the attorney's hand, thanking him for his time.

After Mr. Greenwood left, Shelby came to her feet, staring at Gray. Her eyes flashed and she lifted her elfin chin.

He'd seen that look a time or two. Gram had passed that stubborn gene right down to her granddaughter. Despite the gravity of the situation, he felt a smile forming—and squashed it quickly.

Shelby addressed her family. "Why don't you guys head on out while I have a word with Gray."

Her dad frowned. "You sure, honey? I can stick around awhile. I don't have to work today."

"That's okay, Dad. I'll be fine. Really."

"I'm staying," Caleb said.

Liddy handed him the baby carrier. "No, you're not. You're coming with us." Her eyes warned him not to argue.

Caleb aimed a scowl at Gray as Liddy made her way toward the door.

Then he set a hand on Shelby's arm. "My phone is on. Call me if you need anything. Anything at all."

* * *

The office emptied, leaving Shelby and Gray utterly alone. Only the quiet hum of the air conditioner broke the silence. She brushed back a tendril that had escaped her bun. Her hands were shaking. She folded her arms across her chest. "Is this where you admit to manipulating Gram into giving you half her bookshop?"

"I don't want her store, Shelby. Who do you take me for?"

"You don't want me to answer that."

"Fair enough. But I had no idea she was planning this and no desire to come back here at all, much less permanently."

"Fine, then sign your half over to me and you can be on your way."

He dragged his gaze from hers. Paced the length of the table.

She felt the ridiculous need to scuttle around the other direction just to keep the table between them. But he pivoted and returned to where he was standing before. "You'll need some help around the store until you find a replacement for your grandma."

"I'm perfectly capable of hiring my own staff, thank you."

"I want to help."

"I don't need your help."

His stare was unwavering. "So you're up to speed on the software for the POS system, the bookkeeping, the financials?"

Heat flooded her face. She fought the urge to squirm under his steady gaze. Drat him for being good at such things. And for knowing she darn well wasn't. "That's none of your concern."

His head tilted back a degree. He pocketed his hands. "I want to make you a proposal."

"You're very good at those—not so much on the follow-through though."

Hurt flared in his eyes, there and gone.

She shouldn't have said that. It wasn't as if he'd technically proposed. They'd been too young for that. But they'd promised their hearts to each other. That counted for something.

He offered a nod. "We'll call it an offer then. I'll stick around long enough to do a financial audit. That'll need to be done before you find a new bookkeeper anyway."

"Can't I just hire a CPA for that?"

"Sure, if you want to pay for it. I'm willing and able to do it for free. And I can step into your grandma's position immediately as I'm already proficient in Shopify. I helped her set it up."

Gram hadn't mentioned that. That would solve one problem—one big problem. But the last thing Shelby wanted was to be stuck for days on end with Grayson Briggs. "Don't you have a job back in Riverbend Gap? A life?"

"I can make arrangements. I'm due time off."

"Why would you do this? You hate Grandville."

He smirked. "It's more that Grandville hates me, isn't it?"

"Semantics. Answer my question."

He took his time. "Why do you think your grandma did this?"

"That's a question, not an answer."

"All right, I'll answer it then. She wanted us to put the past to rest. I think it must've meant an awful lot for her to have done this. She loved you and she knew what the bookstore means to you. It wasn't her intention to take it away from you—even a piece of it."

"And yet she did."

"That brings us back to my offer." His gaze sharpened on her. "If you allow me to stick around and help out for a couple weeks—that should be long enough to get things squared away and hire a replacement—I'll sign over the 49 percent."

Shelby's lips parted. She snapped them back together. "Why would you do that? Isn't this your dream—owning a business?"

"If I own a business someday, it'll be because I've earned it."

There had to be some trick here. She just couldn't think clearly enough to figure out what it was.

"I have no desire to own a business in Grandville, Shelby." He regarded her for a beat. "And maybe Gram isn't the only one who wants us to bury the hatchet."

Shelby stiffened. "I'm not interested in some kind of reconciliation."

"I'm only asking for a chance to make things right—as best I can. Maybe if I help you out, maybe if we spend a little time together, we can work through this."

That was exactly what she was afraid of. Gray used to have such a hold on her. She'd fallen fast and hard in a way she hadn't before or since. It had taken over a year to get past the heartbreak. That resentment she carried now was a block wall between them—and it sounded as if he wanted to tear it down.

And yet . . . if he continued to hold 49 percent of the shop, that would tie them together indefinitely. She didn't really have much choice.

She regarded him through a veil of bravery. "You'll sign papers to that effect? Two weeks at the bookshop and you'll sign over your share?"

"Whatever you draw up."

There was nothing but sincerity in those pale blue eyes, in the resolute set of his jaw. But her trust in his word had evaporated ages ago.

She lifted her chin. "Fine. Be at the store at eight o'clock tomorrow. I'll have the paperwork, and once you sign it you can get started."

Chapter 4

Eleven years ago

How had Shelby been lucky enough to score a bookstore job at the age of seventeen? She arranged the seasonal table with beach reads and complemented the theme with various sideline products: a beach towel, a few totes, and some colorful cozies.

Her gaze drifted over Gram's store from the tall wooden shelves, complete with gliding ladders, to the freestanding shelves laden with books.

The brick building, built in 1923, sat near the center of town, set back from the other storefronts. It boasted a small yard and a front porch that welcomed guests to sit and read awhile.

Beyond the front door, a wonderful old staircase led to their second-story shop. At the top it opened up into a lofted space with honey-brown wood floors. Shelby loved every time-scarred plank and familiar squeak. The main room held fiction titles, complete with tables for bestsellers, seasonal books, and a few sideline items. The antique checkout stand sat off to the side next to the front staircase. Behind the stand was the first-editions wall, which contained the store's only used books.

The Nonfiction section took up the smaller middle room, and the back room held the Children's and Young Adult sections, complete with a cozy story-time corner. Gram's office was tucked away downstairs between the back staircase and the rear exit.

Shelby had only been twelve when Gram rented the building and opened the bookstore. Having lost her husband a couple years before, she wanted to use their savings to pursue her lifelong dream. She'd lost the love of her life and needed another purpose. She called it her second story. So when this upstairs space became available, she snatched it up. She wanted the bookshop to be a community hub, and that was exactly what it became.

But the store didn't just cater to residents. Grandville was a college town, so the bookstore enjoyed its share of student business. And the weekenders who came up from Charlotte to enjoy the fifty-square-mile lake often came in search of a beach book or a cozy mystery. Shelby and Gram loved to welcome one and all into their little bookshop.

"Oh, that looks so nice." On her way to the register, Gram stopped, appearing all summery in a sleeveless teal top and a pair of white capris that matched her cropped hair. "You sure have a knack for arranging merch."

"It's so fun. Oh, do we still have those seashell earrings Meg Finlay made? Those would be perfect."

"Over by the register. I'll grab them for you."

"Thanks."

A customer who'd been perusing the Fiction section moved to the next room, browsing covers as she went.

Shelby moved Debbie Macomber's new beach title to the side and slid the ocean-breeze candles to the front. She stood back. There.

"Here you go." Gram handed over the earrings as a lawn mower roared to life outside.

Shelby glanced out the picture window and down to the lawn but didn't see anyone. "Did you pay someone to mow?" Shelby normally tried to beat Gram to the chore. There was only a tiny lawn out front and a square of grass in the back.

"Dorothy asked if I had some work to keep Gray busy this summer. He'll be mowing and landscaping the front yard for us."

At the thought of Grayson Briggs, a strange hum vibrated beneath Shelby's skin. "Oh. Well, you've been wanting to put some flower beds out front."

"It'll be nice to spruce up the yard." Gram snapped a picture of Shelby's display with her phone. "Beautiful. Can you check on the customer when you're finished here? I'm gonna say hello to Gray."

"Sure thing."

Gram went down the stairs and slipped out the door, the bell tinkling after her. A minute later the mower shut off.

Gray, a fellow classmate, used to live in a trailer on the other side of Grandville with his father. But six months ago, halfway through their junior year, his dad was arrested on charges of second-degree murder, and Gray moved in with his grandmother.

Something like that didn't go unnoticed in a town with fewer than fifteen thousand residents. The case was the talk of the town for months, and Ferris's recent conviction only spurred it on. He was now serving time in the state penitentiary.

Rumors had swirled throughout the school about Gray. He was tall and darkly handsome and strutted through Grandville High's halls in weathered jeans and T-shirts, silent and brooding. Shelby had only ever shared one class with him—English—and he'd hardly said a single word all year.

Though one time they'd reached the trash can at the same time, and his blue stare at such close range had made her blood buzz in her veins. Time stood still for a few ticks of the clock before he finally dropped a wad of paper in the trash can and swaggered back to his seat.

The seemingly insignificant moment had left her shaken. Later she told herself her reaction had been based on fear. She couldn't get that direct gaze out of her head. Or the harsh planes of his face. Everyone knew

Gray was rough around the edges, and a violent streak certainly seemed to run in the family—Dorothy Briggs notwithstanding.

Now Shelby wondered how many of those rumors about Gray were actually true. Gram wouldn't have hired a troublemaker, would she? Not even for her best friend.

Shelby finished the display, then checked on the customer who was inspecting the Travel section. After a brief discussion about the best North Carolina guides, Shelby left the woman to shop alone.

She wandered back to the front room where she peeked out the window, hoping for a glimpse of Gray. The mower sat in the middle of the yard, but Gray and Gram were nowhere to be seen. She leaned closer and finally caught sight of him raking out the beds at the base of the porch.

Shirtless.

His summer-bronzed skin gleamed under the morning sun, hugging every delicious muscle. And boy, did Gray Briggs have muscles. He had a body like Michelangelo's *David*, only living and breathing.

His biceps bulged as he worked the rake through an entire winter's worth of decayed leaves and debris. His rippling abdomen mesmerized her for a few long seconds. How did one acquire abs like that? Especially a guy who'd never deigned to join the football or basketball team?

Only when he stopped raking did she tear her gaze away, letting it drift toward his face. Toward his eyes.

Which were aimed directly at her.

She gasped and jumped out of view, heart racing. But she'd been about one second too late.

Chapter 5

Present day

The buttered toast churned in Gray's stomach as he grabbed his key fob and headed out the front door. It was strange to be back at his grandmother's lake cottage. Since shortly after her passing he'd been renting it out as an Airbnb, using a local company to handle the details. Fortunately it was now the offseason and the cottage had been available for his stay.

It was still strange to see the place barren of Granny's personal effects. The family photos, afghans, and stacks of crossword puzzles. She had sure loved those crossword puzzles—and was good at them. When he was a kid he got her a booklet each year for her birthday, and she acted like it was the best gift she'd ever gotten.

He started his Tahoe, blinking against the sunlight sparkling off Cedar Lake. Granny's cottage was one of the few original lake homes still standing. Most of the properties had been bought and leveled to make way for sprawling mansions.

Gray liked Granny's home the way it was—though he'd replaced the furnishings and flooring to bring the place up-to-date. He took a sip of coffee, brewed by the Breville he'd splurged on. Most of his guests appreciated the touch of luxury—as did he. Quality coffee was his one guilty pleasure.

He'd paid dearly for his stop at Latte Da yesterday. Renee Remington had been there with a friend, and her face turned to stone at the sight of him. That familiar old shame returned, tingling his face with heat. It was her son Troy that Gray's dad had killed. An accident, perhaps, but still. Gray was guilty by association.

The Remington family obviously hadn't forgiven or forgotten, and they were a big, influential family. Back when he lived here most folks in town showed their loyalty to them by aiming disapproving looks his way or, if he was lucky, ignoring him altogether. All of the above filled him with shame somehow.

But he was an adult now and able to process his feelings in a more mature way. He wasn't responsible for what his dad had done. Wasn't responsible for the gossip that had fueled his bad reputation. He'd never deserved their derision.

As the caffeine kicked in he pushed the past in its place and thought back to his conversation with Shelby yesterday. He had his work cut out for him there. A lot of making up to do where she was concerned.

She seemed so different from the girl she used to be. He'd known from the beginning she was way out of his league. She was smart and beautiful, the popular girl in school. Not one of those uppity clique girls, but a well-liked, cheerful sort whom classmates rallied around. She was on student council, played on the softball team, and was always willing to lend a sympathetic ear. Classmates flooded to her for advice and encouragement. She somehow seemed more mature than the rest of them. If anyone needed anything, Shelby Thatcher was there to lend a hand.

He gathered all this information from observation throughout their school years. In middle school he'd privately scoffed at her people-pleasing ways. But in high school she'd shot up a few inches, developed curves, and grown into her big brown eyes and wide smile. She always seemed to have a novel in hand, and he often found himself trying to glimpse the title. Somehow this bit of insight into her reading habits made him feel closer to her.

He never actually spoke to her though. Why would Shelby Sunshine want anything to do with a ne'er-do-well like Grayson Briggs? He'd found it best to keep his head down, quietly ace his tests, and focus on planning a better future for himself.

But he noticed her. How could he not? And he later learned she noticed him also.

The memories sent a wave of heat through him. Bad idea to let his mind go there again. He just had to do this one last thing for Viola—and really for Shelby—and then he could put Grandville and its judgmental people in his rearview mirror.

She'd no doubt have those papers for him to sign this morning. Even though the plan had been his idea, he had mixed feelings about it. On the one hand, signing over the store was the right thing to do. On the other hand, he was severing the only connection, however tenuous, he had with her. He had two weeks to make things right with her though. At least there was that.

But in order to fulfill his end of the bargain, he needed to check in with his boss back home.

At a stop sign he placed the call, connecting through Apple CarPlay. Gavin picked it up after three rings. "Robinson Construction."

"Hey, Gavin, it's Gray."

"Hey, buddy. How's everything going?"

"Pretty good. How's the Franke project?"

"The roof shingles came in yesterday. I'm glad you called them. I think the order would've slipped through the cracks, and the Frankes aren't the easiest of customers."

Understatement. The husband was complicated and the wife was indecisive—the pairing made for a very difficult project. But they were nearly done. "Good, good. How's Eric doing?" Gray had recently hired and trained a new project manager as the job had become too much for one person. The company had grown by leaps and bounds the past few years.

"He's doing great. He's out checking the Harding job right now. They love him."

"Good to hear." Gray paused long enough to formulate his thoughts. "Listen, you know how you were recently urging me to use some of my acquired PTO?"

Gavin chuckled. "Let me guess. You wanna catch up with your family and friends."

Gray hadn't exactly opened up to his employer about his family's reputation in his hometown. "Something like that. Can you spare me?"

"I can hardly say no, the way you've poured your heart and soul into this company over the past few years. It's been a tremendous load off my plate. My wife and kids are thankful to have me home for supper most nights."

Gray had been working dawn to dusk since he'd gotten the job. What else did he have to do? "I love my job and I hate taking time off. But I've got some loose ends here I need to take care of. I'm happy to check in—do some scheduling, run interference as needed. I can even manage the bookkeeping from afar."

"I might take you up on that. I'm sure Eric can handle the construction end though, and I can pick up some slack. How long you thinking?"

"A couple weeks?"

"Sure, buddy. We owe you a lot more than that. And the bookkeeping can probably wait till you're back."

Relief swamped Gray. "I really appreciate it. I didn't expect to extend my stay, but something's come up. Don't hesitate to call if you need anything. I'll stay in contact with Eric and step in wherever I'm needed."

"I'm sure we can hold it together till you get back. We still have plenty of mild weather before winter sets in."

"Thanks for being so understanding."

"Just don't go moving back home. I've grown attached to weekends off."

Thinking of his family's reputation in this town, Gray smirked. "Not likely, my friend."

Chapter 6

Shelby spotted Logan Shackleford (biographies and memoirs) at a table for two. A smile spread across his face as he caught sight of her. His short light brown hair was carefully combed, and his businesslike glasses perched on his nose, framing his hazel eyes. His crisp white shirt was fitted to his lean torso, and a maroon tie, fashioned in a Windsor knot, finished the look.

Logan was a loan officer at HomeTrust Bank, which meant that, except for Saturdays, their work schedules were almost identical. Meeting at Becca's Bakery before work on Mondays and Fridays had become a regular thing since they'd begun dating five months ago.

Her chocolate croissant and steaming cup of coffee waited at the table from which he rose and offered her a brief hug. "How are you doing?"

"As well as can be expected, I guess. Thank you for the croissant and coffee," she added as they took their seats.

They'd spoken on the phone only briefly since the funeral. Shelby felt guilty that she hadn't accepted his many offers of company, but she hadn't had the emotional bandwidth to deal with one more thing.

Logan's gaze drifted over her face and shirt. "You look nice."

"Thank you." His expression revealed an assumption that she'd dressed up for their brief date. But he was wrong. Knowing Gray would be at the bookstore had her all messed up. It was a normal inclination, wasn't it?

Since her ex-boyfriend had arrived in town he'd only seen her at her worst.

"So do you," she added belatedly, then tore off a piece of the flaky croissant and tried to enjoy the rich, buttery flavor. They made small talk while they ate and sipped coffee, the conversation mostly revolving around Gram's funeral and plans for Thanksgiving. It was only mid-October, but the holidays would be here before they knew it.

When she finished her pastry, she wiped her hands and dropped her napkin on her plate. "What's on your agenda today?"

"A few meetings, one of which is with Leo . . ."

"About the promotion?"

"I think so, but I'm trying not to get my hopes up."

"You deserve it. You work so hard." Logan came from a prominent family. He was smart and dedicated to his job, but she suspected he was sometimes overlooked. He was an introvert and didn't socialize much with his coworkers—something she'd begun encouraging him to do. "I'll say a little prayer for you."

"Thank you. You're always so encouraging."

He wouldn't like what she had to say next. She should've told him last night during their brief phone call, but she'd still been overwrought about the whole thing. "So I didn't really go into details about the will reading yesterday, but there's something I need to tell you."

He set down his mug, giving her his full attention. "What is it?"

Logan knew her history with Gray—the entire town did. Over the course of her relationship with Logan, she hadn't divulged much beyond the basics. "Everything went pretty much as we expected with the bequeathments except one thing—the ownership of the bookshop. It seems Gram left me only 51 percent of the business."

His brows furrowed. "Did she leave your brother the rest? He doesn't even live here."

"No, she didn't leave it to Caleb." The reality of the situation hit her fresh. Gray was going to be all up in her business—literally—every day for the next two weeks. She cleared her throat. "She left it to Gray."

His head jerked back. He searched her eyes for a long moment and didn't seem to find what he was looking for. "Grayson Briggs? But why? That doesn't make sense."

"I know. I'm still processing it. Gram had kept in contact with him over the years. You know she and Dorothy were lifelong friends."

"I knew that. I just didn't realize your gram still communicated with him."

"I think she felt she owed it to Dorothy to look out for him."

Logan grunted. "There's looking out for him, and then there's giving him half her bookshop."

"I think she may have done that with my best interest at heart. I think she wanted me to have closure." Guilt tweaked at the partial truth. She suspected Gram had hoped for far more than closure. But there was no reason to worry Logan when those hopes would never come to fruition. "I know we were young back then, but his leaving left a mark, and I made no secret of how I felt about the whole thing."

"You have good reason. He was callous. No one blames you for having ill will toward Gray. I guess that explains why he's still in town. People at the bank were talking about it yesterday. Is the will contestable?"

"Not according to Mr. Greenwood."

"So what then? Will you have to buy him out?"

"I don't have that kind of money. And it won't come to that anyway. We made a deal yesterday. He offered to stay and take Gram's place for a couple weeks. Then he'll sign his 49 percent over to me." With that legal document she'd be formally undoing her grandma's final wishes. Maybe Gram had been meddling, but another prick of guilt stabbed her hard just the same.

"Do you really trust Gray with the finances of your business? What if he embezzles money from the shop?"

"He currently owns half of it. Wouldn't that just be stealing from himself?"

"You can't trust him, Shelby."

She didn't trust him with her heart. But according to Gram he'd completed a bachelor's degree in business with a minor in accounting from the University of North Carolina. He was filling a couple of roles for some construction company and apparently doing quite well.

"I'll keep an eye on him."

Logan frowned. "I don't like it."

"I don't either, but I really don't have much choice."

"At the very least I hope you got that deal in writing. He's not exactly known for keeping his word."

"I had Mr. Greenwood draw up the papers. Gray will sign them this morning."

"Would you like me to look them over?"

Shelby glanced at her watch. "Thanks, but I'm supposed to meet him at the store in ten minutes. Anyway, I've already read the contract. It's pretty thorough. I hate to dash, but . . ."

"No, it's fine. I'm due at work too."

They deposited their trash, then exited the bakery.

When she started to say good-bye, he took her hand. "I admit I'm not crazy about the idea of you and Gray tucked away in that bookshop for days on end."

"You have nothing to worry about. I only agreed to this to get the bookshop back."

"Yeah, but why did *he* agree to it? Giving up two weeks of his time plus the ownership?"

That question had been swimming around her head the past twenty-four hours. "I think he wants to respect Gram's wishes."

Logan smirked. "Forgive my cynicism, but I think it's more likely he knows what he's lost and wants it back."

"That's not gonna happen. Even forgiveness seems like a stretch at this point. He'll be sequestered down in the office auditing the books and doing Gram's job while I find a replacement. That's all."

He searched her face and nodded. "Okay. I'm here if you want to talk."

"I'm sure I'll be ready to bust by the end of the day."

At five-nine Logan was only a couple of inches taller than Shelby. So he barely had to lean over when he offered a peck on the lips—as much of a display of public affection as he ever offered. "I'll call you tonight."

"Okay." She headed the opposite direction, pulling her jacket against the cool breeze. She nodded hello to friends and acquaintances, shop owners, and tourists. It was a friendly, bustling little town. She loved the colorful canopies jutting over the walkway and the red, white, and blue Open signs. She adored the brick sidewalks and the pretty lamps and maple trees that lined the street. It was a picturesque sight, captured on many canvases in the art galleries sprinkled throughout town.

The area had become something of an artists' haven in the past ten years or so. The chamber of commerce had done a lot of work toward that end. And the giant mural on the side of the old train depot was one of the most photographed spots in town.

In the distance the lake shimmered under the sunlight. The area was mostly flat but for the small hills surrounding the lake. The deciduous trees on those hills burst with autumn colors, a lovely contrast to the deep green evergreens.

"You sure are pretty today, Shelby," Miss Lucy called as she set a pot of yellow mums outside her florist shop.

"Thank you. Enjoy the beautiful fall day."

"You do the same, honey."

Not likely. She dreaded the hours ahead. Maybe Gray wouldn't show up—he hadn't exactly proven himself reliable in the past. But then she'd be stuck with him as a partner—and what would that look like? She didn't even want to know.

Surely he wouldn't move back to Grandville where he and his dad were town pariahs. People, especially the Remingtons and their elite circle, hadn't forgotten what Ferris Briggs had done. Even before he'd accidentally killed Troy Remington, he practically had his own branch on the town grapevine: public intoxication, drinking and driving, disorderly conduct.

And the antics of the Briggs boy also lived in infamy, some of them gross exaggerations or totally fabricated. Gray had always taken the public scorn with resolute silence—almost as though he felt he deserved it. But the injustice used to drive her crazy.

The grapevine was apparently already abuzz with his presence in town. It surely wouldn't take long for news of Gray's share in the store to circulate. That wouldn't be good for business. Perhaps she should circumvent the possible fallout by sharing news of their deal. She'd mention it in passing to Miss Glenda or Miss Tammy and the rest would take care of itself.

As the sign for the bookshop came into view, Shelby's heart quickened. She clung to what she'd said earlier—that Gray would be down in Gram's office and Shelby would stay busy assisting customers upstairs.

Being a Friday, it would likely get busier in the afternoon, and that's when Haley (fantasy and graphic novels) would arrive. Hiring the eighteen-year-old as a favor to Shelby's former English teacher hadn't been one of her better ideas. But she was grateful she and Gray would have a buffer for the second half of the day.

She passed Cedar Lake Gallery, then rounded the corner of Patsy's Boutique, her gaze going straight to the man standing on the shadowed porch. Gray wore a blue half-zip sweater and khakis, accented with a brown belt and matching suede dress boots. He appeared every inch the businessman, and for just a quick second a bubble of pride swelled. He'd gone off and made something of himself. At one time that had been so important to him.

Then she remembered his sudden departure and her long tear-filled nights. She raised her chin a notch and mentally slid that barrier into place.

He slipped his hands into his pockets as she approached. "Good morning."

"Morning." Her heart thumped like mad as she unlocked the store. Seriously, why did he make her so nervous? It ticked her off. She shoved open the door and flipped on the lights.

She headed up the stairs to grab the office key, Gray on her heels. She breathed in the calming scent of books as she went, the stairs creaking under their feet. Once upstairs she fetched the key.

"This place hasn't changed a bit."

"Only the inventory. As you probably know, Gram wasn't a big fan of change."

"You always had such creative ideas though. I figured you'd have talked her into all kinds of things by now."

"You underestimate her stubbornness."

His low chuckle, as familiar as her reflection, stirred something inside. She used to love the sound of it. Even more so when her cheek was pressed against his chest and it rumbled right through her. She pushed the memory away.

She headed toward the back stairs, Gray following. Once she stood in front of the office, she unlocked the door and moved inside. The citrusy smell of Gram's favorite essential-oil blend filled her senses. Boxes of books were stacked in every available nook since Gram hadn't been here to keep up with inventory.

Shelby could almost see her grandma sitting at the old, scarred desk, her fingers tapping the keyboard, her readers halfway down her nose. It was impossible to be in the bookstore or even think of books without thinking of Gram—she'd passed her passion for reading right along to Shelby.

"A good novel is like a vacation for the mind." Gram's voice rang in her head. *"And who doesn't need a vacation?"* Shelby missed her so much. Her chest gave a hard squeeze.

"You okay?"

"I haven't been in here since . . ."

Gray stepped up behind her so close she could hear him breathe. "I'm sorry for your loss. I know the two of you were close. She loved you so much."

Shelby did not want to talk about this with Gray. The last thing she wanted was to be vulnerable around him. Best keep to business matters. "Thank you. As you can see, things are pretty backed up."

"I'll focus on inventory for now. Once I've caught up on that, I'll start on the audit."

"Sounds good." She opened her purse and withdrew the contract. "I brought the paperwork. After you sign it you can bring it up to the front desk. If you have any questions about our system, I'll try my best to answer them."

"Right. I think I can figure it out, but I'll keep that in mind."

Chapter 7

Shelby handed Theresa Combs (rom-coms) the handled bag and receipt for three new releases. "Happy reading. Enjoy your staycation."

"Oh, I'm planning on it. And I'll make proper use of this." She pulled out the door hanger that read *Go away, I'm reading.*

Shelby smiled. "You go, girl."

A minute later the downstairs bell tinkled as the woman slipped outside. Shelby caught sight of the signed document Gray had brought her and stuck it in her purse. It was a done deal. After two weeks the bookshop would be entirely hers.

She drew in a breath and let relief wash over her. There would be a couple of awkward weeks ahead, but at least this was resolved. Her eyes shot back to the papers as a strange fluttery sensation stirred inside her.

He signed away his ownership to you.

It was impossible not to recognize that this was an act of kindness. Maybe it was only his guilt talking, but it was still an incredibly generous thing to do. And somehow that kindness soothed the ache of pain and grief inside.

The bell downstairs jingled again. Even if the wall clock didn't announce it was four o'clock, the arrival of Daryl Lundstrom would have. The twenty-five-year-old man with Down syndrome was always a bright spot in her day. He reached the top of the steps, his brown bangs hanging in his eyes, and beamed when he caught sight of her behind the counter. "I got your newspaper, Miss Shelby!"

"Thank you, Daryl. You're so helpful. Is that a new shirt?"

"Mom got it for me. She said I look good in blue. Do you think I look good in blue, Miss Shelby?"

"Indeed I do. It matches your eyes."

He slapped the paper on the counter. "My dad had blue eyes. That's how come I got them." His parents had divorced when he was a baby, and his father had taken off for greener pastures.

"Would you like to do some stickers for me today?"

"Will you give me ice cream money?"

Shelby chuckled. "You drive a hard bargain."

"I'm not allowed to drive, Miss Shelby."

"Good point. And yes to the ice cream money. It shouldn't take very long." She settled him at the far end of the counter with the books and discount stickers.

He'd completed this task enough times in the past that he needed no instruction. So she left him to check on the customers who'd come in earlier while she was assisting Theresa.

She spotted Haley tidying the bookshelves again and gritted her teeth. Shelby had spoken with her about assisting customers a few times in the month she'd worked for the store, to no avail. She only wanted to move books around and straighten displays. God forbid she'd actually have to answer the phone. She wasn't cut out for retail, but her mother had been so desperate to find her a job. And now she was Shelby's problem.

Shelby approached the girl who was straightening the Women's Fiction endcap. She stood barely over five feet, her thick brown hair in a messy bun framing the birdlike bone structure of her face. "Haley, have you checked on the customers in the Nonfiction section?"

"Oh, I didn't see them come in."

"Can you see if they need help finding anything?"

"Okay."

Shelby watched her approach the man and teenage boy who were perusing books in the Sports section. Haley spoke so softly her words were inaudible, but the man said they were doing fine and they went back to browsing on their own.

As Haley went off to tidy the children's area, Shelby's gaze drifted toward the back staircase. Gray had been down there all day, leaving only to grab lunch around one o'clock. Not that she was paying attention. Fine by her. He had plenty to do, and the less time they interacted, the better.

The phone pealed from the front desk. Shelby tossed a frown in the general direction of the children's area and went to answer. Felicia Borden (literary fiction) wanted to order seven copies of *Shelterwood* for her book club. After Shelby disconnected the call she placed the order and was checking on Daryl when footfalls sounded on the front stairs.

Liddy appeared looking like a fall fashion model in an olive-green sweater, trendy pants, and black leather boots. Her gaze fastened on the New Arrivals table. "Ooh, the new Kristin Hannah book. I didn't realize it was already out."

"It's really good. Liddy, have you met my friend Daryl? He helps out at the store sometimes. Daryl, this is my sister-in-law, Liddy."

Liddy smiled at him. "Hi, Daryl."

He barely glanced up from his task. "Hi there. I'm doing stickers."

"I'm sure you're doing a great job."

"I am."

Shelby and Liddy traded grins.

"Where's Ollie?" Shelby asked.

"At your dad's house with Caleb." She picked up Kristin Hannah's new release. "I had an errand and couldn't resist stopping in."

"You should take that home with you. You're eligible for Gram's family and friends discount."

She spared Shelby a glance. "I'm not taking it for free."

"Fine, leave it here then. I'll bring it over after work."

Liddy sighed but tucked the book under her arm. "That's very kind of you. Thank you."

"I'm bursting at the seams to discuss it with someone, so read fast." Shelby joined her by the table and lowered her voice. "How are Dad and Caleb getting along? Sorry I haven't been around to help run interference."

"No need for that. They're actually getting along very well."

Shelby did a double take. "Really?"

"They're bonding over their mutual dislike of Grayson Briggs."

"Terrific."

"From my perspective it's working out great. Did he show up today?"

"He's down in the office."

As if summoned by their conversation, footfalls sounded on the back staircase, then Gray appeared at the top. He moved toward them with that fluid stride that bordered on a strut.

"Holy cannoli," Liddy whispered.

"Shut it. You're supposed to be on my side."

"I'm 100 percent on your side, but he sure is pretty to look at."

Gray's gaze flickered Liddy's way before settling on Shelby. "I'm about to call it a day. We're caught up on the inventory."

"Already?" There'd been dozens of boxes.

"Gray!" Daryl's stool crashed behind him as he bolted to his feet and rounded the counter. He lumbered toward Gray, beaming.

What in the world?

"Daryl. Hey, good to see you, friend. What are you doing here?"

"I work here, Gray! Well, sometimes I do. Don't I, Shelby? I get ice cream money. Do you live here again? We can shoot hoops at the park. I still live by the park. Do you still live by the park?"

"Not anymore. I'm just here for a visit." Gray's gaze skated to Shelby. "I'm helping out at the store for a while."

These two had obviously spent time together years ago before Gray had moved in with his grandma. He'd never mentioned it. But Gray must've made quite the impression for Daryl to remember him all these years later. She tried to imagine sixteen-year-old Gray voluntarily shooting hoops with thirteen-year-old Daryl and failed.

"Can we play basketball again, Gray? It's not too cold yet."

"No, it's not too cold. Sure, buddy. Let's meet up tomorrow night at five thirty. We'll have a little time before the sun sets."

"Sure, Gray. Let's meet up then." He turned toward Shelby. "Gray is my friend. We're meeting up."

It was impossible not to be charmed by his excitement. "So I hear. I'm sure you'll have fun."

He scooted back to the counter. "I'm almost finished and then you'll give me ice cream money."

"That's right."

Liddy stuck out a hand to Gray. "Hi, I'm Liddy, Shelby's sister-in-law."

"Nice to meet you." Gray offered a cautious smile and shook her hand.

His smile and demeanor when meeting someone new had always reminded Shelby of a wounded animal that anticipated rejection. It had broken her heart to see it then, and she didn't love it now. He'd never deserved the poor treatment he'd gotten around here. But sticking up for him hadn't exactly worked out for her in the long run.

"Here's the key." He set it on the counter.

"Okay."

"Well . . ." Gray's baby-blue eyes locked on Shelby.

She felt it down to her toes. A long second ticked by. Two. Heat prickled beneath her armpits while thoughts pinged around her brain like pinballs. He had that stare that made you think he could see right into your mind.

"Unless you need something else from me, I'll see you in the morning."

"Uh, sure," she croaked. Cleared her throat. "Sure. I'll see you at eight."

As he descended the steps her breath eased from her lungs. One day down, thirteen to go. She nearly moaned.

Liddy gave her a pointed look. "What was *that?*" she whispered.

"What was what?"

"*That.* That thing sizzling between the two of you. I thought you were going to spontaneously combust."

The bell downstairs jingled with Gray's departure.

Shelby straightened an endcap book that might've already been straight. "That was just anger and bitterness."

"Ha! Keep telling yourself that. He is not over you, friend, and I'm starting to wonder if the same can be said for you."

Remembering the effortless way he'd slid into her heart all those years ago, Shelby resolved to fortify her defenses. "That . . . is not happening."

Chapter 8

Eleven years ago

A strange sense of anticipation built inside Gray as he loaded the lawn mower into the truck bed of his dad's old GMC. The tailgate squawked on the hinges as he shut it. He wiped sweat from his brow. It was at least eighty degrees at only nine in the morning. He crossed the freshly mown lawn, his mind already on the day ahead.

For the past week he'd been working on the bookshop's landscaping for a few hours a day. The scraggly old bushes had been deeply rooted, making progress slow. But today he'd start preparing the beds for new plants and flowers. He was new at this sort of work, but he was learning from YouTube videos.

Initially he hadn't been thrilled when his grandma informed him he'd be working in the middle of town this summer. But he hadn't yet run into anyone from school, and he was actually enjoying the work.

But that wasn't the reason for the anticipation making him all squirrelly.

He rolled his eyes at himself as he took the porch step and poked his head inside the lake house. "I'm taking off now, Granny."

His grandma glanced up from her coffee and crossword puzzle. "All right. Don't forget the sunscreen."

"Yes, ma'am." He wouldn't forget it. He just wouldn't wear it because he never burned.

"Oh, can you pick up some 2 percent milk on your way home?" Granny asked just before the door fell shut.

"Sure thing. See you later."

"Have a good day, honey."

Granny's smile lingered in his mind as he made his way to the truck. In some ways living with her was a huge relief. Since his dad was incarcerated Gray no longer had to worry when he left the house at night. Didn't have to lie awake waiting for a phone call from Dirty Harry's, the hole-in-the-wall bar his dad frequented. He'd bet Dad felt no relief, however. Guilt pricked at the thought of his dad locked away in that cell, and he pushed the image away.

Moving to Granny's side of town hadn't changed everything. His dad's bad reputation still followed him like a nasty scent. And no matter how hard he tried to keep a low profile, trouble always seemed to find him. Somehow his academic performance flew under the radar, which was just as well. When it came to the Warner Scholarship, he hoped being underestimated would work in his favor.

The truck started with a rumble and he backed from the drive and headed toward the bookshop. He thought of that first day when he'd caught Shelby Thatcher checking him out from behind the store's window. The way she'd jumped belatedly out of sight. The thought never failed to make him grin. A weight lifted at just the thought of her.

Oh, he wasn't stupid. She was way too good for him. And ogling him didn't mean she liked him. Only that she liked what she saw. There was an ocean of difference. Some girls were attracted to his bad-boy image. Some kind of thrill, maybe. A chance to tick off their fathers, perhaps—he counted Darcy Colbert in that last group. She was an old friend from the trailer park. They hung out sometimes.

He didn't take Shelby for one of those girls though. She was just curious. No doubt with her perfect family, sterling reputation, and immense popularity, she could never understand someone like him. Much less lower herself to befriend him. He suspected she might even fear him a little. Just as well.

She was going out with Brendan Remington, the biggest tool he knew, so she obviously had terrible taste in boys. Just because the guy was top of the class, star of the basketball team, and from a prominent family didn't mean he was an honorable person.

It would be a real pleasure to steal that scholarship right out of Brendan's greedy little hands. He didn't need it anyway, what with his rich parents. His dad owned a business in town, which would likely be handed to Brendan someday, just like everything else was.

Taking the scholarship from Brendan was just a bonus though. The financial aid was Gray's ticket out of this town, the only way he could afford college. He wanted to own his own business someday. Wasn't sure what kind, but he'd be his own boss, make his own success. He wanted autonomy and job security, and he didn't want to answer to people he had no respect for, no trust in. And he wanted to do it someplace far away from Grandville.

As he entered town he pushed the thoughts from his mind. He needed to focus on his task today. He was looking forward to the work almost as much as he anticipated catching a glimpse of Shelby Thatcher and her beautiful doe-brown eyes.

* * *

In the Young Adult section Shelby set up a table featuring books by Jenny Han, an author she'd discovered her freshman year. She enjoyed spreading the word about her favorite books and authors.

The phone pealed up front and Gram called out from the office. "Shelby, honey, can you get that?"

"Sure thing, Gram." Shelby bustled to the phone and took the call, someone inquiring about their hours. After disconnecting she made her way to the New Fiction bookcase to freshen the shelves—or so she told herself. It was possible she was mainly drawn there by the view along the way.

Gray had been working outside all morning, shirtless since about ten. Not that she was keeping track. He was currently putting down a weed barrier along the sidewalk, but that wasn't what drew her attention now.

Brendan was out on the street with his friends Devon and Drew. Devon appeared to be talking to Gray as he worked.

Shelby didn't like the sneer on Devon's face. She'd once seen him shove a freshman boy into a locker for seemingly no reason. She wasn't sure what Brendan saw in the guy. But she couldn't imagine him standing by while Devon was cruel to anyone, even Grayson Briggs. Even so, she rushed down the stairs and stepped outside.

At the sight of her, Brendan's face broke into a smile. He was handsome with bronzed skin, crystal-blue eyes, and sandy-blond hair that dipped over his forehead in an adorable way. He headed up the sidewalk, carrying two Styrofoam drink cups from the Dairy Bar. "Hey, gorgeous. Brought your favorite—extra-thick chocolate malt with chocolate chips." He handed it to her.

Her heart warmed at the thoughtful gesture. "Thank you. That's awfully nice. I took an early lunch, so this'll hit the spot." She peeked around him as she drew the thick shake up the straw. Drew and Devon seemed to be engaged in conversation on the sidewalk, ignoring Gray altogether. Maybe Shelby had misread the situation.

Of course she had. Brendan would never be a party to bullying. They'd only been going out five weeks, but she'd known him for years. He had a solid reputation, was well liked, and had never been anything but kind to her. Besides, Brendan's father would never tolerate that kind of behavior. Barry was difficult to please, but that didn't stop Brendan from trying.

"We're on our way to Drew's house to ride the Jet Skis. His dad just bought a third one, so now we can all ride together."

"Sounds fun." She was surprised he didn't have a summer job yet. He'd mentioned holding out for a lifeguard position, but it seemed a little late in the season to score that job.

"Come on, Brendan," Drew called. "The day's wasting."

Brendan offered a charming grin. "Better run." He kissed her on the cheek.

"Thanks again for the shake."

"You're welcome. Have a good day."

"Have fun."

He took off down the sidewalk, meeting up with his buddies. Shelby gave them a wave just before they disappeared around the corner.

Her gaze returned to Gray, who hadn't so much as glanced up. He looked formidable, those muscles rippling across his back as he pulled the weed barrier tight and secured it. If he knew she was still standing there, he gave no indication. But somehow she knew he knew. She could feel it in her bones.

She couldn't get the image of Devon's sneer from her mind. And it gave her the courage to speak. "Doing all right out here?"

"Fine."

"Sure is a scorcher. Need anything? We have drinks in the mini fridge."

"No thanks. I've got water." He swiped his face with his forearm and went right back to work.

Shelby stood there for a few seconds trying to think of something else to say, but nothing came to mind. Why was she so drawn to Gray? Maybe because he was such an enigma. He was a loner at school, always eating by himself, walking the halls alone. He never spoke up in the classroom and slumped in his seat like he was just waiting for the bell to ring. And yet she'd caught a glimpse of his graded expository essay before he could shove it in his book bag. A 98 percent—three points higher than her own grade.

Then there was that time at the class garbage can when he'd held her mesmerized for a helpless second.

Gray sat back on his haunches and frowned at her.

She'd been staring. Her face warmed. And still she couldn't think of a thing to say. Why did he always make her so tongue-tied?

"There something else?"

His droll tone had her backing up a step. "Um, nope. I'll let you get back to it." She slipped back inside with her melting shake.

The next day Shelby exited the bookshop and nearly balked at the sweltering late-June heat. She had just enough time to run to the Savory Spoon Café for a big slice of their pie of the month: Dutch apple. Maybe she should text Brendan and see if he wanted to meet up.

She admired the fresh landscaping while she tried to decide. Grayson had left a few minutes ago—she'd been waiting for him to go before taking her lunch break. She'd been avoiding him ever since he'd caught her staring yesterday—*for the second time*.

A grinding sound caught her attention as she met up with the sidewalk. Her gaze followed the noise just down the street to where Gray's old GMC sat in a diagonal parking slot. He was trying, unsuccessfully, to start the vehicle. A moment later he got out and lifted the hood. He wore a Braves ball cap and a resolute frown.

And no wonder. After working in the insufferable heat all morning, he probably wanted nothing more than a nice cold shower.

Shelby's heart quickened as she considered what to do. She'd had possession of her family's second vehicle ever since Caleb went away to college. It was parked just down from Gray's truck.

There was that slice of Dutch apple, served à la mode, waiting for her, but it wasn't the thought of the pie that had her stomach clenching. It was the idea of offering Gray Briggs a ride home.

As she approached he was tinkering with something under the hood. A trickle of sweat dripped down the back of his neck and disappeared under the collar of his white tee. His neck was shaved smooth and summer bronze. Three freckles dotted the landscape.

She wet her suddenly dry lips. "Car trouble?"

He nearly bumped his head on the underside of the hood and spared her a scowl. "Sneaky much?"

"You should be nicer to the person who could offer you a ride home."

"And why would you do that?"

She considered. "Because I'm on break, you're obviously stuck, and I'm nice that way."

"I can probably fix it."

She stared for a good ten seconds as he continued to tinker. Finally, she hitched her purse higher on her shoulder. "Suit yourself." She continued down the sidewalk. Why did she feel let down? Why did the pie suddenly seem like a sad backup option? She'd just wanted to do a good deed, that was all.

"Hey, wait a minute."

Shelby turned, shaded her face with a hand as she regarded him.

"You'd really give me a ride?"

She rolled her eyes. "Why wouldn't I?"

He stared at her for a long second, seeming to consider. "Thanks."

He dropped the hood and followed her to the old Civic. The one time her boyfriend had ridden with her, she'd been so embarrassed. He drove a shiny new BMW his parents had gifted him for his sixteenth birthday. The old Civic was in pretty rough shape. The interior had definitely seen better days, and the mats were long gone, exposing the worn, stained carpet.

But she had no such qualms with Gray riding along, given that he drove that old beater and, until recently, had lived in a run-down trailer park in the worst part of town.

She started the car and lowered the windows to let out the hot, stuffy air. Her hands shook as she put the gear in Reverse and backed out. Gray made the space feel small and cramped. His muscular leg was *right there*. His earthy smell filled the interior and she drew in a long breath full.

"Romance, huh?" He held her copy of *My One and Only*.

She snatched away the Kristan Higgins novel, going warm all over. "One of the many genres I read. Anyway, there's nothing wrong with romance."

"Didn't say there was."

"Your tone said plenty. Romances are hopeful and inspiring and feature strong protagonists who fight for what they want. They examine deep-rooted issues and promote healthy relationships and, laugh all you want, but love happens to be an emotion common to the human experience, and exploring it is a worthwhile endeavor. You'd know that if you ever bothered to read one."

He glanced her way, the corner of his mouth tilting with amusement.

"What?"

"Nothing. I just wondered when I'd finally see that spark of yours, that's all."

Shelby frowned. "What are you talking about?"

"I don't know. It just seems like you're Little Miss Sunshine around school, and ever since I started working for your grandma you've been slinking around—"

"Slinking?"

"—the store. I knew you had it in you. Are you finally going to ask me now?"

The boy made no sense. She gave her head a shake. "Ask you what? What are you even talking about?"

He smirked. That steady gaze seemed to penetrate through her irises and into the neurons of her brain where all her secrets resided. "If the rumors are true."

She dragged her gaze back to the road and couldn't even pretend she didn't know what he was referring to. "If you really did all those things, you could just lie about it."

He shrugged. "Guess you'll just have to believe whatever you want then."

"Guess I will." She slowed for the light but it turned green so she continued on.

"I live on Juniper, down near Timber Bay."

"I know where you live." She could practically feel the arrogance rippling off him and resisted the urge to roll her eyes. "I know where *Miss Dorothy* lives. She and my grandma have been friends for, like, fifty years, you know. I couldn't care less where you live."

He chuckled.

The low rumble ran right up her spine. "What? What is so funny?"

He stared at her for a long minute. Not that she even glanced his way, but his laser-like attention made her skin prickle. Just when she thought she couldn't take it another second, he spoke.

"Little Miss Sunshine's all riled up. Why do you suppose that is?"

"Oh, I don't know. Because you're condescending and boorish?"

"Boorish?"

She notched her chin up. "It means ill-mannered."

"I know what it means, Sunshine. I'm just not sure what I've done to deserve such an insult."

She spared him a withering look. "Stop calling me that."

"Most people consider sunshine a positive thing. It provides light and warmth. Life on planet Earth wouldn't exist without it, you know."

"It's quite obvious you have nothing but disdain for me."

"Oh, you think it's disdain, do you?" Amusement laced his voice.

Shelby huffed. The boy was maddening. Why had she offered him a ride? Sometimes she was just too darn nice! She should've left him there, broken down in the heat. Should've let him walk home. She just wouldn't engage him. A few more minutes and she'd be dropping him off and she wouldn't have to speak to him ever again.

"Got no answer for me?"

Nope. Wasn't going to do it. She clamped her lips shut.

"Just going to sit there in silence for the rest of the ride, huh? It'll be a long few minutes . . ."

He sure wasn't kidding about that. The speed limit around the lake was fifteen miles per hour, and with all the turns in the road, she couldn't exactly speed.

She raised the front windows.

Gray jerked his arm out of the way.

Her lips twitched as she kicked the air on high. She slowed for a kid who ambled across the street in a pair of neon-green trunks, heading toward the lake with an inner tube twice his size.

"Still not talking to me then?"

That stupid slow drawl of his jangled her last nerve. She glared at the boy and his ridiculously large tube as she drummed her fingers on the steering wheel. *Any day now, kid.*

"So you've got a stubborn streak too. Good to know."

Once the boy made it across, she accelerated only to slow down again for a speed bump. This ride would never end. This was what she got for doing a good deed. For thinking that maybe Grayson Briggs was just a poor, misunderstood youth. That everyone deserved a chance.

"Well, since we've got the time and you're not up for conversation, guess I'll fill the gap. I'd like to circle back around to that word you used before—*disdain*. 'Cause, see, it's not *disdain* I feel at all, Shelby."

What the heck was he implying? Heat climbed her neck and flooded her cheeks. So maybe she'd stared at him a time or two. He was interesting to look at, that was all. And she was maybe a little intrigued by him. He had an air of mystery about him. But that was it. That was absolutely it.

His gaze burned into the side of her face.

Do not respond. She gritted her teeth together.

"See, what I'm feeling is altogether different from disdain, and for the record, I suspect I'm not alone here." He paused as if waiting for her reply. When it didn't come, he continued. "This is where you tell me you have a wonderful boyfriend and the two of y'all are just so in love. But I happen to know a little about your boyfriend. He's actually a total jerk. You just don't know it yet."

Shelby pressed the accelerator harder, took a speed bump too fast, and the car rattled. She couldn't care less. Maybe it'd shake some sense into Gray. All she cared about was getting him out of her car as quickly as possible.

And *thank You, Jesus*, she could see Miss Dorothy's cottage straight ahead.

"Not going to defend him?" He paused. "All right. I'll take that as a sign that you're more perceptive than I gave you credit for."

Now in front of the house she pressed the brake, bringing the car to a bracing halt.

Gray took his time releasing his seat belt, then eased out of the car. He turned and flashed a grin. "Good talk, Sunshine. Thanks for the ride. See you tomorrow." He closed the door before she could respond.

Not that she was going to. He swaggered toward his grandma's house, and she growled as she put the car in Drive, then muttered a few things she was sure Gram wouldn't approve of. Her tires spit gravel in her rush to escape. Tension throbbed at the base of her neck, and her palms were slick with sweat. She wiped them one at a time down the length of her shorts. Thank God that was over.

Chapter 9

Present day

Shelby went soft at the sight of her father on his porch swing with Ollie. The baby wore a knit cap and fleece sleeper to stay warm in the cool October evening. Her dad was staring off into space, his salt-and-pepper hair ruffling in the wind. The lines on his forehead seemed more prominent than they had only a week ago. Her heart ached for him. Losing Gram had been hard on the whole family.

Shelby stroked her gram's wedding set, which dangled from a gold chain at her neck. She hoped her face bore no remnants of her recent crying jag. She'd just left her apartment where the mere sight of Gram's tea service had brought a wave of grief. It didn't seem to take much. One minute she was fine; the next she was falling apart in the middle of her kitchen.

Dad caught sight of her coming up the sidewalk and his expression warmed. "Hey, puddin'. What brings you by?"

"Can't I just want to check on my dear old dad?"

"I suspect this little package might be the real draw."

Ollie blinked wide brown eyes at her as she placed a kiss on Dad's cheek. "It doesn't hurt." She scooped the baby from Dad, who gave him over willingly. He scooched over to make room for her on the swing. "Hi there, buddy. Oh, you are so sweet. I could just eat you up." There was something purely therapeutic about new life. When she held Oliver all her troubles seemed to wash away. "Where's Caleb and Liddy—and if I ran off with this little guy, do you think they could catch me?"

Dad's lips twitched. "The town hall meeting ended early, so they took advantage of my free time by grabbing supper out. They're probably expecting their son to be here when they get home."

"Just as well. I've got my hands pretty full at the shop." She'd placed ads trying to find someone to fill Gram's job, but she hadn't had a single qualified applicant, and Gray would be leaving in one week.

She shook away the stressful thought and regarded her dad. "Nice of you to give them a break. They probably don't get out very often on their own." Shelby couldn't imagine trying to find a trustworthy babysitter in a big city like New York.

"They could get all the breaks they wanted if your brother would just move back home."

This again. She resisted the urge to roll her eyes. "You know it's not that simple, Dad."

"It could be. He could do his artwork from anywhere, and now that Liddy's home with the baby, she doesn't have a job to leave."

"He might be able to paint anywhere, but the big galleries are in New York." She was beginning to suspect Dad's disappointment in Caleb had less to do with his choice of occupation and more to do with his geographic location.

"He could travel for the showings and ship his artwork if he wanted."

"I'd love to have them here too, but it would be hard for him to paint his urban landscapes if he's living in North Carolina. Besides, he's a grown man. He has a right to live where he wants."

Dad's gaze dropped to Oliver. "How am I supposed to know my grandson if he's growing up halfway across the country?"

"I guess we'll just have to go see them more often. Maybe they'll come around here more too"—she gave him a pointed look—"if we make them feel welcome when they visit."

Her dad shrugged off the comment. "Well, they'll have their own house to stay in, thanks to your gram."

"Have they decided what they'll do with it?"

"Not that they've mentioned. They've been over there boxing up some things. We're supposed to go get the rest of what's ours and anything else we'd like to keep." His voice cracked on the last word.

Shelby offered a sympathetic smile. He'd been close to his mom and he'd never see her again this side of heaven. "How are you doing, Dad? I can't even imagine losing a parent."

"You did lose a parent."

"Not like this." When she was seven her mom had taken off for Hollywood with dreams of fame. They'd barely heard from her after that—and certainly hadn't seen her on TV or the big screen. It seemed their mom had given up her family for nothing. Shelby wished she couldn't remember her at all. But she did. She remembered her glossy dark hair and expressive brown eyes. She remembered soft hands and melodious laughter.

And she remembered the night when her mom hadn't come home from work. It grew late. The sky darkened and they ate supper under a cloud of concern. Then the phone rang and Dad sent Caleb and her to their rooms. But they sat in the hallway instead trying to hear Dad's end of the conversation.

A while later, eyes red-rimmed and voice wobbling with emotion, he brought them the bad news.

Ollie squirmed in her arms. She shook the memory away and placed a kiss on the infant's head, soaking in the soft baby smell of him.

"Going back to work this week has helped," Dad said. "You know, staying busy."

"I'm glad."

"How've you been this week? You were close to her, too, and accustomed to seeing her every day. Now you're cooped up in the building with that Briggs boy. It's all I can do to stop myself from going down there and hauling his rear end out of there."

"Just remember this was all Gram's doing."

He scowled. "I don't get it. She always had such a blind spot for that kid."

An image of the five-o'clock shadow on Gray's jawline as he left the store this evening popped into her mind. "He's hardly a kid anymore."

"That's what worries me."

"If it makes you feel any better, he stays downstairs all day—crunching numbers, I guess. I hardly see him." But every second of the day she was aware of his presence, always wondering when he'd come up to ask a question.

At first he'd tried to teach her some things related to the POS system. At her reticence he eventually offered to make her a detailed tutorial, and she latched onto that idea. The less time she spent with him the better.

Even so, Gray seemed to have grown increasingly quieter as the week progressed. Maybe he was just locked in on his task. Fine by her. Sooner he got it done, sooner he'd leave.

"What if he doesn't know what he's doing?"

"Come on, Dad. He has a business degree with a specialization in accounting. I'm pretty sure he's qualified for the task. And this'll get him out of the bookstore for good. It's a small price to pay to regain 100 percent ownership."

"I don't trust him."

"I know you don't. I don't either. That's why I put it in writing. We're all covered here. We just have to get through this, and then he'll leave town and this will all be behind us."

Dad's gaze sharpened on her face. "It's your heart I'm worried about. There are no legal papers that can protect it."

She'd once been hopelessly in love with Gray. And the summer he left, it had been all she could do to get out of bed. Breathing seemed like a struggle. Then fall came and she went off to Belmont University where she struggled through a semester, too forlorn and distracted to make a real go of it. Why was she struggling so hard to become an English teacher when everything she needed was back home? She missed her family. Missed the bookshop. Missed home.

Most of all she missed Gray, but he was gone.

None of them wanted to see her return to that dark place. "Don't worry, Dad. I don't need a legal document for that. My heart has a ten-foot wall around it where Gray Briggs is concerned. Besides, I'm seeing Logan, remember?"

His eyes softened. "I like Logan. How does he feel about all this?"

"He trusts me. But like the rest of us, he'll be glad when it's over." Right now that seemed like an eternity away.

"Amen to that."

Chapter 10

Gray stared at the computer screen. It didn't add up.

Well, that wasn't entirely true. The numbers added up just fine. He'd been here almost two weeks, and that was long enough to see a clear picture of the store's current finances. What wasn't making sense was that Viola Thatcher was operating in the red, and Shelby didn't seem to have a clue.

Viola hadn't paid rent on the building in two months, and he'd found some bills locked away in a drawer. Those would have to be paid for the store to remain in business, but there wasn't enough money in the account to cover those costs.

Shelby had received a pay increase a few months ago—but starting that same month, Viola had taken a pay decrease in the same amount. Shelby never would've willingly taken money from her grandmother. Which indicated she didn't know the true state of the store's financial affairs.

Which would make him the bearer of some very bad news.

He could clearly see Miss Viola had overspent in areas. She gave away books too often—charitable donations. She left inventory on the shelves too long. The store didn't have a website—an unpardonable sin in today's business climate. Their social media accounts were largely ignored.

Shelby could turn things around, but it wouldn't be easy. And she wouldn't have much time since she was behind on rent. She'd also have to hire Gram's replacement, and that wouldn't be cheap. He glanced at the cell showing Gram's salary and scowled. No way would Shelby find someone for that paltry sum.

The store did a steady business. People came and went all the time—even shut off in the office he could hear the bell's continual tinkling throughout the day. But he'd been upstairs enough to know the place was somewhat of a community hub. People often dropped by just to shoot the breeze. Viola had loved that. He suspected that had been more important to her than any profit she might make. But a business wouldn't survive with that mentality.

And he wanted Shelby's business to thrive. She shouldn't have to worry about stretching dimes and staying afloat.

He wished he had better news for her. He glanced at the clock. It was closing time, but he'd seen on the sidewalk board that a romance book club met tonight. That was another thing. They gave their members 25 percent off book club selections. And with seven book clubs running out of the store, that really cut into their profits. Shelby would have to change some things if she wanted to keep the doors open.

He glanced around the office at the nine boxes of books that had arrived from UPS today. He'd stick around, scan the books into the system, and adhere UPC labels. After her book club he'd break the news to Shelby.

* * *

Great insight, Katherine," Lucy, the discussion leader, said. "I agree Harper could've been an unlikable heroine, given her jaded beliefs on love and marriage. She could even be abrasive sometimes."

Shelby shifted on the wooden seat. They were out back in the courtyard, discussing *My One and Only* by Kristan Higgins, their October book club selection and one of her favorite romances—even if it did remind her of Gray.

"Her sense of humor made her character likable for me," Elizabeth said.

"That definitely helped," Emma said. "But for me it was finding out about her mother. Those flashbacks were so heartbreaking. I wanted to give young Harper a big hug."

"And the way those wounds impacted her relationship with Nick. *Oh*." Margie pressed a hand to her ample bosom. "It just made so much sense. I could see their childhood hurts wreaking havoc on their marriage, and it just about killed me. I read it in one day and went through half a box of tissues."

"Did anyone else just want to grab Dennis by his little rattail braid and throw him off the wharf?"

"A little harsh there, Sherry, but yes. In the end he was just a big oaf standing in the way of true love."

"Can we just take a minute to swoon over Nick Lowery?" Lucy said.

The group seemed to draw in a deep breath and sigh as a whole.

Shelby couldn't blame them. The first time she'd read the story she'd only dreamed of finding a man like Nick. Ironically, that had been when Gray entered her life. After he left, it had taken her three full years to pick up another romance novel. Even now she rarely read one. She no longer craved the kind of over-the-moon, helplessly-in-love feeling those books depicted. She'd experienced the painful side of being madly in love, and it wasn't pretty. Now she mostly stuck to women's fiction, suspense, and the occasional memoir.

The group moved on to the last question and had plenty to say about the epilogue. She loved these discussions—the way everyone offered their opinions and brought insight and passion to the reading experience.

It always made her realize afresh that fiction was about so much more than entertainment. It offered readers a unique way to learn about themselves and others. The protagonist's journey illuminated a reader's own experiences, her own struggles.

And when she slipped into the skin of someone different from herself, she experienced compassion and understanding that translated to people around her. She became a more empathetic human being.

It made Shelby proud of what she did. She wasn't just a bookseller. She dealt in hope and healing. The warm glow of that reminder carried her through the club's wrap-up and good-byes. While the others headed out she stayed out back, tidying up after them, cognizant of her dreamy smile.

All was quiet inside as she stowed the chairs and turned off the yard lights. She stepped into the hall, frowning at the light burning behind the frosted glass of the office door.

A shadow moved behind the glass and the door swept open. Gray stepped out and came to a sudden halt within inches of her.

Shelby stepped back as her heart gave a heavy thump. She pressed a hand to her chest, startled to find him here so late. He always left at closing.

"Book club over?"

"Working late?" They spoke at the same time.

And answered at the same time. Their gazes locked. The air seemed to weave a spell around them.

She dragged her gaze away and swept past him. Her legs trembled as they carried her to the front where the space was brighter, less confining. Why did she let him fluster her so? It really ticked her off. This was her store, her domain. He was a guest here—uninvited at that, at least by her. She'd gotten over him years ago and he had no hold on her anymore.

He has no hold over me anymore.

"Who are you trying to convince, Sweet Girl?"

"Shelby? You have a minute?"

She squeezed her eyes closed as she approached the front door. It was past eight and she really just wanted to go home and soak in the tub with her Colleen Coble novel. "Can it wait till tomorrow?"

Chaucer, the store's unlikely mascot, sauntered past, gray tail high and flickering like a flag.

Gray stuffed his hands in his front pants pockets. "It can, but I'm not sure it should."

That sounded ominous. And the somber expression on his face didn't help matters. Dread inched its way up her spine. "Something wrong?"

"Maybe we can sit on the porch and talk a minute."

This didn't sound good. She didn't need bad news. Gram's passing—and let's face it, Gray's presence—had left her feeling vulnerable. But she'd never been one to bury her head in the sand, and she wasn't about to start now. "Let me shut off the lights and close up."

She went through the motions, bracing herself for whatever he was about to say. He'd better not be backing out of their deal. He'd signed those papers! He had to abide by the terms.

She locked up the store and found Gray leaning against the porch railing just outside the glowing cone of light.

She crossed her arms. "You can't get out of our deal, if that's what you're trying to do. The paperwork is ironclad. Mr. Greenwood made certain of it."

Something shifted in his face. "That's not what this is about."

Her lungs emptied. She could handle just about anything else. "What then? It's been a long day and I want to get home."

"Sorry to keep you. But I felt you should know sooner than later." He met her gaze. "I finished up the audit. Did you and your grandma discuss the store's finances?"

"A little. Some. Not really. She liked to handle that part, and as you know, that's not really my strong suit. Why? What's wrong?"

His gaze remained steady on hers, but she couldn't read his expression in the dimness. "The store's struggling financially. She never said anything?"

"Struggling?" That couldn't be true. "What are you talking about? We do solid business here. Do you know how many books we sell a week?"

"I know exactly how many. But there's a lot of overhead: rent, staff, utilities. It adds up."

A new thought occurred and Shelby shook her head. "The finances must be okay. Gram just gave me a raise a few months ago. She wouldn't have done that if we were struggling. You've done something wrong. You need to check your numbers again."

"I already did. There's no mistake. And your raise . . ." He broke eye contact. Palmed the back of his neck.

"What?"

He seemed to take forever to answer. "Your grandma took it out of her own salary."

That was ridiculous. "No, she didn't. I didn't even ask for the raise. It was her idea."

"I'm sorry, Shelby, but the same month you received an increase, she took a pay cut of the same amount."

Shelby shook her head. "She said it was past time for me to receive a salary increase because I'd assumed more responsibilities, plus inflation . . ."

But a conversation they'd had while sipping tea in Gram's kitchen came back to her. Shelby had mentioned the expensive repairs on her broken-down Mazda. She was fretting over it because the repairs had taken her entire nest egg.

How had she not put that together before—her personal financial woes and Gram's offer of a raise? If the store was in bad shape financially, that was exactly the kind of selfless thing Gram would've done.

Shelby's eyes burned. She pressed her fingertips to her temples, hoping to stem the tears. Her breaths came quick and hard. This couldn't be happening. The store was all she had. All she had left of Gram. She forced herself to ask the question. "How bad is it?"

He straightened from the railing, his expression softening. "Hey, listen. Maybe we should follow up on this in the morning. It's getting late and—"

"Like I could sleep after this! Tell me. I need to know what I'm dealing with here."

He sighed. "You're two months behind on rent and some other bills. There's very little money in the store account."

Behind on the rent? Very little money? "How much?"

"Two hundred twelve dollars and change."

Shelby gaped. "That can't be right."

"Unfortunately, it is."

"Could there be another account?"

"I've seen no evidence of that."

She cupped her forehead. Rent alone was steep. There wasn't enough to pay October's rent, much less the two months she was in arrears. And those other bills. Shelby wished she could take it out of her personal account, but she was still trying to rebuild from the Mazda repairs. In general, she barely got by, and she'd been okay with that. She'd chosen this job because of her passion for books, not because she ever expected to get rich.

But she did have to get by. And the store had to turn a profit—or at least break even—or she wouldn't have a job at all. Nor would all her booksellers. If she couldn't make rent, they were dead in the water. The building was owned by some out-of-state entity, so it wasn't as if she could beg a neighborly favor. "How long do I have?"

"Your lease says three months. They've sent a couple delinquent notices. I can call and explain the circumstances. The store has leased this space for years, so they might be willing to work with us through a difficult time."

"But if things are as bad as you say, how will I ever get out of the hole?" Her last words quivered with emotion. She bit down hard on her lip.

He took a step closer, lifted his hand, then dropped it as if realizing she wouldn't welcome his touch. "Listen, there's a lot you can do to turn things around. I have some ideas and I'm sure you will too. This isn't a hopeless situation."

"Really? Because it feels pretty hopeless to me, Gray. The store isn't earning enough to pay basic bills, and pretty soon we could lose the *building*. I could lose everything Gram worked for all these years." She was taking her anxiety out on him, but she couldn't even care.

He touched her arm. "Hey. This isn't your fault. And we're not gonna let that happen."

She flinched away. "There is no 'we' here. You'll be leaving now that you've done your part, and it'll be my problem. It's my business—my problem. So just leave, Gray. It's what you do best." She hitched her purse on her shoulder and fled down the steps before the tears burning her eyes trickled down her face.

Chapter 11

Eleven years ago

Shelby fumed as she placed the Nora Roberts novels on the New Fiction shelf. Giving Gray a ride home yesterday had been a huge mistake. He'd gotten under her skin and she couldn't even figure out why. He was just so . . . so *maddening*. So arrogant. Who did he think he was, calling her Little Miss Sunshine, disparaging her boyfriend, insulting her reading material?

Speaking of which, she'd gotten home last night only to discover her book was missing from her car. She'd planned to finish it last night, but no. Gray had stolen it, and that left her with nothing to do except play chess with her dad. She was terrible at the game, and her dad went on a tangent about his long-lost wife the way he did sometimes when he was sad and lonely. Shelby got it. Mom had deserted Caleb and her, too, after all. But at some point you had to move on. Boredom and the depressing topic had gotten the best of her—she ate two sleeves of Double Stuf Oreos and went to bed early.

And it was all Gray's fault because if Shelby had had her book, she would've been tucked away in her room, enjoying a satisfying happily ever after.

"You got some grudge against Nora, honey?" Gram's voice startled her from her thoughts. "You're damaging those dust jackets."

Perhaps she'd been shoving the hardcovers onto the shelves with a little too much vigor. "Sorry, Gram."

"Something on your mind?"

Gram seemed to have a soft spot for Gray, so complaining about him would hardly do any good. Besides, he wouldn't be hanging around the shop much longer. He was almost finished with the landscaping, and then he'd only mow once a week or so. "Nothing worth sharing."

"If you say so. Well, when you're done there, see if you can do something about that front table display, would you? It needs your artistic touch."

"I'll get right on it."

Ten minutes later she was rearranging the display near the window when Gray pulled up to the curb. So he'd fixed his truck. Good for him, because she wasn't offering him a ride home ever again. Even if the rumors about him weren't true, he sure didn't do himself any favors, going around exasperating people.

She waited until he was strutting up the sidewalk before she bounded down the stairs and exited the store. The July heat sucked the air from her lungs, but she was too focused on her mission to be distracted.

His eyes caught on her as he dropped his backpack on the grass. Then that cocky smile curved his lips.

She strode down the walkway. "Where is it?"

"Where's what?"

A family came up the sidewalk, heading toward the bookstore.

She moved aside to let the group pass. When they'd mounted the porch steps, Shelby turned back to Gray. "You stole my book from my car."

"Relax, Sunshine. I just borrowed it."

"Whatever for?"

"Even we Neanderthals can read, you know."

She huffed. Crossed her arms. "You expect me to believe you actually want to read a romance novel?"

"Not want to read. Already read." He withdrew the book from his book bag and gave the cover a once-over. "It's not Lee Child, but I'll admit it exceeded my expectations. That Harper chick was tough as nails, but man, did she have some issues. Nick was one patient dude. The bear scene was comical." He extended the book.

She took it, scrambling for a response. She stared at the book as if it might hold the key to eternal life.

"Cat got your tongue, Sunshine?"

Face warming, she met his gaze. "You expect me to believe you read the whole thing? In one night?"

"Well, I did stay up past midnight, but more or less. Even the touchy-feely stuff was well done. Good humor. And I appreciate a well-done character arc as much as the next guy. Don't worry, I won't spoil the ending since you're only on page 155." He shook his head and tsked. "Does your grandma know you dog-ear pages?"

She couldn't believe he'd read the entire book. Not only read it but wasn't denigrating it or playing it off like he was too masculine to appreciate something as insipid as love.

"Well, I can see I've shocked you. Either that or you're having heatstroke—a distinct possibility today."

Shelby didn't know what to say. Gray seemed to catch her off guard at every turn. She glanced back at the store. "I have to get back to work."

"That makes two of us." He grabbed a shovel and proceeded to spread mulch around the bushes. "Have a great day, Sunshine."

* * *

Gray stepped into his dad's old truck, put down the windows, and turned the key. It started with its usual unsteady rumble. The thing was well over a decade old and on its last legs. The air didn't work, which made a scorching day like today a real pain.

He'd finished his work at the bookshop for the day and then gone to his other part-time job at Lang's Hardware. Joe Lang wasn't exactly thrilled to be his boss. He'd stuck Gray in the garden center because no one else wanted to brave the heat. But Gray preferred working with the plants to encountering people who looked down their noses at him.

Plus it gave him time to think. And today he'd spent most of that time thinking about Shelby. Remembering the way she'd strode toward him this morning all hot and bothered brought a smile to his face every time. He loved that sassy side of her. And her obvious shock that he'd read her book was equally gratifying. Even if the story hadn't been pretty good, it would've been worth finishing just to knock her for a loop like that.

He stuck his elbow out the window as he turned onto Main Street, the heat licking his skin with a hot, sticky tongue. The sign for the Dairy Bar appeared ahead. It was almost suppertime, but the thought of something cold and refreshing had him slowing as he neared the entrance. He'd bring Granny her favorite—a strawberry shake with lots of whipped cream and a cherry.

Apparently he wasn't the only one willing to spoil his supper—the lot was half full. He pulled into a slot near the ordering window, shut off the engine, and jumped from his truck. He was nearly to the line when he spotted Shelby at one of the bright red picnic tables—along with Brendan, Devon, and Drew.

His gaze met Shelby's, locking for a solid five seconds. Then Brendan turned to see why she'd stopped licking her cone. His gaze followed hers, finding Gray, and his expression soured.

Gray's gut twisted. He wanted to turn right back around and leave. But Devon and Drew had also spotted him, and no way was Gray turning tail now. He got in the line.

"Hey, Briggs," Devon called. "Nice truck." A round of laughter followed.

Gray pretended he hadn't heard, but heat climbed his neck and settled in his face. He could handle being harassed, but having it happen in front of Shelby amplified the humiliation. Mostly he tried to avoid these situations, but he didn't see a graceful way out at this point.

"Looks like you got a pretty nasty scratch on it though."

"You can hardly see it for all the dents." More laughter rang out.

When he'd left the broken-down truck in town overnight, "someone" had keyed it on both sides. Should've known.

They were speaking too quietly now for him to make out their words, but judging by the occasional snickering, it was safe to say they were talking about him.

The couple in front of him moved aside and Gray stepped up and placed his order.

His first run-in with Brendan had been in sixth grade when he'd entered the boys' restroom to find him dumping Patrick Ballard upside down into the trash can. Gray pushed Brendan away and rescued Patrick. The poor guy, probably dying of humiliation, darted out of the restroom just as the fight ensued. Devon and Drew came to Brendan's rescue, and Mr. Willard came to see what all the ruckus was about.

Mr. Willard was Devon's uncle, so when the boys ended up in the principal's office, he believed the other boys' story. Despite Gray's insistence it was a lie. Ever since that fight, Brendan, Devon, and Drew had done their best to make his life miserable, and somehow they always got away with it.

It had been his first realization that he would never overcome his dad's trashy reputation. Normal kids with upstanding parents and money would always come out ahead here. And that sure hadn't changed when Dad was sentenced to sixteen years in prison. Even Gray's grandma's good name couldn't save him. She was aware of the challenges he faced, but he tried to downplay them as much as possible. She'd suffered enough with everything his dad put her through.

Drew's cackle broke into his reverie.

What was Shelby doing with these clowns? She was too good for the likes of Brendan. Not that Gray deserved her either.

At least they'd stopped calling out to him, but that was probably for her benefit. Brendan couldn't give away what a complete tool he was. Shelby might pretend to dislike Gray, but she wasn't cruel. She was the type to stand up for the downtrodden.

And let's face it, that was him right now.

"Chocolate malt, strawberry shake," the teen called.

"Thanks." Gray collected his order and headed toward his truck.

"You have a real good evening, Briggs," Devon called.

Laughter trailed him, making him grit his teeth.

The embarrassment lingered the whole ride home. He had to stop thinking so much about Shelby. He couldn't rescue her from those idiots any more than she could rescue him from this town. He'd do the latter part himself with that scholarship. For now he'd just finish his work at the bookshop and put all thoughts of Shelby Thatcher behind him.

* * *

Shelby resolutely kept her eyes inside the shop even if business was slow today. She'd been unboxing new arrivals, which put her in the front of the store—in sight of where Gray put his final touches on the landscaping.

Last time she checked he'd been dripping with sweat though it wasn't yet noon. She couldn't eradicate the image of his back muscles and biceps flexing as he shoveled mulch around the new shrubs.

He'd come into the store early on, but Shelby made herself scarce. She was mortified about the incident at the Dairy Bar yesterday. Brendan's friends had acted like a bunch of bullies. After she expressed disapproval Brendan made them stop, but initially he'd been laughing right along with them.

It seemed so out of character. He was such a gentleman with her. He said the sweetest things and always offered to help Gram or Dad when he came to the house. Sometimes it seemed he was a different person with his friends than he was with her. Which person was the true Brendan Remington?

She finished shelving the new Lisa Wingate novel. She'd had the chance to read the advance copy and was excited to hand sell it to readers. She already had it on hold for several regulars. As she began placing Lee Child's new release on an endcap, she couldn't help but remember a couple days ago when Gray had mentioned the author as they discussed Shelby's romance novel.

"It's not Lee Child, but I'll admit it exceeded my expectations."

Gray might be annoying, but at least he had good taste in literature. She placed the last book. But before she could withdraw her hand, she grabbed the hardcover edition and stared at the cover. Gray would probably love to read the new release.

Would he be able to afford it? As far as she knew he'd never come into the store to purchase books. Even if he couldn't afford it, his grandma would probably buy it for him—though Gray didn't seem like the type to ask for much.

There was always the library though. She placed the book back on the shelf.

Although a Lee Child novel would undoubtedly have a waiting list—possibly months long. But waiting wouldn't kill him, would it?

Her thoughts returned to the Dairy Bar. To the way his neck had flushed as Brendan's stupid friends poked fun at the old truck everyone knew had been his father's. He'd been silent and stoic. And even though she didn't partake in the harassment, she felt guilty by association.

She grabbed the book off the shelf and went to the checkout where she gave herself an employee discount and put her cash in the drawer. At the thought of handing him the gift, her heart trampled her lungs. She could just leave it in his truck—it was parked right in front of the store. He'd surely know it was from her, but she could live with that. She wanted him to have the book—a sort of peace offering.

She placed the novel in a brown paper bag and waited for an opportunity. Today would likely be his last day at the shop, so she didn't have much time. After today she'd only see him when he mowed, if then. When he took a lunch break, she had her chance.

* * *

Gray left the comfortable shade of the live oak and left the park. He preferred to be finished at the bookshop by lunchtime so he had time to go home and shower before his shift at the hardware store. He didn't dare show up late as Joe Lang would love an excuse to fire him. Gray wished he had other options. But he'd applied all over town for a summer job and only got that one because his grandma pulled in a favor.

He only had one more bed to mulch and the front of the store would be complete. He dumped his garbage as he passed a trash can. The store was only a block away, so it was a quick walk back.

On the way he mentally tallied the money adding up in his bank account. Even if he got that scholarship—and he would—he would incur other costs at college. It didn't cover books or lodging. But between what he'd saved this summer and what he'd make while working part-time at college, he should be able to swing it. He'd narrowed down his choices to three colleges: Vanderbilt, Rollins, and Appalachian State. All of them were close enough he could check in on his grandma regularly.

Granny had offered to take out a home equity loan for college, but he'd never allow that. She'd already taken him in when he had no place to go. And his dad had taken advantage of her generosity many times before he went to prison. Gray refused to be that kind of person.

If he was going to make something of himself—and he was—he'd do it on his own.

When he reached the bookstore he went back to work and finished just over an hour later. Miss Viola had said she'd settle up with him at the end of the week, so there was no reason to linger. He packed up his tools.

A few minutes later as he headed toward his truck, he thought of Shelby inside the store. They didn't exactly run in the same circles, and he'd miss those random encounters. The chance to push her buttons. He enjoyed getting her all riled up. It was so opposite to the sunny personality she normally exuded. He loved that she was such a paradox.

He dumped his tools in the truck bed, then opened the door to get in the cab. His gaze caught on something sitting on his hood. He frowned at the brown bag as he walked around the open door. It was leaning against the windshield, the top folded over several times.

A couple months ago someone had left a gift bag on their porch. He assumed it was for Granny from one of her friends and made the mistake of bringing it into the house. The stench quickly alerted him to his mistake. The bag was literally full of crap.

Gray surveyed the area for some clue as to who might've left today's "gift." A lady was headed into the bookshop. Miss Patsy was outside putting up sale signage for her boutique. Other than that, no one was around.

Gray returned his attention to the bag. He wasn't afraid of a little dog crap, but he wouldn't put it past Devon or Drew to gift him with a copperhead snake, and that could end badly.

He grabbed a rake from the bed and used the handle to knock the sack from the hood. It landed on the pavement with a thud. He watched it for a sign of movement but the bag remained still, so he set the rake aside, glancing around once again for anyone loitering. Seeing no one, he cautiously opened the sack, then widened its mouth.

Not smelling anything, he peeked inside. A book. He lifted the bag and pulled out a hardcover copy of Lee Child's new release—one he'd been anticipating.

His thoughts went back a couple of days to when he'd mentioned the author to Shelby. His gaze darted toward the second-story window. A shadow darted away. Or maybe that was just a trick of the light.

Recalling the spectacle he'd just made of himself, he hoped it was the latter. But as he got in the truck, still clutching the brand-new book, he could only think about one fact.

Shelby Thatcher had given him a gift.

It didn't even matter that she probably hadn't even had to pay for it. Or that it was likely some kind of guilt offering for the way her boyfriend and his minions had treated him the day before.

The only thing that mattered was that Shelby had remembered his love of the author and taken the time to do something kind for him. Interesting that she'd left it for him to find rather than giving it to him directly. Maybe she was afraid of making him feel like a charity case. Or maybe she was just too shy to . . . extend an offer of friendship? Was that what this was? He glanced at the book, the notion giving rise to a bubble of hope.

He scowled at his reaction. Ideas like that were sure to get him in trouble. But that didn't stop him from taking one last glance at the bookshop window as he pulled away.

Chapter 12

Present day

Gray's empty stomach churned as he headed slowly through town. There were a few places open on a Friday night, but he didn't feel like meeting with opposition. He'd make do with the frozen pizza he had at home.

He leaned an elbow out the window as he braked for a red light. The refreshing fall breeze carried the aroma of grilled burgers from Scully's Tavern. Tempting. But after that talk with Shelby about the store's finances, he was depleted. He felt somehow responsible even though that was unreasonable. He hadn't caused the problem, only discovered it. Still, the look on her face, the tremor in her voice . . . It about killed him. Made him long to *fix* it.

He still felt so protective of her. And also guilty for the heartache he'd caused in the past. He'd been meaning to bring that up. To beg her forgiveness. He'd been waiting for the right time. But his time was up and now she probably hated him even more.

The tavern door swung open, emitting loud rock music—and a dog exited with the help of the business end of a broom. "Scat! Get outta here." The door fell shut again.

The mutt scampered away, tail tucked. The medium-sized dog reminded him of Bullet, his childhood dog, with his light, long-haired coat and floppy ears. Dad hadn't allowed him inside the trailer, but Gray spent many hours playing with him in their small yard. Sometimes he seemed like Gray's only real friend.

The light turned green.

The dog wandered to the trash can near the beauty salon's entry and jumped up, sniffing the contents. How long had it been since the dog had a decent meal? Was his owner searching for him?

With a resigned sigh, Gray pulled his SUV to the side of the road. He shifted to Park, grabbed a beef stick from his glove compartment, and jumped out. As he neared the dog, he slowed. "Hey, buddy. How you doing? You hungry?" He peeled off the plastic and held out the beef stick.

The dog dropped to the ground, tail tucked, and lowered his head almost to the sidewalk. He seemed as if he wanted to sink right between the slabs of concrete. But he eyed the treat and licked his chops.

Gray sank to his haunches. "It's all right. I'm not gonna hurt you. Come here, I got a nice little snack for you."

The dog took two cautious steps forward, his eyes darting from the beef stick to Gray and back.

"That's it. It's all yours. Just come and get it."

The dog inched closer until he was near enough to snatch the treat from Gray's hand. It was gone in mere seconds.

Gray held out his hand for the dog to sniff. His fur was darker on his back and ears. "Where's your owner, huh, friend? You get lost?" But a quick scan revealed no collar.

The mutt dropped to the sidewalk and rolled over for a belly scratch. Gray chuckled, obliging. "A little treat and now you trust me, huh? Fair enough, I guess."

The poor guy could probably use some water. What should Gray do now? He couldn't just leave the dog wandering the streets where he was likely to get hit by a car. Maybe he had a microchip. It wouldn't be much trouble to take him home for the night and have him scanned in the morning.

He gave the dog one last belly scratch and stood. Would the dog follow? He had another beef stick in the glove compartment to coax him if necessary. But when he started back to the SUV, the mutt was right on his heels.

Gray glanced down at him. "We're buddies now, huh?"

The dog wagged his tail, gazing up at him with something like adoration.

"Don't be getting attached. I'm helping you find your family, that's *all*." He couldn't believe he was taking a dog back to Granny's house. He didn't even allow pets at the Airbnb. What a sucker. He shook his head as he opened the passenger door and let the dog jump inside. He was just closing it when flashing lights caught his attention.

A police cruiser approached, its blue and red lights strobing silently. The car pulled up behind his vehicle.

Unease leached into his blood as Gray met the uniformed policeman between the vehicles. The officer appeared to be in his upper thirties with broad shoulders, a shaved head, and a stonelike expression. Close-spaced eyes and a prominent brow line gave him an eagle-like appearance. "Can I help you, Officer . . ." He glanced down at the man's badge—*Remington*. His stomach bottomed out. Great.

"Are you aware you're parked in a fire lane?"

Gray glanced at the red-painted curb beside his SUV. "I'm not really parked as my vehicle is still running. I just stopped for a minute to—"

"Whether or not your SUV is running is irrelevant, as is your reason for parking there. Have a seat in your vehicle."

Gray pressed his lips together as their gazes locked. The officer knew exactly who Gray was. He really had no choice in the matter. Anyway, it was just a measly parking ticket. Hardly enough to get up in arms about.

He returned to his SUV where the dog waited, head hanging out the driver's-side window. When Gray opened the door, the dog jumped into the passenger seat and sat, regarding him expectantly.

"You're gonna cost me at least fifty bucks, pal. I hope your owners appreciate it."

Gray glanced in his rearview mirror. The cop seemed in no hurry. No doubt he'd draw this out as long as possible. Now that Gray had a minute to reflect, he recognized the man as Mason, Brendan's older brother. Not only had Gray's dad killed their uncle, but of course Gray had stolen Brendan's girl.

Then there was the whole test scandal. When news of that went public, Gray felt he had no choice but to leave. Then the town added *broke Shelby's heart* to the list of his sins. He just couldn't win.

He glanced in his rearview mirror. Didn't seem to matter that all of that was eons ago.

Tired of dwelling on the past, Gray pulled out his phone and answered a few texts from Gavin and Eric about the fiber-cement siding for a difficult customer. Long minutes later, at the sound of a closing car door, he set down his phone.

Mason Remington swaggered up beside his SUV.

"From what I can figure, your two weeks in Grandville are about up, Briggs."

Gray regarded him silently. He had nothing to add. No reason to engage.

"It's time for you to hightail it out of town. Nobody wants you here."

"That a threat?"

"Just a little friendly advice." Mason flicked the ticket at him, a sneer curling his mouth. "Consider this our little parting gift."

Chapter 13

"Know what, pal? You reek." Gray carried the mangy mutt into the guest bathroom and set him down inside the claw-foot tub.

The dog quivered, his tail tucked between his legs, head down, gazing up at Gray with pitiful eyes.

"Sorry, gotta be done." He pulled the curtain around them and turned on the shower. The dog scrambled, attempting to leap out, but Gray held him still. "No way, buddy. You're not staying tonight unless we get that stench off you."

As the water rained down, Gray got the dog good and wet, then lathered him up with Dove shampoo. His coat was matted and the water beneath his paws ran brown with dirt for a good five minutes. How long had this guy been lost?

Some family would be relieved to get their pet back. At least, that's what he told himself as he struggled to scrub the ungrateful dog. When he finished rinsing, he shut off the faucet and the mutt gave a big shake, spattering Gray with water.

It was late by the time he finally settled in bed with the biography he'd brought from home—*The Accidental President*. He glanced down at the dog, who hadn't left his side for two seconds. Even when Gray had taken his own shower, the dog waited right by the tub. Gray had fed him leftovers from the café and set down a big bowl of water that he lapped right up.

Now the dog was curled beside his bed, making some kind of huffing noise in his sleep. He'd tried to jump into bed with Gray, but that's where he drew the line. The area rug would have to do. And apparently the lack of bedding hadn't impeded the dog's slumber. He'd fallen asleep seconds after Gray retired. Was probably exhausted. What a journey the runt must've had.

He stared at the words on the page, but his thoughts returned to Shelby and the bookstore. It was time for him to leave Grandville. But how could he leave her with the store's finances in such a mess? The memory of those tears welling up in her eyes was like a sucker punch. She was in the throes of grieving her grandma and now she had to face the possibility of losing the store.

But the thing was, that store could be saved. He saw a clear path to profitability if Shelby was willing to make some changes. And it wasn't as if she had much choice at this point.

If he could just stay for a while, get the business turned around and profitable through the critical holiday season, Shelby would be set on a solid path for the future. But he'd need at least a couple months. He hated to beg Gavin for more time off. Would he even be amenable to that? They weren't overly busy now, but come the first of January, they'd be dried in on several big projects and the interior workload would keep Gray busy.

The Airbnb had a few bookings, but thankfully it was low season. He could find them comparable places on the lake.

But would Shelby even agree to let him help? She'd barely tolerated his presence these past two weeks. She had her walls up—no surprise. Was she desperate enough to save the shop to put up with him for an extended period of time?

Her family surely wouldn't like the idea. They wore their aversion to him like a neon sign. Caleb had stopped in three times over the past couple of weeks, checking on his sister. Her dad had made an appearance this week also. They weren't exactly subtle. Not that Gray could blame them.

He thought of his confrontation with Officer Remington and the man's veiled threat. Shelby's relatives weren't the only ones who wouldn't be too pleased if Gray stayed on.

But he'd never been one to back down out of fear.

He made up his mind. He'd talk to Shelby first. If she was willing to let him help, he'd request a leave of absence.

The dog sat at Gray's feet in the veterinary lobby, trembling. Every so often, he turned pathetic eyes up at Gray. Clearly the mutt was getting some bad vibes from this place. Or maybe he could just smell the fear rolling off the quivering Chihuahua across the way.

"Grayson, you can go on back to room two," the receptionist said.

He stood and led his canine friend with the makeshift leash—a rope from the back of his SUV. The room was down a short hall, first one on the left. He entered and took a seat in one of the plastic bucket chairs. The dog jumped into his lap and, Gray suspected, would've taken refuge inside him if that were possible.

"Geez, calm down, buddy. This'll be quick and painless, and then you'll be reunited with your family."

The dog tucked his nose in Gray's armpit.

"Get out of there, weirdo."

The dog settled for licking him on the cheek.

While they waited Gray read the posters on the walls. He'd just about exhausted his reading materials when the door opened.

The man who entered was about his age with brown eyes and a fadeaway haircut. He wore a white lab coat and had a toothpaste-commercial smile. "Hi, I'm Dr. Patrick." His eyes narrowed in recognition. "Gray Briggs?"

Great, the guy knew him. Or maybe just knew of him, as Gray didn't recognize him. Tensing, Gray stood to shake his hand—and hopefully make the best of the situation. "Thank you for seeing us on such short notice."

Dr. Patrick was still smiling. "You don't recognize me. I'm Patrick Ballard. We were in the same class at Grandville Middle until my parents moved me to Emanuel in eighth grade."

Patrick Ballard—the guy he'd once rescued from a trash can. Gray's muscles relaxed and he widened his smile. "Yeah, man. Sorry, I didn't recognize you."

Patrick gave him a wry glance. "Braces, contacts, and a healthy diet."

"Well, you look great."

"Thanks. I'd heard you were back in town. I sure hated to miss Viola's funeral, but I had an emergency call." He squatted down and held out his hand for the dog. "Hey there, buddy. I hear you might be lost." He glanced at Gray. "I don't recognize him. Cute little guy though. Seems like a terrier mix."

The canine sniffed his hand and gazed up at him with that familiar woeful look.

"Well, let's get you up on the table and see if you're chipped."

Gray lifted the reluctant dog onto the table and comforted him with a few strokes behind the ears while Patrick grabbed a scanner from the countertop.

"What have you been up to since you left town?" Patrick asked.

"I did three years in the Army, then went to UNC for my bachelor's in business. I'm a project manager and bookkeeper with a construction company in Riverbend Gap."

"That's great. I always wondered what became of you."

"The local grapevine didn't keep you up to speed?"

He ran the scanner over the dog. "Yeah, that's about as accurate as the supermarket tabloids."

"It's good to see you doing well. A veterinarian. That must've taken a lot of schooling."

"And student loans, I'm afraid. But I wouldn't trade it." He set the scanner down and scratched the dog behind the ears. "Well, I'm afraid this guy's not chipped."

Gray's spirits drooped. "Not what I was hoping to hear." Now what would he do? He'd thought of getting a dog one day when his work absorbed less of his time or he got married and had a family. He'd definitely been thinking something a little manlier: a black Lab or a German shepherd.

Patrick was already checking the dog's chest with the stethoscope. After that he palpated the neck and abdomen. Checked his paws, his ears. A few minutes later he gave the dog a good scratch. "Good job, buddy. Well, he's a little thin but he's bright and alert and seems to be in pretty good health overall. You thinking about taking him back home with you?"

"I really hadn't thought beyond returning him to his owners. I'm staying at my lake cottage, which is now an Airbnb. I don't even allow my guests to bring pets. I don't suppose you'd know someone who might like to adopt him?"

"Sadly, there's an overabundance of dogs in the area, which is why I recommend spaying and neutering. How long will you be in town?"

"That's a little up in the air right now."

"Well, if you could foster him for a bit, I could keep my eyes open for a good home. He'd make someone a great pet."

Gray sighed as he scooped up the dog and set him on the floor. He really had no idea whether he'd be driving home later today or settling in for a couple months. But it seemed like he was stuck with the dog, at least for the time being.

"I'd appreciate that. Thanks. I'll let you know if I end up going back home sooner than later."

"Sounds good." Patrick extended his hand. "I'll give you a call if I find a home for this guy. And hey, if you stay awhile we should grab coffee, catch up."

Gray shook his hand, smiling at the thought. "That'd be great, Patrick."

Chapter 14

Shouts, laughter, and the clamor of crashing pins dominated the Lakeview Lanes Bowling Alley, but Shelby was a million miles away. Or really only a few miles away, back at Gram's bookstore.

Gram's dying bookstore.

The pizza she and Logan had eaten earlier churned in her stomach. The store had been busy today. It was hard to reconcile that with the news Gray had delivered last night.

How was she going to turn things around quickly enough to save the store? Even if she could get a couple months' grace from her landlord, how would she ever catch up on rent? She had yet to even read Gray's tutorials on keeping the books. And her efforts to find someone to take Gram's place had been futile so far.

Gray must've taken her at her word and gone home—she hadn't heard from him all day. That he'd left without so much as a good-bye should've come as no surprise. But somehow it had left her feeling abandoned yet again.

So much for all that therapy.

And now she would face a failing business all by herself. How like him to dump the terrible news and leave her to deal with the fallout.

"*You actually told him to leave, Shelby. And you were quite direct about it.*" It was Gram's voice in her head. But for once she didn't want her grandma's input.

The sound of applause broke through her reverie. Logan had just bowled his third strike in a row. She added a belated whoop as their gazes connected, and she hoped he hadn't noticed her lack of attention.

On his way back to his seat, he stopped to chat with a teammate and she settled back in her chair, sipping her Diet Coke. The smells of pizza and floor wax permeated the building. She'd become familiar with the aroma since she'd begun dating Logan, who was loyal to his Saturday night bowling league.

Moments later he dropped into the seat beside her, beaming. "You must be my good luck charm."

"You're having a great night."

"The whole team is. We'll definitely make the playoffs this year. I even like our chances for the championship."

"That would be amazing." Shelby was new to the bowling scene, but it was something Logan loved so she was trying to be supportive. Though his efforts to teach her to bowl had only proven she had no natural skill at the sport.

Her phone vibrated in her pocket and she checked the screen. "It's Caleb. I should get this." She made her way toward the exit as she picked up the call. "Hey, how's it going?" she called over the racket.

A beat of silence passed. "Are you at a bowling alley?"

"Logan's in a league. I'm heading outside. There, that's better. Everything okay?"

"Depends what you mean by okay. I've been going through Gram's papers and found out she took out a home equity loan five years ago that she hasn't paid back. You know anything about that?"

"An equity loan? For how much?"

"Forty grand."

Shelby pressed her hand to her chest. *"What?"*

"You heard right. I don't get it. Why would she have done that?"

"I—I don't know." Unless the store was even worse off than she thought. Had Gram been dipping into her reserves to keep the store afloat? She should tell Caleb what she'd learned. But he distrusted Gray and would recommend she hire someone else to do an external audit—like she could afford that. The thought of dealing with another conflict made her temples throb.

"I've been stewing over this all day—didn't want to bother you at work. Liddy wondered if maybe she could've been scammed."

"Like, phishing or something?"

"Unless you have some idea where that money could've gone, I don't know what else to think. It's not like Gram bought a new vehicle or took that trip to Ireland she always talked about."

Shelby didn't want to think about what it might mean. She needed to look through the store's records and see if she could figure this out. She hated to hope Gram had been scammed, but it actually seemed better than the alternative. If Gram had taken money from the house and put it into the store, would Shelby owe her brother forty grand? Her stomach turned to lead at the thought.

"Are you there?" Caleb said.

"Yeah. Let me do a little digging and I'll let you know if I find anything."

Two hours later Shelby sat pretzel style on the office floor knee-deep in records, skimming the building's lease. Seeing the triple-net lease agreement jogged her memory. The bookstore was responsible for all building maintenance, and five years ago their roof had begun leaking. By the time they noticed it, a lot of damage had already been done. The roof and sheeting had to be replaced.

Had Gram taken out an equity loan to pay for it? The timing would suggest so.

Shelby planted her elbows on her knees and covered her face. *Oh, Gram. Why didn't you tell me things were this bad?* She just wanted to cry. But she was too distressed to do so. She had to make a plan, but she didn't even know where to start.

Her strengths were curating the book selection, selling books, staffing the store, and training booksellers. Why hadn't she taken the time to learn Gram's end of the business?

Because she'd been dreading it. And because neither of them ever dreamed she was so short for this earth.

You were supposed to live to a hundred, Gram. I need you here. Now the tears came. Because she missed her grandma's cackling laughter. Missed her blunt manner and her sweet encouragement. Most of all she missed the way Gram had believed in her.

Because right now Shelby felt completely unequipped for the task at hand.

Chaucer slunk into the room and sidled against her knee. The cat's rare show of affection made the lump in Shelby's throat swell. It was as if he knew she was missing Gram and wanted to offer comfort.

Shelby set her hand on his sleek back, feeling the ridges of his spine as he passed by. "You miss her too, don't you?"

Chaucer meowed on his way back out the door.

"I know just how you feel."

A knock sounded from far away. Who'd be knocking on the front door at this hour of the night? Maybe her brother. She wiped her face and pushed to her feet. The light from the office lit her way as she headed to the door.

As she neared the entrance she caught sight of a familiar figure standing in the exterior light under the store's canopy. But it wasn't Caleb.

It was Grayson Briggs—who apparently hadn't left town after all.

Chapter 15

Great. Just what she needed—her ex-boyfriend seeing her in despair yet again. She unbolted the door and jerked it open. "Aren't you supposed to be gone by now?"

His gaze sharpened on her face, no doubt taking in her racoon eyes. "What's wrong?"

She gave a mirthless laugh. "Are you kidding me? Gram's gone forever, the bookshop's a financial disaster, and now I probably owe my brother forty grand. Other than that, things are fan-freakin'-tastic."

"Forty grand?"

She gave a sigh that seemed to come from the depths of her soul. "What do you want, Gray?"

"I was passing by on my way home. Saw your car and the light."

"Yeah, well, I'm finished up and I just want to—" Her gaze dropped to a dog that edged closer to Shelby, tail wagging warily. Her heart softened at the hopeful gleam in those brown eyes. "You have a dog?" A pet seemed like an awfully big commitment.

"Nah, he's lost—or maybe abandoned. Don't suppose you'd want to take him in."

"My apartment doesn't allow pets. He should be on a leash."

"He hasn't wandered farther than three inches from my side since I found him."

She could hardly take her feelings for Gray out on the cute little pup. She squatted and let him sniff her hand. Then he jumped up and licked her face, evoking a smile. "Hi, buddy. You're a friendly guy." It was kind of nice to be adored for nothing more than being present. "Where'd you find him?"

"In town last night, scavenging for food. I took him to the vet this morning, but he's not chipped."

"Patrick Ballard?" That was where they took Chaucer. Patrick was also a customer and would read just about anything but sci-fi. "He's great. Why don't you just keep the dog?"

"I'm not really in the market."

"Well, I'm not in the market for a failing bookshop, but here we are." She gave the dog a final scratch and stood, pinning Gray with a suspicious look. "Is he the reason you're still here?"

His eyes roved her face. Those eyes were like a blue flame and she was about to melt under the heat. She squirmed. Crossed her arms.

"I have a proposition for you, Shelby."

The low hum of his voice rumbled down her spine. She smirked to cover his effect on her. "This is getting to be a habit."

"You need to turn this place around, and I'm sure you have ideas about how to do that. I do too. I have experience implementing changes for profitability. I know your financials and can help you get comfortable with the POS system."

She was betting this "help" came at a price. Probably a share of the store—possibly the 49 percent he'd just signed back over to her. Too good to be true. She notched her chin up. "And what do you receive in return, pray tell?"

His perceptive eyes took her in and no doubt read her every thought. "This shop was Miss Viola's pride and joy—her second story. And according to her, this is where you belong."

"Is that why she willed half of it to you?"

"We both know why she did that."

Shelby tore her gaze from his. She hadn't exactly cooperated in his reconciliation efforts.

"Because you're too stubborn for your own good, young lady."

You know, Gram, you could take my side for once.

"I am on your side. You're just too stubborn to see it."

Shelby shook her grandmother's voice from her head.

"You deserve to carry on her legacy. She would've wanted you to run this place for as long as you desire."

"So your motive is purely altruistic?" Her voice teemed with skepticism.

His steady gaze cut right through her. "Believe it or not, I loved your grandma. I care about what she wanted."

His sincerity made her twitch with guilt. Just because he hadn't loved Shelby didn't mean he was incapable of loving others. The thought stung.

Regardless, she wasn't at all sure she could pull the shop out of this downward spiral on her own. Gray's offer was tempting, even if it meant putting up with him for a longer period of time. Speaking of which.

"How long are you talking about? And what about your job? Surely you're needed back home."

"I'll be honest, that might be an issue. I haven't spoken with my boss yet. But if you're willing to take my help, I'll ask him for the time off. The Christmas season is coming up. If we implement some changes and have a profitable holiday, I think we can get things back on track."

"What kinds of changes?"

"There's actually a lot we can do. I'd start with a website, then expand the sideline inventory: puzzles, stationery, literary-themed clothing and hats. I know reading is your passion, but there's a higher profit margin in sidelines. Now's a great time with the holidays coming up. We can do some thoughtful rearranging and stock more of the genres that are selling better right now—romance and fantasy and also the classics. In general, the inventory could use some refreshing. If it isn't selling, it needs to go.

"We could do a better job of utilizing social media. And we should build up your email database. You have a lot of loyal customers, and email is the cheapest, most effective way of reaching your customers with special offers and sales.

"Speaking of cheap . . . It seems there are a lot of books given away for this or that cause or charity. I love your generous spirit, but you should hold off on donations for a while. And I understand why you give the book clubs a discount, but it's too steep. You're losing your margin."

Ouch. Her book club members were some of her most loyal customers. And people hit her up weekly for donations.

"I know it won't be easy, but we can turn this place around, Shelby."

He had some sound ideas. She had some of her own but didn't know which ones would actually increase profitability. And she couldn't afford to take risks when the store was on the verge of disaster.

Shelby thought of the forty-thousand-dollar equity loan and winced. He might as well know the full extent of the situation. "Things might be worse than you think." She told him what Caleb had discovered and her suspicions about the roof.

"I'll investigate that. Go further back in the records and see if that's where things went off the rails."

He was so much smarter than folks around here gave him credit for. They'd studied together—back when they couldn't keep their hands off each other long enough to focus. Just the memory of those stolen kisses and tender touches warmed her through.

Two months of Gray Briggs? Terrible idea.

And yet, what choice did she have? She didn't possess the skill set to turn this store around. Hadn't even found Gram's replacement yet. "I obviously can't afford to pay you."

"I'm not looking for compensation. I just want to do right by Miss Viola." He regarded her for a long moment. "If I can get the time off, will you let me help?"

Shelby took in those sculpted cheekbones and deep-set eyes, staring so steadily. Her heart waved a red flag, but her brain screamed that she—and the bookshop—was sunk without him. She hated to admit it even to herself, but she needed his help.

Having him in close proximity was a real risk. She'd just have to keep those walls good and high. He'd slipped through the cracks before, but she was older and wiser now. Knew how to protect herself.

Still, her heart tremored as she submitted to the plan. "All right. If you can get a leave from work, I'll accept your offer."

A flicker of something flared in his eyes. Relief? Satisfaction? "Good. I really believe we can turn things around."

"I sure hope so." Because if they didn't, Gram's dream would go up in smoke—and Shelby's future with it.

Chapter 16

Eleven years ago

Rain chased away the remnants of fireworks hanging in the night air. Thunder rumbled in the distance, and the wipers of Brendan's BMW worked double time as Shelby stewed in the passenger seat.

What was supposed to have been a romantic viewing of the fireworks over the lake had turned into a spontaneous party with Brendan's friends. Or maybe not so spontaneous. She suspected her boyfriend had invited the others. The secluded beach became a party scene: loud music, beer, making out.

But she hadn't made out with Brendan, and at this point he wouldn't even receive a good-night kiss.

She glanced down at her new sundress, the one she'd been saving for. What a waste. She'd wanted an evening alone where she and Brendan could talk. After almost seven weeks of dating, she still didn't feel as if she knew him very well. She was tired of his cronies hanging around all the time. Tired of their bad influence and arrogance.

"You should go to the party with me," Brendan said.

She'd only been to one party at Drew's house, and it had gotten out of hand. "Not tonight. I'm tired and I have to work in the morning."

A lone figure appeared ahead on the roadside. Their headlights caught on a white tee and drenched dark hair.

Grayson.

He passed in a blur. Shelby whipped around.

"It'll be a lot of fun. Drew's parents are out of town and everyone's coming."

"Wasn't that Gray Briggs?"

"What?"

"That was Gray back there, walking on the side of the road."

"So? Why don't you want to come to the party? Your curfew's not for another hour and you don't have to be up that early for work. Just come hang out for a little while."

Gray's truck must've broken down again, and he was still several miles from home. "We should give him a ride."

"Like I'd let that lunatic around my girlfriend. He'd probably take us down to the gravel pit and they'd never find our bodies."

Shelby rolled her eyes. She wasn't so sure anymore that Gray deserved his reputation. From what she'd seen he took a lot of abuse and showed a great deal of restraint. She hadn't seen him since she'd left that book on his truck a week ago.

But there was no sense arguing with Brendan. Anyway, Gray would probably rather walk home in the rain than accept a ride from him. She couldn't really blame the guy. She turned back around in her seat.

"Come on, Shelby. Go to the party with me. Don't be such a killjoy."

Shelby sighed. "Just take me home, Brendan."

Shelby waited just inside the front door as Brendan's taillights faded into the distance. Her dad and brother hadn't noticed her arrival. They were too busy arguing in the living room.

"You've got a full year in. Why would you quit school now?"

"Because it's not what I want, Dad. How many times do I have to tell you that?"

"Grandville U has a wonderful art program. I could get you in. You need an education before you pursue an art career. Do you have any idea how competitive that field is?"

"Thanks for the vote of confidence. I have a once-in-a-lifetime opportunity and I'd be stupid to turn it down."

"Some friend in a gallery? That's not an opportunity; it's a sidenote. If you want to pursue a career in art, you need—"

Shelby slipped outside and dashed down the porch steps through the deluge to her car. Those two had been at it all summer. If she needed additional motivation to head back out into the night, that was plenty enough. She was tired of playing man in the middle with them. She saw both sides. But ultimately it was Caleb's life, his decision.

She jumped into the car, soaked to the skin and shivering despite the warm temperature. She started the vehicle and pulled from the drive, recalling the way Brendan had pulled to a stop moments ago in front of her house.

"It's pouring down rain. No sense in both of us getting drenched."

She pulled onto the street. "No sense, indeed. Never mind that we just left a guy walking by the side of the road in this storm."

She pressed on the accelerator, wanting to reach him more quickly. Turned up the windshield wipers, which squeaked and shuddered against the glass.

She recalled Gray's strange reaction to the gift she'd left on his truck last week. He'd knocked the bag to the ground like he thought it might strike him dead. What other "gifts" had been left for him that he was so suspicious?

Maybe Gray could be irritating and arrogant. But those weren't crimes. Knowing others had treated him so poorly hurt her heart.

According to his grandma, he'd been judged unfairly all his life. And of course his own grandmother would defend him. But Gram was a good judge of character, and she'd trusted him enough to hire him at the bookshop.

Through the years Shelby had heard plenty about Gray's mean streak. About his laziness and his devil-may-care attitude. She'd always bought into it, at least to some degree. Heaven knew his dad's actions had done nothing to recommend the family.

But gossip was often exaggerated or completely fictitious. And nothing she'd observed from Gray so far suggested any of it was true. He was hardly lazy. He'd worked hard at the store in the oppressive heat and even had another job at the hardware store. A troublemaker wouldn't have ignored Brendan's friends when they berated him at the Dairy Bar.

And she couldn't forget the way he'd stared down at the book in his hands like he couldn't believe someone had left him a gift. For the first time she wondered how it might feel to be him, raised motherless on the wrong side of town by an alcoholic dad who landed himself in prison. Taken in by his grandmother, looked down upon by his peers.

Was Gray the real victim here?

Her headlights caught sight of him just up ahead, walking toward her. She let off on the gas and slowed to a stop beside him.

He kept walking.

She put her window down an inch. "Gray! Hop in!"

"No thanks," he called over the downpour.

Pressing her lips together she swung the car around in the middle of the deserted road. The poor turning radius required a three-point turn. Water dripped down the back of her dress, which clung to her like a second skin. Her wet sandal squeaked as it slipped on the gas pedal.

Gray's long legs had eaten up quite a distance. She advanced till she came alongside him and lowered the passenger window. Rain poured in. "Don't be so stubborn. You're getting soaked."

"Go to your party, Sunshine."

"Do I look like I'm heading to a party?"

He spared her a glance as the car chugged along beside him. The wipers' rhythmic *squeak-slap* sounded over the rain.

"Guess I'll just follow you home then. Might as well. Got nothing better to do."

He kept walking.

Rain poured through the window. Lightning flashed. Thunder cracked. "Do you have a death wish?"

His white shirt was nearly transparent, his tanned skin showing through. The material clung to the curves of his biceps and the flat ridges of his stomach. Beads of water dripped down the thick column of his throat.

"You're ruining the upholstery on my car. It's Italian leather. Worth a fortune. Cost me a ton of money to replace it."

At the bald-faced lies he stopped and regarded her with a mock scowl.

She applied the brakes and checked her rearview mirror to make sure a car wasn't approaching. "Stop being so stubborn and get in already. I can have you in a warm shower in five minutes flat."

He lifted a brow as a teasing light flickered in his eyes.

Her body temperature increased by ten degrees. "You know that's not what I meant. Get in the car already, Grayson Briggs."

After a long pause he opened the passenger door and slid inside. Then he closed it and put up the window, shutting out the storm's noise.

The sudden hush and his large presence seemed to shrink the coupe in half. Her heart thumped in her chest as she accelerated. "There's a blanket in the back."

He reached behind the seat and grabbed the blanket she'd last used for a picnic with Brendan. That date hadn't gone according to plan either. A Braves game, live streaming on his phone, usurped his attention.

Gray was easing the blanket beneath him.

"You might as well dry off with it. The seats are beyond repair."

He started with his hair, then dried his face, neck, and arms. She tried not to think about those arms. What did he do to achieve muscles like that? He didn't play sports at school and he wasn't a gym rat. If he stepped foot in there, the jocks in the weight room would harass him to death.

"Did your truck break down again?"

"Over on Halverson. Thought the repair would get me by for a while."

Halverson. His old neck of the woods. Darcy Colbert lived over that way. It was no secret Gray and Darcy hung out. She probably had a great view of the fireworks from her place. "You and your girlfriend watch the fireworks together?"

He tossed the blanket into the back seat and caught her eye for a split second. "Jealous?"

She rolled her eyes. "The ego on you. It's called making conversation. It's what polite people do. They also thank each other for gifts."

"You gave me a gift?" He raised an eyebrow.

"You know I did. I almost gave you a romance novel since you enjoyed the other one so much." Somehow her words came out smooth and effortless, even though her respiration struggled to keep up with her heart.

"Saw you pass by with your boyfriend a while ago."

She smirked. "Jealous?"

"He doesn't deserve you."

Her gaze caught on his at the honest assessment. A zap of electricity held her captive for a long moment. The current sizzled between them with a low hum.

She jerked her attention back to the wet pavement. She didn't bother asking what he meant. Didn't necessarily want to hear the answer. She was beginning to draw her own conclusions about Brendan anyway.

"No comment?" he said when she remained silent.

"That's a matter of opinion, I guess."

"If you say so."

She drove on, not needing directions. The last time she'd brought him home she'd sworn never again. And here she was just a week and a half later doing the same thing. And gifting him with a book.

What is it about this guy?

She just felt bad for him, that was all. He'd gotten a raw deal. He was misjudged or at the very least the victim of exaggerated gossip. He didn't deserve to be talked about and harassed by his peers.

That didn't really explain why her hands were shaking as she turned the wipers down a notch. Or why butterflies the size of pelicans fluttered about her stomach.

She gave him a sideways glance. Okay, yes, he was . . . appealing. Plenty of girls at school gave Gray a once-over when he passed in the halls. It was the allure of the forbidden. Gray was the town bad boy and certain girls were attracted to that.

Not Shelby though.

The quiet inside the car grew oppressive. She made a right turn as she searched for some neutral topic of conversation. "My grandma likes the landscaping you did. She'd been wanting to get that done since she opened the shop."

He sent her a smirk. "Atta girl—a nice safe subject. I knew you'd find one."

She pressed her lips together. It was downright irritating the way he read her mind sometimes. "What do you want from me?"

"How 'bout something that matters, Sunshine? Tell me something real."

"You *bother* me."

The corner of his lip curled up. "There you go. What else?"

"I don't know. Why don't you choose the topic since you seem to know what we should be talking about."

"All right then. How about this—we have something in common, Shelby Thatcher."

"What? I bother you too?"

He let out a low chuckle. "Well, yes, you do, now that you mention it."

He made it sound like *bothering* might be a good thing. A warm flush crawled up her neck and into her cheeks. Thank God it was dark.

"But that's not what I was referring to."

And of course, with that leading statement, he just went quiet. She rolled her eyes. Shifted in her seat, suddenly twitchy. *"And . . . ?"*

"I was talking about our childhoods. We both grew up without mothers. That's not exactly common."

Shelby turned onto his street. Gray's mother had died in a car accident when he was little, back when his family lived in Tennessee. They'd moved to be near his grandma because his dad was suddenly raising a young boy alone. "I'm sorry that happened to you. Children shouldn't have to grow up motherless. I guess we do have that in common, even if the circumstances are very different."

"Because your mom's still living?"

Maybe or maybe not. "No, because your mom died and my mom chose to leave us."

"My mom might've died in an accident, but she wrecked because she was drunk. So the argument could be made that she had a choice in the matter."

Oh. The grapevine had been silent on that one. Shelby's heart twisted. "I didn't know that."

"She and my dad were both alcoholics. They met at AA, which is pretty ironic since alcohol ended up wrecking both their lives."

All their lives. Gray hadn't exactly gone unscathed. She could hardly believe he'd brought up the topic. He was such a lone wolf. He didn't chat with friends and he certainly didn't divulge his deepest secrets to girls he hardly knew.

She slowed the car and turned into his grandma's drive. The lights were off except for the one on the porch. Behind the house, a bloom of green exploded over the lake despite the rain.

She put the car in Park.

He unbuckled his belt and turned to regard her with his steady gaze. "Why'd your mom leave you guys?"

No one had ever asked her that. Maybe because word had quickly spread around town back then so people already knew. "According to my dad she wanted to be an actress, a big Hollywood star—like that was going to happen. She regretted getting married so young and getting saddled with kids—my words, not Dad's."

"How old were you?"

"Seven."

"You remember her then?"

"Vaguely. She used to make pancakes on Saturday mornings. And she had a really pretty voice. She used to sing to me. And she smelled like sunshine and cotton. Sometimes I smell her when I'm doing laundry." The memories, though old and tarnished, put a knot in her throat. "What about you? Do you remember your mom?"

"Nah." His hands rested on his thighs. Nice strong hands with squared fingertips. "I was only two when she died. My dad never stopped loving her though. Did you ever hear from your mom?"

"She sent some postcards when we were younger. I kept them on a corkboard in my room and reread them until I had them memorized. They had these scenes from California and some generic drivel on the back about what a great time she was having. Like she was on vacation or something. I kept thinking she'd come home."

"When did you realize she wouldn't?"

"I guess when I was about twelve. We hadn't heard from her in a couple years, and one day I just grabbed every postcard off that board and chucked them in the garbage. I decided then and there if she wasn't thinking about me, I wasn't going to waste time pining after her."

"Adults can sure make some stupid decisions."

No doubt. And though they'd both grown up without a mom, Shelby had at least had a steady, loving father while Gray's dad's poor choices had landed him in prison.

Childhoods could vary drastically, from idyllic to uneventful to downright traumatic. The playing fields were unlevel, leaving some children so disadvantaged. Including Gray. The thought planted a dull ache in her chest. "I'm sorry for all you've been through." She set a hand over his. She'd meant it as a gesture of comfort. But the instant their bodies connected, it turned to something else.

Their gazes locked in the dimness of the car. She couldn't make out much. His eyes gleamed in the darkness. Moonlight skated over his cheekbones, nose, and lips.

He turned his hand over and their fingers wove together, the sensual slide connecting them on levels way beyond the physical realm. She couldn't have let go if she tried. Couldn't tear her eyes from his. Couldn't breathe. Somehow they were so close the warmth of his breath whispered across her lips.

"I thought about you while I was reading the book."

His words sent a shiver up her spine. "What were you thinking?"

His gaze fell to her mouth and lingered there. "I probably shouldn't say."

Her lips tingled. She wet them. "I thought we were being real." Who was this bold creature who'd taken over her tongue? Whoever she was, Shelby wanted the answer—and she hoped he'd show rather than tell her.

He leaned in by inches. She watched mesmerized as the fringe of his lashes fell. Their breaths mingled in the space between them, set to the frantic rhythm of her heartbeat. Then their lips met in a soft, sweet brush. Just one touch made her heart stutter. Squeezed the oxygen from her lungs. Made her want to climb inside him.

And yet, one touch was not nearly enough. She returned the kiss. Their lips moved in a dance that seemed brand-new, as if the two of them had just discovered kissing. She set her hand against the warmth of his neck. His pulse thrummed against her palm.

You make Gray Briggs's heart race. She was heady with the impossible thought.

He cupped her face, angled his head, took control. His touch anchored her in the here and now. Everything else ceased to exist as she yielded to his mastery. Because, yes, Gray was a master at kissing.

A boy didn't reach this level of expertise without plenty of experience. She swatted the thought away, wanting to recapture the oblivion of complete surrender. But the notion nagged like a pesky fly swarming her dinner plate.

Darcy Colbert.

He'd just been with her tonight. Had he kissed her too? And Shelby was also in a relationship. Though thoughts of breaking up with Brendan had been swirling for days, she hadn't yet done so. And here she was making out in her car with another boy.

Not just any boy—Gray Briggs. She'd never even known him to be in a committed relationship. What was she doing?

The reality check was unwelcome but persistent. It ushered in awareness of the outside world. The rain pummeling the roof. The console digging into her ribs. The guilt worming a hole in her gut.

She pressed a hand against his chest. Instantly there was space between them. Ragged breaths. Questioning eyes.

Oh, those half-lidded eyes could suck her right back under if she gave it half a second. "This is a mistake," she all but blurted.

He put another few inches between them, still palming her face.

"I—I'm dating someone. And so are you."

He pinned her with an unswerving look. "She's not my girlfriend, and that was no mistake. You know it wasn't." His thumb swept a path along the curve of her cheek. Their gazes tangled, his eyes smoldering. "Tell him you're with me now."

Her heart clenched at his words. No one had ever said anything like that to her. No one had ever looked at her this way. As if she was everything he'd ever wanted. "Is that what you want?"

"Yes."

He was everything she'd ever wanted. It wasn't knowledge gleaned from information or research or even time spent together. It was a *knowing* rooted deep within her soul. A connection she'd never shared with another person. And there was only one thing she could say in response.

"All right."

Chapter 17

Present day

"What in the world is this?" Between pinched fingers, Shelby held up a . . . raccoon hat? *Ick.* She dropped it into the trash pile and wiped her hands down the length of her shorts.

"Gram sure collected some odd things." Liddy held up an abstract painting of a face melting into a table. "Please tell me Caleb didn't create this abomination."

"Not a chance. But you can see why I insisted on decorating the store." Shelby pulled a band from her wrist and swept her hair into a quick bun. Autumn had not yet alerted the attic of its arrival. She'd promised Liddy she'd help clear out the musty space after church.

Dad was at home tending Ollie, and Caleb was outside putting meticulous stripes in the yard with the mower. Because when you were an artist, the lawn was your palette.

Shelby opened another box, unearthing old Christmas decorations she'd never set eyes on. *Goodwill.* The next box contained what appeared to be costumes and wigs. Back in the day her grandparents had gone all out for Halloween, turning their home into a favorite stop for trick-or-treaters.

Gram is gone.

The thought was like a frigid wave. This house would soon be on the market and another family would move in. It didn't seem right. She fondled the rings around her neck, seeking comfort.

"Time moves on, sweetheart. Changes come. It's a natural part of life."

You hated change.

"Guess my stubbornness isn't the only thing you inherited from me."

Time to think about something else. She shifted her thoughts to Caleb and her dad. Better to think about someone else's problems right now. "How's it going at the house, between Caleb and Dad?"

"Not terrible. Not great either. Your dad keeps dropping not-so-subtle hints about us moving to Grandville. It's pushing Caleb away."

Shelby sighed. "He should know the harder he pushes, the faster Caleb will run."

Liddy scrapped a pile of mangled hangers. "You know, when Gram left him this house, I was kind of hoping . . ."

Shelby's gaze darted to Liddy. Hoping they'd move here? The thought buoyed her spirits.

"Well, shoot, you think I wouldn't love living near my best friend and favorite sister-in-law? My son's only grandparent?"

"But I thought you loved living in New York."

"I do, I do. It's done great things for Caleb's career and we have close friends there. But our family's here. And his career is to the point where he could make it work if he wanted to."

Shelby digested this. "Have you told Caleb how you feel?"

"Not in so many words. He's so averse to the idea—and the more your dad pushes, the more he digs his heels in. I think he's afraid your dad will only exert more control over him if he moves back."

"He's an adult. Dad doesn't have any control over what he does."

"Tell him that."

"I'll talk to Dad. He needs to stop pressuring him."

"That would help. Thanks."

The thought of having Liddy, Caleb, and Ollie in town warmed her through. "It would be a dream to have you guys close by. Or you could just leave Ollie and I'll raise him as my own."

"Twenty-one hours of labor says he's mine."

"Sure, throw that in my face again." Though Shelby's own mom had endured twenty-three with her and had no trouble leaving her behind.

Liddy moved over to an old bureau by the window and gazed out to the lake, which shimmered under the clear blue sky. "This would be a great place to raise a family."

If only Caleb would get on board with the idea. Shelby dumped a box of old clothes into the Goodwill pile as Liddy sorted through the drawers of the bureau. "More old westerns."

Gram and her westerns. "Set them aside. I might read them later."

"Heard from Gray yet?"

Shelby had already caught Liddy and Caleb up to speed about his potentially staying to help resurrect the business. "Nope. But I'll be surprised if his boss lets him take so much time off."

Liddy quirked a brow. "Is that disappointment I hear in your voice?"

"Only because I'm not sure if I can do this alone."

"You don't give yourself enough credit."

"I know where my strengths are—and where they aren't."

"You're smart, Shelby. You could figure this out on your own."

Why hadn't she insisted Gram at least train her to do her job? Digging the store out of the hole would be overwhelming enough on its own.

"And we're here to help however we can."

"You guys might not be here long, and you have this house to deal with. Caleb's got a show coming up, and Dad's busy teaching. As much as I dread the thought of Gray hanging around till the end of the year, it's my best chance of turning the store around. I just can't believe Gram let things get this bad."

"Clearly she made some poor decisions." They'd talked about the equity loan, but Shelby hadn't yet mentioned where the money might've gone since she didn't know for sure.

"She probably thought she'd get it all squared away and I'd never find out. I just wish I knew what her plan was, because it all seems pretty daunting right now." Shelby felt so much pressure to rescue the store. It was Gram's legacy. What if she lost it?

"You've got this—Gray or no Gray." Liddy winked. "But I'm kinda hoping for Gray."

"Hey." Shelby swatted her with a ruffled apron. "You seem to have forgotten that once upon a time he decimated my heart."

"You were both young and foolish. He seems to have grown up quite nicely, and for all his apparent reputation, he did relinquish his share of the store. That says something."

"It says he doesn't want anything to do with Grandville."

"Yet he offered to stick around long enough to help you."

"He's doing it for Gram."

"Keep telling yourself that." Liddy smirked.

Shelby shot Liddy a wry look. "Whose side are you on?"

"Hey, speaking of hot ex-boyfriends, Caleb and I saw Brendan Remington at the hardware store. For some reason I thought he'd moved away."

"He did for about two minutes, but he moved back after his divorce. He's working at his dad's investment firm. I heard Barry's getting ready to retire, so Brendan will be taking over, which is what he's always wanted."

Her phone buzzed with an incoming text. She fished it from her pocket. "It's Gray."

Talked to my boss. I can stay till the end of the year. See you in the morning.

Shelby's stomach did some kind of twitchy thing, like a body in the lingering throes of death. It was official. He would be staying for the next two months.

Two. Months.

She'd be working side by side with Gray Briggs for eight weeks, six days a week. Forty-eight days. Her math skills faltered at the calculation of hours—but it was a lot.

"Have some faith, Sweet Girl." Shelby heard Gram's voice in her head. *"Everything will work out just fine."*

Easy for you to say.

"Well?" Liddy said. "Don't keep me in suspense."

Shelby turned her phone toward Liddy, who scanned the text and turned a smile on her. "And there you have it."

"Why do I suddenly feel like my life is about to spin out of control?"

"Don't worry." Liddy placed an arm around her shoulder and gave a squeeze. "You've got this all under control, girl."

But that was just it. Shelby didn't have it under control. Not the store—and certainly not her stubborn feelings for Grayson Briggs.

Chapter 18

Nerves quivering, Shelby unlocked the store and slipped inside. The familiar smell of books welcomed her as she flipped the Open sign and headed up the staircase. *It's just another Monday at the bookshop.*

Gram's cackle reverberated through her skull.

Not funny, Gram.

At the top of the stairs Shelby stopped to straighten the hardcover books on an endcap. She got distracted by the beautiful cover of Elizabeth Berg's latest novel, and while she read the back cover copy, Chaucer wove through her legs, emitting a loud meow.

"Hi, buddy. Don't worry, I didn't forget you."

She set the book down and set out Chaucer's food behind the counter. The cat gave her a dismissive glance and waited for her to leave. He didn't like an audience.

"You're very welcome."

The bell jangled downstairs and a minute later Gray appeared, looking handsomer than any man had a right to. The sun flooded through the plate-glass window, chiseling shadows into his perfectly sculpted face. The blue button-down stretched across his broad shoulders and hugged his thick biceps.

Really, God? He couldn't have grown a paunch or lost some hair in the past ten years?

"Morning." His raspy voice scraped the corners of her heart.

She'd been staring. She dragged her eyes away and made herself busy behind the counter. "Morning."

"I was up late last night making a list. I'd like to get your thoughts on where you want to start."

"Uh, sure. But I need to call Sturgis first thing and see if they'll give me some grace with the rent. If they won't . . . all of this will be a moot point." She'd tried hard to put that possibility from her mind.

"It's in their best interest to work with us. And the store has a long history of financial stability. I like our chances."

"Fingers crossed." She checked her watch. "They open in half an hour."

"We might as well get rolling then." He dumped his messenger bag under the counter.

It hit her fresh that he'd taken off the rest of the year from his regular job to help her. How could he afford to be away that long? Was he risking his job? Gray's text yesterday had been brief and to the point. "Hope you didn't have to sell your soul to get this leave of absence."

He spared her a glance. "Just my firstborn."

"Probably would've looked like you anyway."

His lips twitched. "Should we go down to the office?"

Shelby thought of the cramped space that would put them up close and personal. "Let's stay out here since we'll be talking about the displays and merchandise." Her gaze caught on the file in his hands. "Okay, let's see your list."

He handed over a document that resembled a Peter Carey novel more than a list. "You did all this last night?"

"Well, over the course of the past several days really. Plus Dog kept me awake till one."

"*Dog?*"

"Have to call him something."

"You could give him an actual name."

"That would suggest ownership and I'm just fostering him till Patrick rehomes him."

"Keep telling yourself that."

He stood silently while Shelby scanned the document. There were a lot of ideas here. Ideas that would require a lot of change. A lot of work. By page 3 her head was spinning. Had she mentioned work? Would all of this really save the store, or would it just put her in an early grave?

Gray slipped the document from her fingers. "I know it's a lot. Let's take one thing at a time. The merchandise is something we should get right on. Black Friday is less than a month away. How do you feel about ordering clothing, hats, and such related to literature? Like I mentioned, the margins would be healthy. Do you think your customers would go for that kind of thing?"

"Sure. I mean, I would." Gram had been resistant to sidelines. She'd kept them to a bare minimum. "But this is a bookshop first and foremost. I don't want to turn it into a novelty store."

"Agreed."

Shelby's gaze drifted over full shelves that were somewhat crammed together. The store had a few rooms, but it wasn't exactly spacious. "Where exactly would we put all this additional merchandise?"

"I thought we'd clear out—or at least minimize—the genres that aren't selling. I have spreadsheets that show us what those are, but I'll bet you already know."

"Historical fiction, poetry, and . . . westerns," she admitted reluctantly. Gram had loved westerns and stocked copious copies of all her favorites. She glanced at the shelving bearing those beloved titles as tears stung her eyes. Would this even feel like Gram's store by the time they finished revamping it? These changes would feel like losing Gram again, bit by bit.

Gray touched her arm. "I know it'll be hard making changes to your grandma's store. But we have to think of the greater good. We're honoring her by making the store a success. Besides, if we don't make the hard decisions, there won't be a store left at all."

She winced. "Harsh."

"There's an entire bookcase of westerns and you only sold one in the past month."

She remembered the sale. She'd actually kind of pushed the guy into it. Okay, fine, westerns weren't exactly flying off the shelves.

"That's how we'll make space for inventory that'll turn a profit and bring us back into the black."

"You're really warming the cockles of my heart there, Briggs."

"What are cockles anyway and how exactly are they warmed?"

She wasn't sure about her cockles, but her arm was actually heating up. Because, yes, his hand still rested there, burning her skin like a hot coal. She shifted until his hand fell, then aimed for her pockets with trembling hands.

Oh, right. No pockets.

A shuffle sounded and Logan appeared at the top of the stairs, his gaze quickly landing on her. And Gray. Her and Gray.

Logan frowned.

Because she might've forgotten to notify him that Gray was sticking around town for, oh, the rest of the year or so. Whoops.

Logan's gaze toggled back to Shelby. "I was waiting for you at the bakery . . ."

The bakery. Where they'd had plans to meet before work. She slapped a hand to her forehead. "I'm so sorry. I completely forgot."

Gray shifted away. "I, uh, have a phone call to make. We can pick this up later."

"Right, yeah."

Logan's brows lowered beneath the rim of his glasses as he watched Gray's retreating form until he disappeared down the steps.

"I thought Gray left," he said when Gray was gone.

"So did I. It was— A lot has happened since we last spoke." Well, okay, they'd texted but hadn't spoken on the phone or in person. "The audit turned up some problems. The store's in trouble financially, Logan. I mean deep trouble." She explained the dire situation and told him about Gray's offer of help.

Logan regarded her with pressed lips, and when her words finally petered out, he pushed his glasses into place. "He's staying here for two months and you didn't think to mention it to me?"

Well, golly gee, she'd had a few things on her mind this weekend. Things like salvaging her grandmother's business—and her own career for that matter. Hadn't she just mentioned her entire future was on the line? "I told you, Logan. It slipped my mind." The words came out stiffly. Which was fine because she was feeling a little starchy about the judgy stare he leveled on her.

"Yes, I recall. The same way you forgot we were meeting at the bakery, as we do every Monday morning, because your ex-boyfriend is hanging around town in hopes of winning you back."

"That's ridiculous. He's here to help save Gram's store, nothing more."

"I saw him touching you."

"He was touching my *arm*. Offering consolation because I've just lost my grandmother, and I'm in danger of losing her store as well."

"I'm sorry for your troubles. Truly. But you could've asked *me* for help."

"I don't need a bank loan, Logan. I need to turn this business around, and quick. And if that means accepting Gray's help, that's what I'll do. It's my shop, my decision. I'm sorry I neglected to inform you and sorry I missed our meeting, but I was—"

"*Date*."

"—in the middle of some—" She gave her head a shake. "What?"

"You missed our *date*. Not meeting."

He was quibbling over semantics? "Yes, fine. I missed our date. And again, I'm sorry. I've been pretty distracted and anxious as you might imagine."

"I accept your apology." He glanced back toward the staircase. "But I can't say I'm too thrilled about your ex-boyfriend skulking around for the next two months."

He was jealous. Which was absurd because Gray was the last man she'd trust with her heart. However, she wasn't exactly feeling warm toward Logan now either. He didn't seem to grasp the gravity of her situation. "It's business, Logan. That's all."

He regarded her for a long moment. "All right. If you say so."

"I do."

"Okay, good." He checked his watch. "Sorry to dash off, but I have a meeting in fifteen minutes. I'll call you later."

"All right."

He gave her a peck on the cheek, then turned and strode from the store, his loafers silent on the wood floor.

Their first argument, if you could call it that, had ended with an apology and forgiveness. But somehow it had left her feeling . . . what? She couldn't put her finger on it.

She shook away the thought. Didn't matter. She had much bigger problems to solve and they had nothing to do with Logan.

* * *

Gray hadn't expected to be heading home before noon. But his neighbor Mrs. Lyons called shortly after Logan Shackleford left the store to inform him that Dog hadn't ceased barking since Gray left this morning.

As he exited his SUV he could hear the animal barking like a maniac. When he opened the front door, Dog fell on him like he'd been gone for months, all waggy tail and floppy tongue. "All right, all right. Yes, hello,

I'm home. Was it really so bad—the air-conditioning, comfy couch, bowls of food and fresh water?"

Dog clambered in a happy mess all over Gray's feet.

His gaze sharpened on the wood floor—or more specifically the hundreds of scratches the dog had clawed into the threshold. He gave the dog a withering look. "Really? You ruined the floor?"

Ruined might be a bit hyperbolic. He could fix it, but geez. Last thing he needed right now. The joyful gleam in the dog's eyes tamped down his frustration. Yeah, all right. He knew a thing or two about loneliness. Still. He gave the floor one last frown.

He couldn't exactly leave him home all day to damage his floor and God knew what else. There were dog crates, but it seemed cruel to lock the creature up all day. Shelby had given him permission to bring the dog back to the store, but Gray wasn't happy about the inconvenience. Or the distraction. They had a lot of work ahead of them.

Now he was arranging his life around the mangy mutt. "Don't get used to it." He grabbed the rope-leash from the hook on the wall. "Come on."

The dog trotted at his side, then hopped into the vehicle and sat on the passenger seat like he was human. Except for the tongue lolling out the side of his mouth. The dog was grinning at him, he'd swear it.

He turned onto the road that led to the store, his mind going back to Shelby and her confrontation—if you could call it that—with her boyfriend. He didn't remember Logan from his years in Grandville, but Gray recalled the Shackleford family. His mom and dad owned the local supermarket. Hadn't Logan's dad run for town council a time or two? He couldn't remember if the man had won, but probably. The Shacklefords were well respected in the community. They lived in one of the McMansions on the lake. They no doubt adored Shelby. Who wouldn't?

It had been obvious Logan wasn't too keen on Gray's continued presence in Grandville.

Welcome to the club, pal.

Logan was a professional, judging by his crisp white shirt, red tie, and pressed pants. He hailed from a fine, upstanding family. Pillar of the community. The guy couldn't be more Gray's opposite. Maybe Shelby had finally figured out what she was looking for.

The thought rankled. No sense dwelling on it though. He wasn't here to cause her problems. He was here to help solve them.

When he entered the store he headed back to the office, Dog in tow. Shelby was behind the desk and just ending a call. She beamed at him as the dog begged shamelessly for her affection, which she gave. "That was the rep from Sturgis. I explained about Gram passing and my inheriting a bit of a mess. She seemed reluctant to cut us a break at first, but she came around. She's giving us till after Christmas. Normal rent payments will have to resume in January, and we'll have to pay what we owe in back rent then too." Her smile faltered. "And now that I'm saying it out loud, it sounds kind of impossible."

"No, no, that's great. The holidays are where it's at in retail—you know that. We'll implement some changes and make it bigger than ever."

"You really think we can do this?" Shelby said.

"We'll give it everything we've got."

Chapter 19

Eleven years ago

In the end Shelby didn't tell Brendan about Gray as she broke up with him. She was too worried about how Brendan and his friends might respond. She didn't worry she'd break Brendan's heart. In fact, she suspected he'd move on quickly—he was never without a girlfriend for long. Once he had another girl on his arm, maybe he wouldn't care who Shelby was with.

She ended the relationship during her lunch break the day after the Fourth of July. He responded with a curled lip and a *who cares* attitude, making her wonder why she'd even been with him at all.

He and his family had such a great reputation in the community, but she was beginning to see he didn't live up to it. Conversely Gray, who'd been all but condemned by the town, seemed the bigger person.

I broke up with him, she texted Gray as she walked back to the bookshop, her steps light now that she'd done the deed. Gray had texted her first thing this morning and she scanned the simple text as she awaited his reply. *Good morning, Sunshine.*

Her lips curved into a smile as warmth stole over her that had nothing to do with the hot sun high overhead.

A minute later his response appeared. *How did it go?*

Uneventful. I didn't tell him about you though. Thought it might be better.

I'm glad. I was worried about how he might respond toward you.

He was worried about her. Shelby's heart turned over in her chest. Who knew Gray Briggs could be so sweet?

Have you told anyone about us? he texted.

She could hardly believe there was anything to tell. But every time she remembered his kiss, every time she remembered the way he touched her, the way he gazed at her, she craved him yet again.

Not yet, she replied.

Okay, good. Let's talk first. Can we meet up before my shift at the hardware store? Around 3:30?

I can meet you behind the bookshop for a few minutes. It was a scraggly yard, sheltered by buildings on both sides, that went unused. She'd tried to talk Gram into glamming it up for book club meetings but hadn't had any luck so far.

Perfect. See you then.

The minutes dragged by as Shelby anticipated seeing him again. Would it be the same as it had been last night, or had the storm and darkness woven some kind of magic spell around them?

Maybe in the light of day the magic would be gone. Maybe he would wonder what he'd ever been thinking. They were so different. He was exciting and interesting and *real*. She was a little . . . boring. She read books and got good grades and excelled at small talk. Suddenly all that seemed so trivial.

As her nerves jangled, she worked out a plan that would allow her a few minutes' privacy. Her grandma was working downstairs in her office. Shelby would offer to take the empty book boxes to the dumpster behind Cedar Lake Gallery—a daily task Gram hated. No one would notice if it took Shelby a few extra minutes. Charlotte could easily cover the store.

At three fifteen she entered the office to find Gram scanning new books into the system. "Things are a little slow upstairs. I'll take the boxes out for you."

"Bless you, dear. That's so thoughtful."

Guilt pricked as Shelby gathered the broken-down boxes, took them out the back door, and hauled them to the dumpster they shared with the gallery. Deed done, her heart thumped heavily as she approached the bookshop from the alley. When she rounded the corner, there was Gray, sitting on the back porch, legs dangling over the side.

* * *

At the sight of Shelby, Gray dismounted the porch and headed toward her, his gaze sharpening on her as they closed the space between them. He was drawn to her as if she were magnetized. Didn't stop until she was in his arms and his lips were on hers.

She seemed just as eager for him. Relief enveloped him, quickly followed by desire. She embraced him as he kissed her with the same fervor she brought out in him.

By the time he put some space between them, they were both breathing heavily. He framed her face with his hands as he consumed her with eager eyes. "I missed you."

Her luscious lips turned up. "I missed you too."

He placed a soft kiss on her mouth and found her lips warm and soft. "You are far too distracting."

"Me? You're the distracting one."

His gaze dropped to her mouth. "How much time do you have?"

"Just a few minutes."

Not enough time for what he had in mind. He sighed and put space between them, then took her hands, mostly to keep his own from wandering. But also because he was kind of afraid she might not like what he had to say, and he was loath to mess up something that had barely begun. "Listen . . . What would you say if—what if we kept this between us for a while?"

She nodded. "I was actually thinking the same thing."

He blinked. But why should he be surprised? She was probably ashamed to be seen with him.

"I started worrying this morning about how Brendan might respond. That's why I didn't tell him about us. I was afraid he'd feel as if you'd taken something away from him. He and his friends have already badgered you so much—I don't want it escalating. Brendan will move on quickly enough, and when he does . . . we can let people know then."

A weight lifted from his shoulders. She didn't want to make him her dirty little secret. She was worried for *him*. She truly saw who Brendan was now. It was such a relief for someone else to see it too. Such a relief to have someone on his side for a change.

Her gaze drifted over his face as if she were trying to decipher his thoughts. "What?"

"That's really sweet of you. But I don't care about Brendan and his goons, Shelby. I can take care of myself."

"I know that. But there's no reason you should have to put up with that needlessly. If that wasn't your concern, why were you wanting to keep this on the down-low?"

He twisted the words around in his head, hoping he could express himself in a way that would make her understand. "We both know my social standing leaves a lot to be desired. I just don't want this dragging you down."

She tilted a smile at him. "I'm not worried about that."

That was only because she'd never been anything but loved and adored. It was hard to understand what being an outcast felt like until it happened to you. "I don't want to take that chance."

"I don't want to keep us a secret forever, Gray. When people see that we're together, they'll give you a chance. And once they get to know you, they'll see you for the great guy you are."

Oh boy, was she deluded. He tempered his words. "That's a great thought, Sunshine. But it doesn't really work that way."

"How do you know?"

He gave a brittle laugh. "I just do."

Her chin hiked up. "Well, I think you're wrong."

He kind of loved that little stubborn streak she had going. He gave her a peck on the lips. "We might not have the same reasoning. But at least we agree that we should keep things quiet for a while. So let's just do that. We can worry about the rest later."

"I can't think when you kiss me."

"Good," he said. And kissed her some more.

Chapter 20

Present day

Gray glanced at the clock—closing time—then back to the screen that confirmed more bad news. He heaved a sigh and pushed back from the computer.

Between customers today Shelby had ordered sideline products, including literary-themed clothing. In the afternoon she'd begun going through the store's shelves, eliminating books that weren't selling and reducing inventory of less popular genres. The office now housed boxes full of books to be returned. Slowly but surely, she was making space on the shelves.

His goal was not only to allow room for more profitable products but also to reduce the overall cluttered appearance of the store. Walking into an overcrowded space could make customers feel overwhelmed. Still, he saw these changes were difficult for her. He wished he could do something to soften the blow.

Dog approached, tail wagging, as if he sensed it was time to go. Gray opened the door and the dog bolted out and charged up the back staircase. By the time Gray reached the top, Dog had found Shelby, who was tidying up the Children's section.

He glanced around the shop on the way over. "You got a lot done today."

"I had Janet come in to help with customers so I could focus on de-cluttering."

"I wondered why there were three of you." Though there were really only two as Haley seemed to just drift around the store doing as little as possible.

Shelby squatted to give the dog the affection he practically begged for, then glanced up at Gray. "What's wrong?"

"Why do you think something's wrong?"

Shelby rose to her feet with a heavy sigh. "Just tell me."

"I looked back in Viola's records. Things had been fairly stable for years, though not very profitable. Then the roof failed and business slacked off. The economy took a toll. You were right about that equity loan. Five years ago there was a forty-thousand-dollar deposit into the account, and shortly thereafter, a check in the same amount was written to Home Guard Exteriors."

Her expression fell. "Now on top of everything else, I owe my brother forty grand."

"He might not see it that way."

"We all assumed he inherited the house free and clear. Gram and Pop paid it off years ago."

"And you thought you'd inherited a thriving bookshop. This isn't your fault."

She pressed her fingertips to her temples. "I hate this."

Dog caught sight of Chaucer across the room and charged after the cat with a happy yap.

Chaucer screeched as he scrambled away, then leaped onto a high shelf out of Dog's reach. He turned and perched on the edge, head low, back arched, peering at the dog with a predatory gleam in his eyes.

Dog let out a bark, his entire back end wagging.

Chaucer hissed.

"Hey, be nice," Shelby said. "He just wants to play with you."

The dog was lonely for friends and the cat was wary of someone new and intimidating. "Kind of reminds me of us when we met."

Her gaze darted to him.

Oops. He hadn't meant to say that out loud—even if it was true.

"Am I the dog or the cat in this scenario?"

He smirked, remembering those early days. "As I recall, you didn't exactly put out the welcome mat for me."

"I was never mean to you."

"No, maybe just a little . . . standoffish."

"You were arrogant and irritating."

He'd been insecure and hopelessly attracted to her. "Even so, we managed to become friends."

She snorted. "Is that what you call it?" She shelved a board book someone had left out while his mind went back to all the ways they'd been so much more than friends. Like the way her eyes used to soften just before he kissed her. The way she seemed to melt under his touch. When she fell into his arms, he felt like the luckiest guy in the world.

"I don't want to talk about the past. We have plenty of work right here in the present to keep us busy."

He blinked away the sweet memories. This thing between them was like an invisible force field. He, too, wanted to put the past where it belonged, but at the very least he needed to apologize. He'd tried to be patient because she'd been dealing with so much, but they'd be working closely for weeks.

"We'll need to be on the same team now more than ever. And I can tell you're still angry about what I did."

"Well, Gray, you up and left me after making certain promises."

He absorbed that accusation. "I did. You deserved more from me. I should've told you what I was planning. I'm sorry I didn't."

"Should've *told* me? We should've had a discussion about it."

"You're right." He swallowed hard. "I never meant to hurt you, Shelby."

She spared him a glance. "Why do people always say that? Intention or no, it still had the same effect. Did you ever consider my feelings even once?"

At the end of his senior year, frustration and helplessness had welled up inside like a toxic plume. "I honestly didn't know what else to do. I was just a stupid kid. I didn't know I'd lose you. I didn't know you'd hate me for it."

She whirled on him. "I didn't hate you. I loved you, you idiot. I thought you loved me too."

He took a step toward her, then stopped when she stiffened. "I *did*. I did, Shelby. I thought— I don't know, I thought you'd—"

"Just sit around Grandville waiting for you to return—or not return at all?"

He winced. Yeah, he'd been a dumb kid. Because basically, yes, he'd expected her to just get on board with his plans. And he'd given little thought to the actual danger he might be facing. "You're right. I didn't consider your feelings at all. I was thoughtless and you didn't deserve that. I soon regretted my selfish decision when you wouldn't take my calls."

"Can you blame me?"

Yep, he'd been an idiot all right. There was really nothing more he could say for himself. It would only sound like excuses anyway. "I'm sorry. I wish I could do things over. I'd do them differently."

She gathered a stack of books and faced him, a deep breath making her shoulders rise and fall. "I appreciate your saying so. But I don't want to talk about this anymore. It's in the past and I've moved on. I'm grateful you're staying to help. That means a lot. But can we please put this away for good? *Please.*"

He didn't feel much better about it than he had a few minutes ago.

In fact, he felt even worse. But pushing her wouldn't be fair. And it sure wouldn't do any good. He'd apologized. There was nothing more he could do. "If that's what you want."

"Great. I'll put these in the office with the other returns, then we're done for the day."

* * *

Shelby was shaking as she turned the Closed sign. She watched Gray walk down the sidewalk toward his SUV. Why did that stupid breakup haunt her so many years later?

So she'd had her tender little heart broken. So what? It happened to just about everyone. She'd finally gotten that apology she'd been waiting for all these years, but instead of feeling better, she felt as if he'd just ripped off a fresh scab.

"You know why, Sweet Girl."

Shelby gave a deep sigh. All that therapy hadn't been for nothing. So, yes, Gray's sudden exit had reawakened all those feelings of abandonment from her mother's departure. But she was over all that now. She'd worked through the feelings and come out the other side.

Gray was sorry. She was ready to move on. She *was* moving on—with Logan. Maybe he wasn't as exciting as Gray, maybe his touch didn't exactly set her on fire. But it was nice. Comfortable. Worthwhile. Shelby would not be like her mom, blowing off something good for the hope of something better.

She and Logan could have a wonderful future together.

"Shelby Shackleford?" Gram's voice again.

Can't win 'em all, Gram.

She checked her watch. Maybe she could catch Caleb and Liddy at home. Shelby had to come clean with them about that equity loan.

Twenty minutes later she made herself comfortable in Dad's living room. Her dad was out with friends and Liddy was at the grocery store. Ollie was sound asleep in the Pack 'n Play and ESPN blared from the TV.

Caleb used the remote to turn it down, then settled in the chair across from her. "What's up?"

"A lot has happened in the past few days. I'm not sure how much Liddy has told you."

"I know the store's not doing as well as you thought—and that Gray's sticking around to 'help.'"

She'd ignore the tone he used on that last part. "'Not doing well' doesn't quite cover it. I'm in arrears with the rent and there's practically nothing in the account. The situation's fairly dire."

"How do you even know that's true? Just because Gray said so?"

"He's a competent accountant. He showed me the books, went over the numbers."

Caleb shoved his glasses into place. "I don't trust him."

"Well, I do—at least with this." Her heart was an entirely different matter.

"If I were you, I'd hire someone else to do an audit."

"With what money? And anyway, I don't need another audit. He wouldn't lie to me about this. He wants Gram's store to succeed."

Caleb leaned back in his seat, seeming to shrug it off. "It's your store. You're going to do what you want."

"I wish you could let go of the past."

"I wish you could see he's still into you."

She rolled her eyes. "This is about Gram's business and nothing more. But I'm not here to discuss all that. I found out where that equity loan went. The store had a roof leak back then. Gram used that money for repairs."

"*Forty grand*? For a leaky roof?"

"Believe it or not. It was pretty far gone by the time we discovered it. I have the receipt."

"Okay, well, at least that explains the mystery."

He didn't seem to understand. "Caleb, you were supposed to get the house and I was supposed to get the bookshop. And now the bookshop owes you forty thousand dollars. I can't pay it back right now, but—"

"*Whoa.* Hold up. You don't owe me anything, Shel."

"I actually do. You should talk it over with Liddy."

"Please. As if she'd disagree. This house is worth a ton of money, and if it's true that the bookstore's in the red, *you're* the one who got the short stick here, not me."

"Still . . ."

"No way. I'm not taking any money from you." He shook his head. "In fact, if the store's truly in jeopardy, we could take out another equity loan to help you get things—"

"Absolutely not. This house belongs to you and Liddy. That's what Gram wanted."

"I wish you'd reconsider." He gave her a wry look. "The accountant *and* the equity loan."

"I'm comfortable with both decisions. So I guess we'll have to agree to disagree."

Chapter 21

Gray's efforts to escape the store before the romance book club arrived had been in vain. At the last minute he had to take Dog out back to relieve himself.

He did his best to avoid townspeople in general, but crowds in particular. There were newcomers who didn't know him, of course, but the old-timers seemed to have long memories and short fuses.

The dog seemed more interested in sniffing each bush than actually doing any business. "Hurry up already."

The backyard had changed over the past eleven years. The basic layout was the same: a grassy area set in the U-shaped space between the brick buildings flanking the shop. But now shrubbery and colorful perennials graced the periphery. A fire flickered in a center pit and white lights twinkled overhead. The cozy space and fall weather made the perfect setting for a book group.

A clatter of laughter and chatter sounded just before the first readers arrived. He braced himself for rejection. But when the three sets of eyes fell on Dog, squeals of delight followed as the women gathered around the mutt like he was the best thing this side of heaven. They were friendly, asking him questions about Dog. Gray tried to talk them into adopting him, but they all had excuses.

Even so, they did their best to get Gray to stay for the book club, at which they would be discussing a rom-com. It was nice to find a little acceptance. Sometimes people could be kind—even people in Grandville apparently.

Shelby, who'd entered the yard at some point, just looked on with an amused grin as he tried to extricate himself from the friendly group.

Ten minutes later night was falling when he finally freed himself and made his way to his SUV. He was about to be late for supper with Patrick at Davey's BBQ, a casual spot on the edge of town with outdoor seating.

He scowled down at the dog. "You're a big flirt. And I don't think you had to pee at all."

Dog glanced up at him, grinning, that tongue lolling from the side of his mouth.

It had been exactly two weeks since he'd found the animal, and so far no takers. He'd stopped to see Patrick yesterday at his office, and the man had exhausted all of his options. But he had suggested dinner. It might be nice to have a friend while he was in town. It was easy to trust someone like Patrick, who'd also experienced his share of bullying back in the day. He seemed to have risen above all that.

Gray opened the door and let Dog inside. Even he could admit he was tired of calling him that. It was starting to feel like an insult. But he'd never dreamed the animal would be in his care for two weeks. Recently Shelby had begun calling him Shadow because he followed Gray everywhere he went.

He started the SUV, pulled from the slot, and merged onto Main Street. "All right, Shadow, let's head to supper."

The dog let out a bark as if approving of his new name.

"Yeah, don't get excited—this is still temporary." But even a stray dog deserved a real name.

Cars belonging to Friday night diners and barhoppers filled the street parking spots. Farther ahead a crowd gathered on the manicured town green in camp chairs and blankets facing a giant movie screen. He remembered Movies on the Green. During their senior year he and Shelby had watched some chick flick that had her all cuddly on the ride back to her house.

He shook the thought away as he stopped for pedestrians. Then the crosswalk cleared and he moved on, passing the last streetlight in town before heading into the residential area beyond it.

It had been a long two weeks, implementing changes, rearranging shelving. The shop was more attractive already—even Shelby had admitted it—and their new inventory was selling well. Even better, Shelby seemed to have lit up since his apology.

It was difficult to maintain a distance when they worked so closely together. When they were laboring toward the same goal. He wanted so badly to see their efforts pay off. He hoped the advice he'd given her would turn things around. The biggest test would come on Black Friday and following when—

A chirp sounded behind him. He glanced in the rearview mirror. The red and blue flash of police lights turned his stomach to lead. He wasn't speeding. He eased off the gas and moved to the side, hoping the cruiser would go around.

No such luck.

Gray pulled into the emergency lane and brought his SUV to a stop. He lowered his window and withdrew his license and registration—already on top of the pile from his recent ticket. Which he'd already paid.

A moment later Mason Remington—surprise, surprise—appeared at his window. Still had that same stony expression and perpetual frown.

"License and registration."

He handed them over. "Mind telling me what this is about?"

Mason seemed in no hurry to reply. He took his time looking over Gray's ID even though he'd seen it only two weeks ago. "Wait here."

As if he had a choice. Remington was bound and determined to punish him for existing. No, not for existing, but for having the nerve to show his face in Grandville. What was his problem—him and all the others?

Okay, so his dad had killed Mason's uncle, but it was unintentional and he was serving his time. Of course some believed his dad had committed first-degree murder and that he should be serving a sentence twice the length he'd been given.

But none of that was Gray's fault.

It had started as an argument between Troy Remington and Dad at Dirty Harry's over a stupid game of pool. According to spectators, the disagreement escalated into a fistfight at which point both men had been tossed.

Only his drunk dad served as a living witness to what had happened on the porch of the establishment. He claimed Troy came after him once again and he punched the guy, who then fell and hit his head on the railing—a fatal blow. An accident, according to his dad.

But matters were complicated by the men's history, which included a woman who'd recently dumped his dad for Troy. Her testimony put Dad's motives in question. But the jury decided Dad was guilty of only second-degree murder.

And the townspeople seemed to take great pleasure in taking it out on Gray. The stolen-test scandal his senior year hadn't helped matters much either.

He pulled in a deep breath, held it to the count of five, and let it go. He wished everyone could just put the past behind them. But it wouldn't be that easy. He'd have to lay low through the end of the year. Of course, that was what he'd been attempting tonight, and look where that got him.

Well, he hadn't done anything illegal. Remington just delighted in giving him a hard time.

The sounds of tread on gravel alerted Gray to the officer's return. He shone a flashlight into Gray's face. "Where are you coming from tonight?"

He faced the windshield to avoid the blinding light. "Work."

"Oh, you work here now, do you?"

"I came from the bookshop. Why'd you pull me over? I wasn't speeding."

"The one that belongs to Shelby Thatcher?"

It was the only one in town. "Yes."

"The one you were supposed to help her with for two weeks?"

"The very one." It was impossible to keep the sarcasm from his tone.

"And yet here you still are a month later. I wonder what could be keeping you here."

"Is there a question in there somewhere?"

"Here's a question for you: How much have you had to drink tonight?"

Gray pinned him with a look. "I haven't had any alcohol." He never drank. When your dad needed beer more than oxygen, you tended to avoid the stuff. "I haven't broken any laws. You had no right to pull me over."

"I wouldn't be so sure about that. You crossed the center line a ways back. You were weaving. And now you're acting belligerent, so I'm going to have you step outside the vehicle."

"I didn't cross the center line, and if I'm belligerent it's because you pulled me over without reason."

Remington puffed up his barrel chest. "Are you refusing to exit the vehicle then?"

Gray gritted his teeth. If he refused, Remington would no doubt take great pleasure in removing him from the vehicle. Gray opened the door and stepped out.

Shadow barked.

"It's all right, boy."

Mason directed him toward the front of the SUV where his headlights formed two cones of light. Cars passed by and Gray tried not to think about who might be inside them or what rumors they might start.

Doesn't matter. You don't even live here anymore.

"We'll be doing a field sobriety test. I need you to walk heel to toe on this line for nine steps, turn on one foot, and return for nine steps."

Gray had already begun the test, blood surging through his veins. The man had no right to use his badge to intimidate citizens. "We both know this has nothing to do with alcohol." When he finished the nine steps, he turned on one foot.

Remington was a hulking silhouette in the headlights. "Seemed a little shaky on that turn, Briggs."

Gray started back toward the SUV. "Your eyes need to be checked."

"And you need to pack your bags and get out of town."

"Is that a threat?"

"Oh, let's just call it a friendly little tip. I'm nice that way."

He could mention his stay was temporary. But he didn't owe this guy an explanation. "I have as much right to be here as anyone else."

"You're right, Briggs. It's a free country. And if you think moving back here is in your best interest, you're welcome to do so."

Why did he get the feeling that Remington would make sure it wasn't? Not that Gray would ever consider moving back to this hellhole. But the rumor mill must be saying otherwise if Remington was going to this much trouble. *Eight. Nine.* He stopped a foot from Remington, staring into those beady little eyes.

The officer shone his flashlight into Gray's face and held up a pen. "Keeping your head still, follow the pen with your eyes."

Should he request a Breathalyzer? Those could be inaccurate, but not as biased as this officer. Gray gritted his teeth but did as he was told. He'd just get these stupid tests out of the way and then Remington would let him go.

The officer moved the pen to the side at a glacial pace. Back to the center. Then to the other side. After a long moment he lowered the pen but kept the flashlight on Gray's face as he lifted his lips in a smirk. "Grayson Briggs, you're under arrest for driving under the influence."

Chapter 22

Gray was fuming by the time he exited the police station. It was almost midnight when they finally released him, though he'd passed the Breathalyzer test long ago. "*Paperwork*," the jailer had said with a smirk. Clearly the department was happy to help Remington pressure him to leave Grandville. Nice having a firsthand look at the American justice system at work.

Gray hadn't seen Remington since being placed in a holding cell with nothing but a steel toilet and a hard cot. With bars on two sides of the room, he couldn't help feeling like a caged animal at the zoo.

Or like his dad, who survived each day in a similar environment. Of course, his dad actually deserved the punishment. Still, Gray made a mental note to send him an email. He'd been a little distracted since arriving in town.

Shadow trotted at his side. At least the officers had been kind to the dog. Shadow received plenty of attention and treats from the watch commander and jailer.

Gray shot the happy canine a wry look. "Could've used a little loyalty in there, pal. Those guys are not our friends."

Shadow seemed unconvinced.

Gray came to a stop at the edge of the parking lot. He couldn't even walk back to his vehicle—Mason had gloated about having it towed.

Gray fished his phone from his pocket. Three missed calls, a voicemail, and two texts—all from Patrick. He returned the call and his friend answered after only one ring.

"Hey, is everything okay?"

"It's fine. Sorry to stand you up tonight. I'll explain later. Listen, I hate to ask for a favor when it's so late, but I could really use a ride."

Rustling sounded through the phone. "Sure, of course. Where are you?"

"The police station."

A beat of silence carried over the line. "Okay. Be right there."

Gray pocketed his phone as warmth spread through him. That was the sign of a good friend right there, coming without a single question. Too bad more people couldn't be like Patrick.

His allegiance was almost enough to push away the dark feeling that had set up camp inside him tonight. The whole incident had unleashed that old sense of shame. The shame of being poor. Of having an alcoholic father. Of being viewed as less than. Once again he felt as if he were walking around with a neon *Loser* sign over his head. He shouldn't allow anyone to make him feel that way. But being back here, being subjected to all those old judgments, all those accusers, had brought those feelings to the surface again.

Cars passed by as he walked Shadow in front of the station. The area was well lit and near the road. He should've asked Patrick to pick him up down the street. Anyplace but the police station. But nothing was open this late except the bars, and he didn't want to be seen hanging around there either. There'd been enough speculation that he'd turned out just like his old man.

Ten minutes later Gray's rescue came in the form of a white Audi. The interior light flashed on as Patrick threw open the passenger door. "Hop in."

Gray surveyed the pristine leather seats and carpeted floor mats. "I forgot to mention I have Shadow with me."

"My dogs are in here all the time."

A minute later they were settled and leaving the parking lot. Gray was so relieved to get off the property. He wanted to forget this night ever happened.

"So . . ." Patrick said as he pulled onto Main Street. "I can hardly believe it."

And here came the questions.

Patrick arched a brow his way. "You finally got around to naming the dog."

Chapter 23

Eleven years ago

If Shelby had learned anything in the past three months, it was this: Being with Gray was night and day from being with Brendan. She stared at her reflection, a giddy smile curving her lips, as she fixed her hair using only her bedroom night-light.

They hadn't yet told anyone they were together, and meeting secretly had been challenging. They shared only one class together: chemistry—ironic since she spent the whole class trying to ignore the butterflies in her stomach. It was so distracting she could only be glad they didn't share lunch hour. She couldn't imagine trying to stay away from him.

Her two best friends, Monica and Lindsay, had noticed her staring at him and teased her about her crush on the school's bad boy. She'd been tempted so many times to tell them the truth, but her fears of Brendan retaliating stopped her.

Her ex-boyfriend had begun dating Kelsey Stevens before summer's end. But another matter now pitted him against Gray. They'd both applied for the Warner Scholarship, which would be awarded to the applicant with the highest GPA, and so far the two of them were at the top of the heap. A fact that Brendan and everyone else were now well aware of.

As autumn progressed Brendan's friends amped up their harassment—always done furtively, of course, and meant to stir up Gray's temper.

Somehow Gray rose above it. She was so proud of his academic performance. So proud of how hard he'd worked so he could go to college. She was frustrated thinking of how easy Brendan had it. Maybe his parents couldn't afford the Ivy League school he wanted to attend, but he'd never even bothered getting a job this summer.

Shelby had already earned a partial scholarship to Belmont in Nashville and planned to major in secondary education. She wanted to be an English teacher. Vanderbilt, also in Nashville, was on Gray's top three list, and he'd already been accepted. She dreamed of their future in Nashville, away from the watchful eyes of Grandville.

Sneaking around with Gray took considerable effort. Meeting after school was out since she served on three committees and participated in four clubs. Anyway, he worked after school until the hardware store closed, then he had his studies. He had to keep up his grades if he wanted that scholarship. He joked that sneaking around was sexy. Maybe it was . . . a little. But it came at a cost.

Tonight she planned on broaching the topic. She wanted to tell her family and best friends. She felt so guilty each time she told her dad good night and went to her room—only to sneak out later. Felt guilty when she lied to Gram about who she was texting. Felt remorseful when Monica or Lindsay invited her over and she fibbed about her plans.

She could trust her family and friends to keep a secret, and spending time together would be easier if they knew. Surely she could make him understand that. He was needlessly worried about her reputation anyway. If people refused to see Gray based on his own merits, she didn't care what they thought of her.

It was almost eleven. Dad would be sound asleep by now. A fresh pinch of guilt twisted her insides. Even so, she carefully opened the window and climbed out, grateful the ranch offered an easy first-floor escape.

She dropped to the ground and rounded the house. The October air was crisp, and the scent of woodsmoke carried on the breeze. She searched the shadows for Gray. He insisted on walking with her to the park where he'd left his truck. Sometimes they huddled inside it, and other times they sat in the swings or lay on the creaky merry-go-round. It didn't matter what they did as long as they were together. She lived for these stolen moments.

There he was in the moonlight, approaching her drive with that easy swagger she loved so much. Her face broke out in a smile and her steps quickened. She couldn't get to him quickly enough. They hadn't been alone together in almost a week—forever.

At the edge of the darkened street, they came together like a magnet to steel. Shelby quickly got lost in the kiss. How had she made it almost a week without these lips on hers?

"Glad to see me?" he teased breathlessly.

"I only came so I wouldn't hurt your feelings."

They were kissing again. He pulled her closer, his hands finding the curve between her shoulder blades, the small of her back. Oh, he was so good at this. They should probably move this to the park, but she couldn't bring herself to—

Headlights cut across the night. They jumped apart. She hadn't even heard the engine. The unfamiliar car swept into her driveway and stopped twenty feet away.

"Who's that?" Gray asked.

"I don't know."

There was no sense hiding now. The headlights had already given them away.

The door opened and even in the dim light she recognized her brother's form. Caleb slammed the car door and strode toward them. "Get away from her."

"Caleb, stop. You don't know what you're talking about."

"It's pretty clear what's going on here, Shelby."

"And just what is that?" Gray said with a steely voice.

"Oh, I think we both know the answer to that." Caleb came to a stop in front of them. "Go in the house, Shelby." His eyes never left Gray.

She stepped between them. "No. You don't understand. We're dating. We've been dating for weeks."

Caleb's head whipped her way. "So Dad knows about this?"

Her silence answered the question.

"What are you doing with him? Where's your head?"

"Shut up, Caleb. You don't know him."

"I know enough. He's already got his claws into you, and you're going to wind up with a broken heart or worse." His eyes narrowed on Gray. "Isn't that right, thug?"

"Leave him alone!" Tears prickled her eyes. She was so tired of everyone misjudging Gray. She planted her palms on Caleb's chest and shoved. "Don't you say one bad word about him! You don't know anything!"

"Hey, hey." Gray grabbed her, turned her toward him. His steady gaze locked on her. "Come on, settle down."

A sob died in her throat at his gentle tone.

"It's okay. Why don't you just go on inside with your brother? We'll talk later."

Caleb muttered something and she shot him a death glare. She was so disappointed to have their time together wrecked by a brother who apparently decided on a whim to return from college for the weekend. They never should've kept this relationship a secret for so long. Now it was all going so wrong.

Gray squeezed her arms. "Shelby, look at me."

She gave him her attention, her breaths still coming fast and shallow. "Yelling in the street isn't gonna do any good. You know that. Everything'll be okay. I'm going to leave. Just go on inside, all right?"

A tear spilled over.

He swiped it away with his thumb, his expression softening. "None of that now. Call me tomorrow, okay?"

A lump lodged in her throat. She nodded.

Without another word, Gray walked off, disappearing into the shroud of darkness. When she turned back to Caleb, he was still scowling in Gray's direction. "Dad won't be happy about this either, you know."

"Oh, shut up, Caleb." Shooting him one last glare, she started for the house.

* * *

Gray hardly slept all night. He kept seeing the venom in Caleb's expression, hearing it in the tone of his voice. What was worse, he understood it. If he had a little sister, he wouldn't want her hooking up with a guy like him either.

But Caleb believed Gray was using her. That he'd just take what he wanted and drop her cold. It couldn't be further from the truth. Gray had fallen hard for Shelby. He thought about her all the time. Lived for those fleeting moments alone. What would happen now that her family knew?

His gut clenched hard. There was no way her dad would be any more okay with it than Caleb had been. Especially since they'd kept their relationship a secret for three months. He pulled into the hardware store lot and parked the truck. He assumed Shelby would tell her dad this morning, and Gray prayed he'd hear from her soon.

Otherwise it was going to be a very long day.

Gray never took calls at work—he couldn't afford to upset Lang. But when Shelby's came in just before noon, he slipped behind the bags of mulch and answered. "Are you okay? I've been worried."

"I'm fine." She sounded as if she'd been crying.

She wasn't fine and it was his fault. He was the one who hadn't wanted to tell anyone. "Where are you?"

"At the bookstore. I'm on break, out back."

He wished he could get over there and see her in person, but they were short-staffed today. He'd be lucky to get a break at all. "Tell me what happened."

"My dad—" Her words pinched off with a squeak. "My dad was so upset. I'm grounded forever and he doesn't want me seeing you anymore."

His breath stuttered.

"He can't keep me from seeing you! I'm almost eighteen. I'm not a child anymore."

"Maybe he just needs a chance to adjust to the idea." Even as Gray said the words, his hope ebbed like blood from a jugular wound. What father would want him dating his precious daughter? Especially when they'd been sneaking around behind his back?

"I tried to explain why we didn't tell anyone, but I don't think he believed me. He was so upset. So disappointed in me. He took my car keys—dropped me off at work like I'm fifteen."

"This is all my fault. I shouldn't have let it go on this long."

"It wouldn't have mattered. He believes all those stupid rumors about you and your family. I was so mad at how he talked about you!"

"Aw, honey. I don't want you to fight your dad over me. And they're not all rumors, you know."

"You don't deserve the bad rap you've gotten. It's so unfair."

She was crying now and he longed to get his arms around her. He needed the comfort, too, because the whole situation was feeling pretty hopeless. "Hey, listen. It'll be okay. He just needs a little time."

"You didn't hear him. He was so angry."

"I'll apologize to him." But how in the world would he ever prove himself to her dad? There was only one way he could think of. It hurt just to think about it. "I have a plan. It won't be easy, but . . ."

"What? I'll do anything."

"We should respect his wishes, earn back his trust. Maybe then he'll give me a chance."

"*No*. That'll take forever. You didn't hear him. He won't back down. And I have to see you. I can't stand the thought of not seeing you."

"I want to see you too. But if this is going to work, I have to earn his respect, Shelby. Man to man. That's what it'll take."

A beat of silence passed between them. A knot tightened in his gut at the thought of losing her forever. Maybe she wouldn't believe it was worth all this. Maybe he should be willing to give her up rather than come between her and her family.

But he couldn't. He closed his eyes. *Please, God. She's everything to me.*

"Let's just try it and see, okay? Give it a little time."

"How long?"

"I don't know. But I want this as much as you do. *I love you*, Shelby." The words burst like water from a dam. "I wanted to tell you last night. I shouldn't have said it over the phone, but I couldn't wait any longer."

"Oh, Gray, I love you too. So much."

She loved him. Shelby Thatcher loved him.

The heavy load lifted from his shoulders until he felt so light he feared he might go airborne. "All right then. We're in this together. We'll do whatever we have to do to be together."

"All right." He heard the smile in her voice. "There is one bit of good news in all this—Gram already knew about us."

"How?"

"She saw us kissing outside way back in July. And you know she likes you. She's rooting for us."

His lips curved into a smile. "See there? Maybe she'll have a positive influence on your dad."

"That's what I'm hoping. She thinks he just overreacted and that he might come around."

The good bit of news quenched his soul. There was hope. Maybe he *could* earn Mr. Thatcher's trust. "It's all the more important now that we abide by his rules no matter how hard it might be."

"I don't like it."

"I don't either, babe. But maybe it won't take as long as we fear."

"I'm going to beg Gram to change his mind about you."

His grin widened. Shelby could be so determined when she set her heart on something. He almost felt sorry for Miss Viola *and* her dad.

Joe Lang came around the corner and stopped short at the sight of Gray. His eyebrows crashed together. "*Hey.* Get off the phone. You're not on break and you've got customers waiting up front."

Chapter 24

Present day

Shelby already had the lights on and the store open by the time Gray arrived with his dog. She didn't even wait for them to reach the top of the stairs.

"Morning!" The mutt ran straight for her and she gave him some love. "I had an idea last night I wanted to run by you. Remember Phoebe Bell, our local famous author? Well, she has a book releasing in— Hey, are you all right?" Gray's blue eyes looked tired, as if he'd just rolled from bed. Or maybe like he hadn't slept at all. "Are you sick or something?"

"Just a late night. What's this idea, and please tell me there's coffee."

"Down in the office. You and Patrick stay out late?"

"Something like that."

Did he have a hangover? The old Gray refused so much as a sip of alcohol, but she didn't really know him anymore. "If you have a headache, I have Tylenol and Advil, or Gram kept essential oils in the desk drawer, and she has peppermint that is really good for—"

"That's okay. I just need to wake up." He gave her a sideways glance. "How much coffee have *you* had?"

Maybe she was a little overcaffeinated. "Mind your own beeswax."

The dog spotted Chaucer and dashed after him.

Gray frowned. *"Shadow."*

Shadow, huh? Shelby smirked at him.

When he caught her eye he squelched a grin. "Shut up."

"Someone's getting attached."

"It's only temporary."

"If you say so." The bell jingled downstairs. Shelby tossed Gray a smug look as she headed down the stairs. "We can resume the conversation about my idea when you're properly caffeinated."

Three more customers came and went before Shelby had a chance to hunt down Gray. She found him in the Religion section where he was shelving books that had come in yesterday. "I just sold a *One more chapter* tee and a *Bookmarks are for quitters* cap. Also four novels. I love Saturdays."

"That's great. How'd your book club go last night?"

"The discussion went well. Everyone loved the book." They'd read Annabel Monaghan's summer release. "But as I anticipated, the news about the reduced discount wasn't exactly popular."

"That's to be expected. It won't equate to that much per book, but it'll add up over time for us."

"Ellen Lyons all but threatened to buy hers from the evil empire. But when the others came to my defense, she backed off."

"Good job. I know that wasn't easy for you."

Gray's steady gaze and smile warmed her. He seemed almost . . . proud of her. She shook the thought away. "Thanks. How are our numbers looking for the month so far?"

"Up from last November. I'm encouraged." He held his hand up and they high-fived.

"That's great news. We still have a long way to go though. Which brings me back to that idea I had."

"Phoebe Bell, local author of mysteries, if I remember right."

"Local, yes. But in the past ten years her book sales have exploded.

She's hit the *USA Today* list with her last several releases, and she has a zillion fans on social media—even if she does have someone else managing the accounts."

"She has to be, what? At least sixty by now."

"Mid-sixties, I think. Anyway, she's launching her new release here in early January, which will be great for the store."

"I saw that on the schedule but didn't realize what a boon it will be."

"Last launch she sold over 150 hardcovers. We had a line out the door and past Patsy's Boutique."

"That'll be great then."

"So back to my idea. What if we set up a preorder special on the book? Don't scowl. It doesn't have to be huge. Just 10 percent maybe and then Miss Phoebe could get the word out to her following that they can preorder a signed book at a discount. We're only two months away from her release, so we'd have to get right on it."

"What about shipping costs?"

"We could either tack that onto the price or absorb it."

"If we give a discount we can't eat the mailing cost. Even if we ship them via media mail it won't be cheap. What if we sell at price and absorb the shipping cost? Her readers will still get a signed copy and that should excite her fan base."

"We'd sell more copies if it's discounted too."

"But we'd earn less profit per book. And the more books we sell, the more we'll have to package and ship. I can run the numbers if you want, but we'll be better off without the discount."

He was probably right. She was beginning to trust his expertise as it was starting to pay off. He already had a basic website up and running, so this would require minimal effort on the front end. "All right. I'll take your word for it."

"Awesome. And I love your idea."

"Now all we have to do is get Phoebe on board."

A while later Shelby hung up the phone and nearly pumped a fist in the air. Phoebe was open to talking about the idea, but she wanted to do so in person. Shelby wasn't surprised. The woman lived alone—she'd been a widow for years.

Excitement winged through Shelby as she helped a customer, then assisted Zuri (fiction and self-help) with the POS system. This preorder special could be big if Phoebe was able to spread the word to her fans far and wide.

"We've been busy today," Zuri said after the last customer left. The college student majored in ethnic studies at GU and was well read in almost every genre, which made her excellent at hand selling. "The apparel has been popular."

"Gray's been posting photos on our socials. I think it's helping."

"No doubt."

"How are your classes going?"

"Great. I love my professors this semester. And the campus is so beautiful in the fall. We don't get those colors back home."

Zuri was from Florida. "Do you miss your family?"

"Tons. But I need to be here and they're supportive of my education." She checked her watch. "I can't believe it's noon already."

"Why don't you take your lunch break? I'll send Theresa when you return."

"Sounds good." Zuri grabbed her purse from behind the counter. "Aw, when did you put this up?"

Shelby turned and followed Zuri's gaze to the westerns Shelby had pared down to one shelf. The ledge now boasted an engraved gold plate she hadn't seen before.

In memory of Viola Thatcher
"A great book begins with an idea; a great life, with a determination."
Louis L'Amour

She hunted down Gray and found him out back with Shadow. He was texting on his phone while the dog smelled every bush in the yard. Her heart softened at the sight of Gray—and it was pretty mushy already from seeing what he'd done.

"I saw the plaque," she said when he noticed her. "That was really sweet of you to put that up. She liked that quote."

He smiled. "I know. She quoted it to me a time or two."

"Sounds about right."

"I know this has been hard, making all these changes to the store. She'd be really proud of you, Shelby."

"Thanks." It had felt like uprooting Gram one volume at a time. It needed to be done, but gosh, it made her ache to change the shop her grandma had worked so hard to build. Shelby just hoped it worked. Speaking of which . . .

"I got hold of Miss Phoebe. She invited us over to discuss the preorder deal tomorrow afternoon."

"*Us?*"

"If you don't have plans, I could use your help."

He shrugged. "Sure. Why does she want to discuss it in person?"

"She's lonely, I think. But she's also closing in on her deadline and can't afford time away from writing. That's why I offered to bring pizza."

"I could pick it up. Or we could just have it delivered."

Shelby held back a grin. "Um, yeah, that'll work."

Chapter 25

It was almost one o'clock when Gray pulled up to Shelby's grandma's house. He wasn't sure why she'd asked to meet him here. For that matter, he wasn't sure why she wanted his help with Miss Phoebe. But she was the boss and it wasn't as if he minded spending time with her.

Now there was a thought he didn't care to examine too closely.

He'd left Shadow at home in a pet enclosure he'd purchased last night. He was now in for over two hundred dollars on the mutt. He should probably take out an ad in the paper or something. But he'd had a lot on his plate and hadn't gotten around to it. Just getting his SUV out of hock had taken him hours yesterday (plus a hundred seventy-five dollars). *Thank you, Grandville police.*

He'd also checked in with his boss back home. The new project manager was doing well. Gray made a phone call to smooth things over with a particular customer and checked on some siding that had gotten lost in transit. Since he'd offered to do the bookkeeping remotely, he'd also been working on that. It only took a couple hours a week.

As he exited the vehicle he spotted Shelby around back, walking toward a wooden pier. He headed her way. The sun was high overhead against a clear blue sky, providing welcome warmth for the November day. They were in the middle of a nice warm spell, though he'd hardly been outside to enjoy it.

"Afternoon," he called.

She turned from the end of the dock, where she was setting a pizza box inside a fishing boat. "Hey. You're right on time."

The pier shuddered under his footsteps. "Did I miss something? I thought we were going to Miss Phoebe's."

"We are." Humor flashed in her eyes. "Did I forget to mention she lives on Eagle Island?"

"You may have left out that little detail. But now I know why pizza delivery wasn't an option." His gaze skated to the box. "Luigi's . . . Nice." Best pizza in three counties. His mouth watered just thinking about the savory sauce and mounds of melted cheese. "Hop in. I'll untie us."

He undid the knots as she settled in the captain's seat and started the outboard engine. It was the same aluminum boat they'd taken out on the lake many times back in the day. What would the family do with it now that they were selling Miss Viola's property?

He wouldn't mind having the boat for himself. He could keep it at the Airbnb for guests. *And then what, idiot?* Regular visits to the good people of Grandville? Rides in the boat, living out memories of what used to be while watching Shelby fall in love with and potentially marry her banker boyfriend? He felt that one in his gut.

Despite the painful reality check, the memories of those sunset kisses on the lake lingered. She used to set him on fire. He'd been so far gone over her. She was the first woman to sweep him away like that.

Who was he kidding? She'd been the only one to do so. Losing her had left him damaged goods. He'd never wanted to find himself in that miserable place again. After all, you couldn't lose what you never had. Never mind that he'd been the one to ruin things.

He settled in the seat beside her and she guided the boat from the slip and out onto the open waters. There were only a few boats on the lake today despite the beautiful weather. "You do much fishing these days?"

"I still go out with Dad sometimes."

She'd always had great luck with the fish. She called it skill. He wasn't so sure. "There's good fishing back home. When I'm not working you can usually find me casting a line on the French Broad River."

She was quiet for a beat. "What's your life like in Riverbend Gap? Are you close to anyone back home?"

He arched a brow. "Is that your way of asking if I have a girlfriend?"

"Nooo." The word accompanied an eye roll. "I was asking about friends. Besides, most girlfriends wouldn't be too happy about their man helping out an old girlfriend with her business."

He gave her a speculative look. "How about boyfriends?"

"Logan is very understanding. But we were talking about you."

He allowed the dodge. "I have friends back home. I'm closest to the guys I work with since that's where I spend most of my time." He took in the scenery and could almost feel his muscles relaxing at the familiar beauty. For all the folks around here who'd been a thorn in his side, he'd always loved this lake and the wooded hills around it. "The trees still have their color."

"I've been wanting to get out and enjoy fall, but I've been pretty distracted."

"You've had a lot to deal with. But better late than never. The leaves will be gone soon." Autumn had always been her favorite season. She loved the crisp air after the steamy summer. The cool nights, the scent of campfires, and the beautiful foliage surrounding the lake. He couldn't blame her.

As they headed out of the bay and into the main basin, the wind ruffled her brown hair and the sunlight lit it with copper sparkles. He used to be mesmerized by all the colors in hair that seemed plain brown at first glance. It was just like her personality—seemingly straightforward when she had so many layers. You only had to look for them.

She turned and caught him staring.

He looked away. He shouldn't be thinking about her hair or her personality or the lingering kisses they'd once shared on this very boat. Did her boyfriend know they were taking this little excursion today?

"There's a rumor going around about you."

He winced at the memory of being hauled into the back of Officer Remington's cruiser Friday night. "Shocker."

"Miss Patsy heard from Lou Greenwell that you were hauled away in handcuffs Friday night after being arrested on a drunk and disorderly charge. Word has it you did some real damage over at Dirty Harry's."

"Obviously untrue."

She shook her head as she steered toward Eagle Island. "The grapevine sure keeps it entertaining."

"It was actually a DUI."

Her gaze darted to him, the grin sliding from her mouth. *"What?"*

Might as well get it out there. "I was pulled over and taken in—that part's true enough. They took me to the station, but the Breathalyzer proved me completely sober. Good to hear the grapevine's still alive and well though."

"Why didn't you tell me?"

"What could you have done? It worked out."

"Worked out? I could've—" She huffed. "Was this a setup? Was Mason Remington involved in this?"

She'd always been so defensive of Gray. It had been a new and welcome feeling having someone on his side, ready to defend him. But he didn't need her to come to his defense now. She had a business to save and she needed this community's support now more than ever. "Let it go, Shelby."

"They can't arrest you simply because they don't want you here."

Oh yeah? "Seems they can."

"You have to report him."

"Who's going to believe me, Shelby? The folks at the precinct seemed pretty delighted to see me behind bars."

"This isn't right. We should file a complaint."

"It's over and done with. I won't be here long—and until I leave I can fight my own battles."

"You always were stubborn beyond reason."

He stared at her pointedly. "Pot, meet kettle."

She throttled down as they neared the island with only the one house. He didn't like the set of her jutted chin. Didn't want her getting caught in the cross fire. "Stay out of this, Shelby. Promise me."

She cast him a glance. "I don't like it."

"You don't have to. But they can't hurt me. I won't be around long enough for that."

"Famous last words."

* * *

I hope she goes for the idea," Gray said as they mounted the porch steps.

The pizza's enticing aroma wafted over from the box he carried. Shelby gave the box—and Gray—a once-over as she lifted her hand to knock. Her lips twitched. "Well, it never hurts to come bearing gifts."

The author's home was a yellow Cape Cod with white shutters and a quaint front porch. It was rather ordinary except for its island locale, which caused the property to be valued in the millions. It was one of only three islands in Cedar Lake and the only one boasting a house. "I've always wanted to come here."

"Who hasn't? Can you imagine living on an island?"

Birds tweeted from a nearby pine tree and a squirrel scuttled through the leaves. It was the ideal location for someone who wanted to escape the rest of the world.

Gray glanced around the wooded property and spoke softly. "No wonder she's lonely."

"She used to live near town but was having trouble meeting her deadlines."

"So she moved to an *island*?"

"Miss Phoebe's a little . . . eccentric."

The door swung open and the vivacious woman grabbed Shelby's hands. "Sweetheart, I swear you just get prettier every time I set eyes on you."

"You're one to talk, Miss Phoebe." The author had a head full of auburn curls and green eyes that sparkled. She wore brick-red lipstick that flattered her coloring and a light cardigan that skimmed her curvy figure. Her smile could light up a room.

That smile found Gray and her gaze swept over him from head to toe. "Well, *hello there*. Who do we have here?"

Shelby held back a chuckle. "This is Gray, the temporary business partner I told you about. Gray, meet Grandville's famous author."

"Nice to meet you, ma'am."

"Oh, pooh. Who is this ma'am you speak of? Call me Phoebe, honey. Shelby, you didn't mention he was such a handsome devil." She stepped aside, letting them through. "Come in, come in. Have a seat at the table, my sweets. I'll get us some tea. I'm so eager for company. I've been neck-deep in this story for days on end . . ." Her voice trailed as she headed into the kitchen.

Gray followed Shelby into the small dining room and set the pizza box on the table. He leveled her with a stare. "You could've warned me."

Shelby waved him off. "So she's a bit of a flirt."

"She practically purred when I passed by."

Shelby smothered a laugh.

His gaze sharpened on her as she barely held back a smile. "'Bearing gifts,' huh? Could've mentioned I was one of them."

Chapter 26

Eleven years ago

For weeks Gray and Shelby saw each other only in passing at school. There were many fleeting looks, tortured smiles, and whispered greetings. Each night as he lay in bed, waiting for sleep to claim him, it was all he could do to keep from calling her. So many times he'd tapped out texts.

How are you?

I miss you.

I can't take this anymore.

He deleted them all. They had to see this through if he had any chance of winning over her father. She would let him know when and if her father softened. Gray just had to hope and pray it would all work out. Not easy for him—optimism wasn't exactly his default.

A couple days after he and Shelby had last spoken on the phone, Gray handwrote an apology to her father. He poured out his heart in a way he never had before. Assured Mr. Thatcher that his intentions were honorable. That he'd like the chance to earn back the man's trust. He read the note at least ten times before sticking it in the mailbox.

Mr. Thatcher never responded to the letter. But Gray hadn't really expected him to. Still, Gray *was* genuinely sorry—and he hoped it would eventually have a positive effect.

If Gray had thought his feelings for Shelby might fade with time, he would've been so wrong. They only grew deeper. Every time he caught sight of her down the hall or across the room, his chest ached for want of her. At times he was crippled with the fear that her father would never give him a chance and he'd be forced to live without her forever.

It was a suffocating kind of fear. The kind he'd felt last year when his dad was sentenced to sixteen years in prison, and Gray was sentenced to life without a father—or so it seemed.

He'd confided in his grandmother about Shelby and their hopes that her dad would eventually come around. She offered continual encouragement. Somehow when she was around he could believe Mr. Thatcher might learn to trust him. He could even believe he might be worthy of Shelby.

But most of the time he just missed her so much he was miserable and hopeless.

The days dragged by. The grass turned brown, the trees shed their leaves. The weather changed. But their situation remained the same.

The only good thing about their separation was it gave him plenty of time to study. Throughout December when his classmates prepared for the school's Christmas dance, Gray studied. While his peers shopped for the perfect gifts for their friends and family, Gray studied. While the other students attended family gatherings and gift exchanges, Gray studied.

He did buy two gifts: a box of his grandma's favorite toffee and a gold necklace with a heart for Shelby. He left the package in her car when it was parked outside the bookshop on December twenty-third. He hoped wearing it would remind her of how much he loved her.

His spirits were buoyed on Christmas Day when he found a gift from her on his porch: a first edition of *James and the Giant Peach*—the book that had begun his love of reading. He thrilled at the sight of the book.

At the thoughtfulness of the gift. But it was her brief note he pored over every day for weeks.

> *Thank you so much for the necklace! I'll wear it every day and think of how much I love you. We're making progress! I miss you so much.*
>
> *XO,*
> *Shelby*

He spent Christmas break studying for the exams he'd take in January. Spent New Year's Eve at home with Gram, watching the ball drop in Times Square. When school break ended he was both relieved and desolate at the thought of seeing Shelby again. It was a cruel form of torture being so close and yet so far.

By the end of January his GPA had never been higher. His classmates discovered that he'd passed Brendan as class valedictorian. More importantly, the Warner Scholarship was within Gray's grasp. He would head off to Vanderbilt and Shelby would go to Belmont. They'd both be in Nashville. Surely he'd have her father's permission to date her by then.

With his grades on the rise and his future looming large, his hopes mounted. But soon a new kind of torture emerged in the form of Brendan and his goons. One day in late January they caught Gray alone in the gym locker room, and with a ratio of three to one, he had no fighting chance. Brendan's minions held him while Brendan knocked the air from his lungs. Nice and tidy. No witnesses. No bruises.

But the message was clear: Brendan was not about to lose that scholarship to the likes of him. After they left he picked himself up from a heap on the cement floor, seething. He'd like to wring their necks. One on one, none of them would stand a chance with Gray. But he wasn't an idiot.

They were trying to provoke him. Trying to set him up so Brendan would win the Warner Scholarship, which could be revoked for misconduct. Too bad Gray had no proof of what they'd done. No one would ever believe the truth without it.

The scholarship wasn't the only thing keeping him from retribution. He was still trying to win Mr. Thatcher's favor. He couldn't afford to be foolish. He had far too much on the line.

Then finally on a snowy day in mid-February, Shelby texted him out of the blue.

You're invited to my grandma's house for supper this Friday at 6:00. My dad will be there. Can you come?

He stared in disbelief at the text for a long minute, adrenaline pumping nervous energy throughout his body. His muscles tensed. His hands shook. He dissected the verbiage of the text. The stilted tone and marked lack of enthusiasm. Her dad was likely privy to both her invitation and his response.

I'd love to come, he replied. *Thank you for inviting me. Can I bring something?*

He sent the text and waited. Only seconds passed before her reply came. *Just yourself. See you then.*

The tick of the grandfather clock filled an uncomfortable gap of silence. Mr. Thatcher silently forked a brussels sprout into his mouth. Upon Gray's arrival the man had offered him a reserved greeting and a firm handshake. Now his prominent brows were pulled into a frown over cold blue eyes that mostly avoided Gray.

Thank God this meal was almost over. Although that was also awful because nothing had yet been accomplished. He could hardly swallow the roast beef past the tightness of his throat.

Across the table, Miss Viola offered him an encouraging smile.

Next to him, Shelby shifted in her seat. "Daddy, did I tell you Gray is all set to be our class valedictorian?"

"Several times." He spared Gray a glance. "Congratulations on your accomplishment."

"Thank you, sir. But we still have weeks to go and it's a close race."

"You'll get it." Shelby gazed up at him in a way that made him want to stare at her forever. "I know you will."

Miss Viola put her napkin on her plate. "You're planning to attend Vanderbilt in the fall?"

"Yes, ma'am. I'll be studying business. I'm especially interested in accounting and marketing."

"He'd like to own his own company someday."

Mr. Thatcher pinned him with an expectant look. "Whereabouts?"

Clearly the right answer was here in Grandville. But it wasn't the truthful one. "I'm not sure just yet."

"What kind of business?"

Miss Viola scowled at her son. "Stop interrogating the boy, Stanley. He's hardly touched his roast and it's one of my best, if I do say so myself."

"Everything is delicious, ma'am."

"Well, I'm not the cook your grandma is, but I've got a meal or two up my sleeve."

Thankfully the topic turned to Gray's grandma and the secret recipes Miss Viola was always trying to get her hands on.

When they wrapped up the meal Gray offered to help with dishes, but Miss Viola refused. Much to his dismay, she enlisted Shelby's help instead, leaving him alone in the living room with Mr. Thatcher. Gray was glad at least that they were in somewhat neutral territory. He suspected that was Shelby's doing. Though he couldn't be sure since he hadn't gotten her alone yet.

The man gestured to the comfy-looking sofa and settled in an olive-green La-Z-Boy that had seen better days. Miss Viola's home was cozy with colorful throws and rugs and antiques sprinkled among newer furnishings. She had eclectic taste in the art department, but he liked the whimsical pieces.

Mr. Thatcher wasted no time getting down to business. "Have you been seeing my daughter?"

Gray blinked. "I, uh, I see her at school pretty much every day."

"Outside of school. Privately."

"No, sir."

"Not once?"

"Not since October tenth."

"Have you called or texted her?"

"The last we spoke on the phone was October eleventh. The only text since then was her invitation for tonight." Gray gathered his nerve. This was it. He needed to fight for this. He'd waited months for the chance and he couldn't blow it now. "I'd like to apologize in person for the way I conducted myself early in my relationship with Shelby."

Mr. Thatcher's eyes turned frosty as he lifted a brow.

"I mean the sneaking around," Gray said quickly. "As I said in my letter, that was my fault. I take full responsibility."

"Shelby explained your reasoning. About a hundred times, in fact. It seems my daughter and mother are convinced your bad reputation is undeserved."

"I'm not perfect, sir. I'll be the first to admit I have plenty of faults. But neither am I a stranger to false accusations and rumors. I care deeply for your daughter and only want the best for her."

"And that's you?"

Warmth shot to his face, prickled the back of his neck. "I have no doubt she could do better than me. But I think she returns my feelings, and there's nothing I want so much as a second chance with her. I know

I don't come from much, but I have plans for a better future. Plans I'm working really hard on."

Mr. Thatcher held eye contact.

Gray fought the urge to look away. To squirm in his seat. What was he thinking? Had anything Gray said swayed the man? It was impossible to tell with his impenetrable eyes and perpetual frown.

"I didn't appreciate the way you sneaked around with my daughter—"

Gray opened his mouth.

Mr. Thatcher held up his hand. "But I did appreciate your apology. And your efforts since then to abide by my wishes. Whether or not you're deserving of my daughter remains to be seen." He sat back in his chair, steepled his fingers, and leveled a stare at Gray. "But I do believe in second chances. And it seems as if you're currently in the enviable position of receiving one."

Gray's breath escaped his lungs. A ten-ton load fell from his shoulders. "Thank you, sir. You won't regret it."

"See that I don't." He got up and retreated to the kitchen.

The mumbling of voices carried from the kitchen. Mr. Thatcher was saying his good-byes to Shelby and Miss Viola. The side door opened and shut.

The second the man was out the door, Shelby ran into the living room and flung herself into Gray's arms.

Chapter 27

Present day

Hours later Miss Phoebe walked them to the door, setting a hand on Gray's arm for the fourth time. No, "setting" wasn't quite right. The woman curled her long fingers around his bicep and gave it a gentle squeeze.

Then she gave it a final pat as if she couldn't quite bring herself to let go. "I hope I didn't keep y'all too long. You're such delightful company."

"Are you kidding?" Shelby turned at the door. "I love talking books with you. The writer's process fascinates me. And I can't thank you enough for doing this preorder special with us."

"My readers will go crazy for it—and preorders are crucial for me too. I'll sign as many books as we can presell."

"We appreciate it," Gray said. "I'll get the web page set up tomorrow."

"Let me know when it's a go, sugar, and I'll get Lacey to spread the news to all my fans. Thank you for the pizza and the visit. I know it's such a pain to get all the way out here."

"Thank you for having us." Gray leaned in for a quick hug and instead found himself swallowed by eager arms and a cloud of floral perfume. He patted her shoulder awkwardly until she released him.

The woman turned to Shelby and offered her a big hug too. "Let's keep in touch, sweethcart." Then more quietly, "Oh, girl, you'd better snap him up before I do."

Shelby's snort turned to a clearing of the throat. "It's always so nice to visit with you, Miss Phoebe."

"You pimped me out." Gray had to work to keep his scowl from morphing into a smile.

"Now, let's not underestimate the power of Luigi's pizza."

"I swear her hand dropped to my backside during that hug."

She chuckled as he assisted her into the boat. "It did not. And don't tell me you didn't enjoy every minute of her attention. She catered to your every whim."

"I was afraid for my life."

She laughed outright and the sound caught him right in the heart. He'd forgotten how much he loved that sound.

He untied the boat, then grabbed her arm before she sat in the captain's seat. "Let me drive so you can enjoy the scenery."

"I'll take you up on that. Though I'm flying so high, I don't know if I could possibly feel much better."

Once she was seated he started the motor and guided the boat from the slip. The water was as smooth as glass. The sun had disappeared behind the hills. They'd been at Miss Phoebe's house all afternoon, and even he had to admit the time passed quickly. The author's verbal stories were so entertaining he'd already added her latest book to his to-be-read pile.

He'd looked up Phoebe Bell last night. The author was as successful as Shelby had intimated. She'd even had two books adapted for the big screen. Her social media following was impressive—she had over a hundred thousand Facebook followers and even more on Instagram.

"I have to hand it to you, Shel." He increased the boat's speed. "You're a genius. This preorder thing's gonna sell a ton of books."

"Hope you're right."

"Take the win. She's got a massive following and readers love their signed copies. On another note, we'd better line up plenty of help to package and ship all those copies."

"We'll need readers to receive them on January thirteenth. Her avid fans will be upset if they don't have it on release day."

January thirteenth was two months away. He'd be back in Riverbend Gap by then. The thought of going home opened up a pit inside. It wasn't the thought of leaving Grandville or the bookstore. But the thought of leaving Shelby.

Not good, Briggs. Not good at all. He couldn't let himself go there again.

The past no longer stood between them, but there were plenty of other reasons why thoughts like that were unwelcome. She'd never leave the bookstore or her family—and he'd never ask her to. Grandville was her home.

Oh, and there was her boyfriend.

You're an idiot. Here he was, sitting here detailing all the reasons he should control himself, when Shelby wasn't the slightest bit interested in anything he could offer.

The engine sputtered. Gray frowned at the throttle, then glanced back at the engine.

"What's going on?" Shelby was already moving toward the motor when it died.

He tried to restart it three times, but it only sputtered.

"Dad keeps a tool kit on board. Maybe you can fix whatever's wrong."

Gray's eyes drifted over the instrument panel, then landed on the fuel gauge. "I can't fix this."

She turned to look at him. "Why not?"

"Because we're out of gas."

Chapter 28

The boat drifted to a stop. The shoreline was forever away and there wasn't another vessel in sight. Shelby shelved her hands on her hips. "Yep, I'm a genius all right."

"It could happen to anybody. We'll just—" Gray's gaze skated over the boat's interior. "I don't suppose there are paddles tucked away somewhere?"

She lifted the seat well cover even though a paddle would never fit inside. There was some fishing tackle, an old ball cap, and four life vests. She let it fall shut with a huff. She was better than this. But she'd been so distracted by their mission. And, if she was honest, by Gray's presence on a boat they'd once spent so many hours on.

She shook off the thought as she fished her phone from her pocket and checked the screen. No bars. Hardly a surprise in the middle basin. "Nothing."

"Me either." He surveyed the distant shoreline. "Maybe someone'll see us out here."

"If they do, they'll assume we're fishing." A heavy feeling of dread anchored in her stomach. The water slapped the sides of the boat as it rocked gently, drifting slightly with the wind. Her legs were wobbly in a way that had nothing to do with motion. Shelby lowered herself onto the seat.

"The sun's setting."

It would be full dark in half an hour or so. "We'll keep checking our phones. We're bound to get cell service eventually."

Shelby felt much less hopeful forty-five minutes later. To the west, the last light of the day lingered on the horizon. At least the moon had favored them by making an appearance. Starlight twinkled overhead. Gray was a mere shadow on the other side of the boat.

Even though they'd only drifted a bit, she checked her phone again. Maybe a night fisherman would come along. Before the thought was finished, reality drained the optimism. Fishing was good in November, but dusk and early morning were the premium hours—one had passed and the other was still hours away. Also, the deep waters along the shoreline were the best spots, not the middle of the lake—all good fishers knew that.

Gray was pretty quiet over there. Was reality settling in for him too?

No one could see them out here now. The wind was pushing them slowly away from Eagle Island and farther into the center of the basin where they were unlikely to get cell reception. They'd already gone through the bins and found nothing useful for signaling or moving the boat.

"Hand me your phone," he said. "Now that it's dark, maybe the flashlight will draw attention."

"Good idea, but let's use yours. I'm low on battery."

"Mine just went dead."

Her stomach plummeted. "I'm down to 12 percent. We should probably save it in case we get reception."

"You're right. Chances of flagging someone down probably weren't high anyway."

"I'm going to shut mine off for now. I'll check periodically."

A cool breeze blew across the surface of the water. Shelby crossed her arms over her torso. She wore a long-sleeve T-shirt that had been comfortable earlier, but it was getting colder.

The boat rocked as Gray shifted. "Here, take my sweatshirt."

"I'm fine."

He extended it to her. "Take it. I have a shirt underneath and I'm not cold."

When they'd been together she joked that he had an internal furnace. He never even wore a jacket in the winter. "You sure?"

"Positive."

She took the hoodie, slipped it over her head, and threaded her arms through the sleeves. She practically swam in it. But the thick material was gloriously warm from his body heat and smelled divine. "Thank you."

The region might be in the middle of a warm spell, but temperatures were sure to drop into the fifties tonight. And out here on the open water it would feel even cooler. Why hadn't she checked the gas level? Such a rookie mistake. "This is all my fault. I'm sorry."

"I didn't check either. We'll be fine."

"Even if we're out here all night?" Neither of them had said it out loud yet. As if they might speak it into being. But the sun had taken her hope right over the horizon.

"We can pretend we're camping." There was a smile in his tone.

"On a cold November night in the middle of the lake?"

"It's not that cold."

Another breeze cut across the lake, contradicting his words. Her empty stomach rumbled, reminding her it was past suppertime. The pizza they'd had for lunch would have to carry them both for a while. It was going to be a long night. But maybe conversation would make the time pass more quickly. "Hope you didn't have any plans tonight."

"I was supposed to play basketball with Daryl."

That's right. Gray was friends with him too. "How did that relationship happen?"

"When we lived in the trailer park, he was just down the street. He asked me to shoot hoops with him one time, and we just kind of got into the habit. Nice guy."

Daryl wasn't the only one who was nice. Not every teenage boy would take the time. She wondered how Daryl had felt when Gray disappeared so abruptly. She'd been shocked. They'd been so close, and then he was gone. And she knew nothing about how his life had unfolded after that.

"What happened after you left Grandville? What was basic training like? Where did you go from there?"

A brief pause revealed perhaps he was surprised she'd initiated a forbidden topic. "Basic training was as tough as they say. But I didn't really mind. I had a lot of anger to work through. And not a small amount of guilt."

"About leaving?"

"Yes. Also, I was heartbroken. I know I brought it on myself, but that didn't stop me from missing you like crazy."

His words were a balm to her soul. But she didn't let herself linger there. "Where were you stationed?"

"Afghanistan. For a while we conducted operations against the remnants of Al-Qaeda. Then when the withdrawal of troops began, I served by training Afghan forces."

"Was it terrible?"

"Not really. It gave me a purpose. I started building some self-worth, figuring out who I was outside of Grandville."

Because he'd been rejected by the community. "But you never lost sight of what you ultimately wanted out of life."

"I was always clear about that."

"And you did it. Went to college, got a degree, made something of yourself."

Gray shrugged. "I'm doing all right."

"You're doing more than all right. You're very good at what you do.

You should be proud of that—coming from nothing and building a life for yourself."

"I am."

He did seem more at peace with himself. More confident in who he was. She looked way down the lake where Gray's house sat on a little inlet. "Will Shadow be okay at home alone?"

"He'll be fine. My wood floors may not be though."

"I assume you can fix it, working for a construction company and all."

"Sure. It's not that big a deal."

"Do you like your job?" She always thought he'd own a business someday. He'd talked about it a lot, wearing a dogged expression. He'd always had something to prove. To whom, she wasn't sure. Maybe just himself.

"Love it. The owners, Gavin and Wes, are good people. Run a solid business. I feel like I contribute something worthwhile. And they've hinted there's opportunity for ownership there eventually."

"And this leave of absence isn't going to wreck that for you?"

"Nah, I've worked there long enough, built up some trust. The respect goes both ways."

She was so glad for that. Gray deserved respect and trust—something he'd had precious little of here in Grandville. And even though he had little regard for the townspeople, he'd never forgotten her grandmother. She'd thought about that over the years. Mostly when Gram mentioned hearing from him.

"Thank you for keeping in touch with Gram. It meant a lot to her."

"I think it was more her keeping in touch with me."

Shelby happened to know he'd written regular letters. How many men his age cared enough to keep in contact with an elderly woman? "She missed your grandma so much."

"They were quite the pair, those two. Miss Viola always pulling Granny into some crazy activity or event. Forcing her out of her comfort zone."

"And Miss Dorothy always keeping Gram level. They were a good match. I can't imagine having a friend for fifty years, through all of life's ups and downs. What a gift."

He made some noncommittal noise. Did Gray have a friend back home? He'd always had such high walls. She hoped he wasn't quite the lone wolf he'd been in high school. Or maybe he wasn't a lone wolf at all. Maybe it was just a protective mechanism—reject others before they could reject him. She ached at the thought.

Since he'd returned to town he'd met up with Patrick Ballard a few times. That realization soothed the ache. Life was hard enough without good friends to hold you up. To cheer you on. Everyone needed a safe place to land, and Patrick was as loyal and as stable as they came.

Though Shelby still kept in touch with friends from high school, Liddy was her safe place. Shelby had known from the first time Caleb brought her home that she was something special. Those trips Shelby had taken to New York were as much to see Liddy as Caleb—and now sweet little Ollie.

How would Shelby manage those trips now that the store was her responsibility? She had dependable booksellers on staff but no one suitable for management. Janet would be great, but she didn't want more responsibility. Zuri had potential, but she was only part time. And once she graduated she'd be off to bigger and better things.

"What are you thinking about over there?" The darkness seemed to call attention to Gray's deep voice.

"The store. Gram made it all look so easy." But she hadn't exactly been on top of things, had she?

"You have a big role in the business. It was a shared responsibility."

And now she was in it alone when even Gram hadn't been able to make it work. How was Shelby going to manage on her own?

"I can hear you worrying from over here. Have some faith. Businesses go through tough spells. You're doing all the right things to turn it around."

"Hope you're right."

She'd finally submitted to his training her on Gram's end of the business. And while inputting inventory and bookkeeping wasn't really her thing, she was capable of doing it. She just couldn't perform both their jobs, and she'd been putting off hiring someone since Gray was helping. She should probably resume looking though. He'd only be here for another month and a half.

The thought caught her in the heart.

No, not the heart. She was just worried about managing without him. Even if they were able to get the business back on track, would she be able to keep it steady month after month, year after year? It felt like a daunting task. And a lonely one without Gram around, singing off-key. Shelby's throat swelled at the thought.

I miss you so much, Gram. I thought you'd be here forever.

"Nobody lasts forever, Sweet Girl. You'll be just fine on your own."

The backs of her eyes stung and she blinked back tears. Gram had always believed in her. Why was she having such a hard time believing in herself?

She wasn't sure how much time had passed when Gray spoke again. "Why don't you check your phone again?"

The breeze had picked up and she could tell by the lights on the shore that they'd drifted a bit more. She waited for her phone to power up and zeroed in on the upper left corner. "I have a bar!" She tapped on Favorites. Dad put his phone in sleep mode after nine, and it was later than that.

Caleb it is.

She tapped on his name. "It's ringing." Once. Then twice. *Come on, pick up, Caleb.* Three times. *Please, God, don't let me lose the signal.* Why wasn't he answering?

A click sounded. "This is Caleb. I'm unavailable at the moment. Leave a message and I'll get back with you." *Beeeep.*

"Caleb, it's me. I'm in a boat in the middle of the main basin. Currently just west of Inlet Bay and drifting westward. I ran out of gas and hardly have a cell signal and my phone's running out of battery. Please come as soon as you can!" There was no sound on the line. She checked the screen.

"He didn't pick up?"

"No. And the call dropped. I don't even know if the message went through."

All the hopes that had buoyed her the past minute sank like a two-ton boulder, leaving her with a severe adrenaline crash.

"Maybe we'll get a signal again."

"I'm down to 7 percent." She shut off her phone. Even if Caleb later saw that she'd called, her voicemail might not have gone through. He might try to call her back, but that wouldn't do any good. They were likely stuck out here for the night. She hugged herself against the cold breeze.

"We should probably think about getting settled for the night."

She glanced around the small boat. What did "settled" mean exactly? There were two metal benches, too short for even her to stretch out on, and a flat-bottomed hull that was probably cold as ice.

"You'll be warmer when you get down low, out of the wind."

The boat rocked with his movement. A seat well cover squeaked as he lifted it. "We can open up the life vests and lie on them."

"Do you want your hoodie back?"

"Keep it. I'll be fine." He handed her two vests and they made a pallet of sorts in the middle of the boat.

She pulled up the hoodie and tied the drawstring under her chin. Then she lowered herself onto the floor, lying on her back on the lumpy pallet, one of the life vests cushioning her head.

The boat rocked hard as Gray settled somewhere beside her.

Minutes ticked away as the vessel settled in place. Water licked the hull. Crickets chirped and a bullfrog croaked, making it seem as if the boat were just offshore. Funny how sounds carried over the water.

It really was warmer down here though. No wind. And the vests provided welcome insulation from the cold hull.

She was supremely conscious of Gray's body and the heat rolling off it. She could hear his breaths. They were all alone out here. In the dark. Under the stars. Her heart acknowledged that fact with a few heavy thumps.

"I know it's early," he said, "but we should probably try to get some sleep."

She was still trying a while later. Maybe an hour. Maybe two, judging by the drop in temperature. She shivered, then crossed her arms over her chest, hoping to conserve some warmth. It was hard to fall asleep when she was so cold.

Gray had been still for a long time. At least one of them was getting some rest.

Maybe she should check her phone one last time and see if Caleb had gotten her message. It would be worth it, even if it took the rest of her battery. Once morning arrived, other boaters would be about. They wouldn't need the phone then.

She rolled as quietly and gently as she could away from Gray so the light and motion wouldn't wake him. Then she powered up her phone. It was bright in the darkness. There was no signal, and as her gaze flicked to the battery icon, it dropped to 3 percent. Hopes dashed, she shut down the phone.

Looked as if they'd be out here all night.

Chapter 29

This was torture. They were in the middle of the lake, all alone, night closing around them, and he was lying inches from the woman he'd spent his whole adulthood reminiscing about. Sure, he'd been working with her for over four weeks. But this was different. Out here there were no distractions.

There was nothing but time and *her*.

Moonlight draped over her form like an ethereal blanket. He smelled the sweet scent of her shampoo. Heard her shallow breaths. Felt her shivering. He could easily alleviate her suffering by pulling her into his arms. But that would take his own torture to a new level. Anyway, she'd been still for a while. Maybe she'd finally fallen asleep. It was probably his own bedtime by now. Too bad he was wide awake.

She rolled away from him, moving slowly and carefully. A moment later the light of her phone illuminated the boat. She wasn't asleep after all. She was still holding out hope for a rescue. The phone went dark again and her quiet sigh drifted through the night air.

"No signal?" he asked.

The boat rocked gently as she glanced over her shoulder. "I thought you were asleep."

Her chattering teeth disrupted the flow of her words. Shelby got chilled in an air-conditioned restaurant. She used to carry a sweater with her even in the summer. Under the current conditions she was probably miserable.

Guilt sliced through him. "You're cold. Let me warm you up."

"That's okay."

"Your shivers are shaking the boat."

Nothing but silence. He got it. She wanted the warmth but not his nearness. He couldn't blame her. The closeness would serve as a reminder of what they'd once had. He wasn't too keen on jogging his own memory. But it was getting colder. He wouldn't mind a little warmth himself. Maybe then they could both fall asleep and forget they were stuck in the middle of the lake.

"Come on, Shelby. I'm not proposing marriage. Just a little shared body heat."

Water splashed nearby as a fish jumped.

"Well . . . when you put it like that, I guess it would be foolish to say no."

Taking that as permission, he slid over and pulled her against his chest. He tucked his knees into the back of hers and put his arm around her. His hand accidentally fell on hers, and he would've let go except it was like a block of ice. He wrapped his hand around it, half expecting her to jerk it away.

But she didn't. Instead she scooched back into his chest, tucking her head under his chin.

And holy smokes. She felt so good snuggled up against him—and not just her warmth. His heart hitched. *Do not make this personal. All you are is a warm, willing blanket.*

"You really *are* a furnace."

"And you're an ice cube."

"It's colder than I thought it would be."

The frigid water and metal beneath them didn't help. He tightened his arm around her, cupped her hand more tightly. "Maybe we can get some sleep now." That might be true for her, but his chances of sleep had just decreased exponentially. Because the scent of her hair teased his nostrils, and the feel of her soft curves against him made him recall other times he'd had his arms around her.

Like that first kiss on the Fourth of July, for instance. He'd known they had something special the minute his lips touched hers. She was hardly his first kiss, but hers made all the others irrelevant. The way she yielded to him made him downright heady. He couldn't believe Shelby Thatcher was kissing him back and with so much fervor. She was so soft. So responsive. All he wanted from then on was to make her his own and to belong to her in return.

When it actually happened, it was like a dream come true.

Getting to know her was the kind of pleasure he'd never experienced. Having her in his corner brought a wave of relief he hadn't even known he needed. It was no longer him against the world. They were a team. She was on his team.

And when they were alone . . . She had this ticklish spot on the side of her neck. Every time he kissed her there, even if they were half gone with passion, she hitched her shoulder and giggled. He often did it on purpose just to get that very reaction. The sound of her laughter lit him up.

"Thank you for staying in Grandville."

Her words cut through the silence, and the pleasant memory evaporated.

"I know I haven't been very welcoming."

A band tightened around his chest. "It's okay. I definitely owe you big-time."

"I probably expected too much from you back then."

"Nah." He shifted his hand on hers, warming her fingertips. "I was the problem, not you, Shelby."

"We were just kids though. When does that ever work out?"

Maybe that was true. But he'd wanted them to work just the same. Thought they'd have a future. His childhood had just warped him. Caused him to make a poor decision he would later regret.

"But look at you now. You didn't stop reaching for your dreams. And somehow, despite the way you were treated, you became a wonderful person."

Her words warmed a cold spot inside him. "If that's true, it's only because I had good people around me. You and my grandma. Your Gram."

"Still, I'm really proud of you for doing everything you set out to do."

He smiled against her hair. "Thanks."

* * *

For someone who'd been so uncomfortable moments ago, Shelby suddenly felt more at peace than she'd been for a long time. She let the sweet feeling wash over her. Maybe this was the forgiveness Gram had been urging her to find all these years.

"Or maybe it's just those strong, young arms that have you wrapped tight as a burrito."

Gram's voice invoked a smile. She'd always been president of the Gray Briggs Fan Club.

Shelby thought of Gram looking down on them right now. *I guess you must be pretty happy with yourself right now. But don't be getting any ideas.*

Though, yes, those strong, young arms did feel awfully nice—and not just the warmth. A niggle of guilt threaded through her. These were not the arms she was supposed to be thinking about or wishing for.

But while his warmth might not be a matter of survival, who could blame her for wanting to ease her discomfort? At least now she'd be able to sleep, rocked by the gentle sway of the boat.

Shelby shifted in her sleep, snuggling deep into the delicious warmth, and drifted off again. Her alarm was going off but she ignored it. She was so tired. And it was the middle of the night. But the buzzing grew louder.

Go away.

She whimpered, reaching once again for that deep state of oblivion.

"Shelby. Shelby, wake up."

"What . . . ?" She pried her eyes open to darkness. And that buzzing. It wasn't her alarm.

She was on the boat with Gray. And judging by the direction of his voice, she faced him now. Her head rested on his arm, her face pressing into his neck. And her knee— *Ack!* It was tucked between his legs.

She jerked it away, putting a few inches between them. The boat rocked in response.

"Someone's coming."

That buzzing was getting louder. *A boat!* She sprang upright and blinked against the docking lights cutting through the darkness. The spreader lights revealed the craft as a pontoon. *Caleb.* He must've gotten her message after all.

"Looks like we've been rescued." Gray stood and began stowing the life vests.

There was no reason to flag Caleb down as he was already heading directly their way. She crossed her arms against the breeze and waited.

"You okay?" Caleb called over the water.

"We're fine," she said. "Did you bring gas?"

"No, your message cut off so I didn't know what happened. I'll just tow you in."

She didn't have to see his expression. His tone informed her he was unhappy to find her stranded with Gray.

Caleb turned the pontoon and backed toward the front of the boat, then shut off the motor. "I'm throwing you a line."

The rope landed inside the boat with a thunk. Gray grabbed it and knotted it to the bow cleat.

Once it was secure Caleb called, "Hang on." He towed the boat toward the pontoon, and as they grew closer, even the darkness couldn't hide the irritation on Caleb's face.

Which probably accounted for Gray's silence.

"I wasn't sure my voicemail went through at all. We haven't had much of a signal."

Caleb said nothing more as he towed them closer. When the boats connected, Gray stepped onto the pontoon and held out a hand for her. Then she took the line from Caleb and secured it to the pontoon while Gray settled at the stern.

The boat lights illuminated Caleb's scowl—which he aimed directly at her. "Really, Shelby?"

Why did her brother always catch her in the most compromising positions? "It was business, Caleb. We weren't exactly out here for a joyride."

He took in her appearance: Gray's voluminous sweatshirt and her disheveled hair. She resisted the urge to smooth it. She imagined them as Caleb must've seen them just now, popping up from the hull of the boat like—

"Yeah, well, you looked pretty cozy out here to me. Maybe you've forgotten the way he left you, but I haven't. You think he's changed? People don't change. You're headed for heartbreak and you don't even know it."

Shelby bristled. He was wrong about all of it. They *had* been out here on business. Gray *had* changed. And they'd only huddled together for warmth. But she didn't feel like explaining any of that. "I called for help, Caleb, not a lecture."

Their gazes held for a long moment, two stubborn wills meeting and clashing.

"Have it your way," Caleb finally said. Then he headed for the captain's seat.

Chapter 30

Eleven years ago

As winter morphed into spring Gray hardly noticed the changing of seasons. Being with Shelby out in the open brought new feelings: pride and a kind of indescribable joy he'd never before experienced. Having her at his side in the cafeteria and holding hands in the hall had turned heads. Tongues wagged, sure. Everyone wondered what Shelby Thatcher was doing with the likes of him.

While his academic stature hardly overcame the damage to his reputation, his new role as Shelby's boyfriend seemed to make their peers wonder if they'd missed something. Her close friends at least gave him a chance. They even attended prom together with their dates and had a great time.

Brendan and his posse, however, glared daggers at Gray when they passed in the halls. He made a point of avoiding restrooms and locker rooms. No doubt they'd love to get him alone again—they had yet another reason to hate him now.

But the teachers loved Brendan—he sucked up to the men and charmed the women. He was as fake with the faculty as he'd been with Shelby, and they all bought into his pathetic act.

Gray took Shelby out once a week and savored their time alone. Each time he picked her up, her dad was cordial and so was her brother when he was home from college. Gray was finally making headway with her family. Maybe they had a chance after all. He hoped so, because he was falling deeper by the day.

In early May for Shelby's birthday, he spent some of his hard-earned money on a ring. Not an engagement ring, of course. They were only eighteen and had years of school ahead of them. But it *was* a promise. He already knew he wanted to spend the rest of his life with her, and she'd admitted the same in April as they'd talked on the phone late into the night. He wanted to give her a token of that sentiment. Something that would sustain them through college. And let's face it, he'd be so proud to see her wearing that symbol of his love on her finger.

On the evening of her birthday, after he'd treated her to dinner at the Waterfront Bistro, she opened the gift. They were at the park where they'd often met back in the fall. Her lips went slack at the sight of the ring glittering from its navy-blue nest. A tiny diamond nestled inside the gold infinity knot.

"Don't freak out." He spoke into the gap of silence, suddenly nervous. "It's not an engagement ring or anything. It's just a—"

"Promise ring?" She gazed up at him, tears shimmering in her hope-filled eyes.

A relieved breath tumbled from his lungs. "Will you wear it?"

She took the ring from its case. "Of course I'll wear it. Oh, Gray. I love it. I couldn't love anything more. I can't believe you spent so much money. You need to save up for books and such." But those qualms didn't stop her from slipping that ring onto her left hand or smiling like he'd just made her year.

He took her hand and pressed a kiss to her knuckles. "Worth every penny."

The smile in her eyes and the long, delicious kiss afterward carried him for days. But his relationship with her proved to be a distraction. Mid-month he went into an AP chemistry class unprepared for a pop quiz and his grade slipped to a high B.

A few days later, with just two weeks of school left, he discovered that he and Brendan were in a dead heat for valedictorian and the Warner Scholarship. The finals would determine whether or not Gray would go to college. The realization knocked the wind out of him. He couldn't believe he'd let his guard down for a couple of weeks and now everything was on the line.

Since he had two AP classes this semester and Brendan only had one, Gray would win if he got straight A's. He had to nail that chemistry final to raise his grade. He studied every spare minute, forgoing two date nights with Shelby—a huge sacrifice. She'd offered to help him study, but she was too darn distracting.

When finals week arrived he was prepared. He'd aced his first three. Chemistry was Thursday and on Friday, the last day of high school, all he had to do was turn in an English paper.

On Thursday when he finished his chemistry final, he felt invincible. He'd done well. He might have even gotten an A+. That scholarship was in the bag and there was nothing Brendan could do about it. In a celebratory mood, he took Shelby out for ice cream after work and they toasted cones to his bright future.

"Mr. Briggs, can you come with me, please?"

The easy smile slid from Gray's mouth at the sight of the vice principal in the doorway. Why were they calling him from English class? Had something happened?

His teacher, Mrs. Caldwell, glanced at the clock and offered Gray a smile. "It's almost time for the bell. Go ahead and turn in your paper and take your things with you."

"Yes, ma'am."

Mr. Fletcher's grim expression tightened the knot in Gray's stomach as they walked the quiet hall. "Did something happen? Is my grandma okay?"

"She's fine. This is another matter entirely."

"What's wrong then?"

The man didn't answer. Gray was about to ask again when he caught sight of the school principal, Mr. Donovan, standing by Gray's locker, watching them approach. A black plume of dread spread through him.

Mr. Donovan frowned. "Gray, I need you to open your locker, please."

"What's going on?"

"Open it, please."

Fine. He had nothing to hide. Gray put in the combination and opened the door. He'd already cleaned out his locker, so it was empty save his book bag.

"Open your bag, please."

What in the world did they hope to find? Drugs? A gun? It ticked him off to be singled out this way. But it also scared him to death because the future seemed so promising right now. And if he'd learned anything in life, it was that things never worked out his way.

He unzipped the two compartments and set the bag in Mr. Fletcher's outstretched arms. While he held it Mr. Donovan rifled through it. Gray kept a neat bag and knew exactly what was in it. His chemistry textbook, his English journal, a water bottle, his phone and charger, a ChapStick, a gel pen, and two yellow highlighters.

The principal pulled out the textbook and fluttered through the pages. A paper fell out and wafted onto the floor.

Mr. Fletcher picked it up, unfolded it, and aimed a frown Gray's way. "You'll need to come with us."

The paper, Gray found out in the office minutes later, was the advanced test for AP chemistry. A rumor had apparently been circulating that he had the test in his possession, and his teacher confirmed he'd scored an A+ on the final, his highest test grade in the class all semester.

It didn't matter that Gray had never seen that test before or that he'd studied his butt off for weeks for that A+. The school's zero tolerance for cheating meant Gray would get a zero on the final, tanking his grade, costing him the Warner Scholarship—and any chance he'd ever had at a college degree.

Chapter 31

Present day

"How are things going at the bookshop?" Logan asked, once the server brought their food. He'd chosen their favorite seafood restaurant for their date, and it was bustling with tourists and locals even on a Tuesday night. He looked handsome in a button-down that brought out the green in his hazel eyes.

Oh, how Shelby was dreading their upcoming conversation. "Business has been pretty good. The new products have been popular. We have a long way to go, but I'm very encouraged." She dug into her seafood gumbo.

Logan tilted his head. "We?"

"The booksellers and me. It's a team effort, of course. We finished decorating for Christmas today too. The Shop and Stroll will be here before we know it." The whole community turned out to support the retailers on that day. It was like an extra Black Friday. "Did I tell you about Miss Phoebe and the preorder deal?"

"I don't think so."

Shelby explained the idea, going into detail but leaving off the bit about her excursion to the island with Gray, and the midnight rescue. Caleb was still irritated with her over that. In any case, he and Liddy had committed to sticking around until after Thanksgiving—probably just to keep tabs on Gray, but Shelby couldn't be sorry about that. She loved having him and Liddy in town. Loved having her friend stop by the shop at random times. Enjoyed grabbing coffee together on Sunday mornings before church. And she could hardly get enough of little Ollie. Plus the extended visit also seemed to have mollified their father for the time being.

Of course, with Thanksgiving coming up, all that could change. Family holidays could bring out the worst in people sometimes. Shelby hadn't planned to be there. She was supposed to be heading to Charlotte with Logan and his parents to spend the day with his grandmother. But all that was about to change.

Logan swallowed a bite of blackened salmon. "Sounds like you have things under control."

"I wouldn't go that far, but I'm hopeful. Even once we avert this crisis, we still have to maintain steady sales. We're working on ways to ensure that."

Last week she'd implemented another idea with Gray's help: to-go orders. Their customers could order and pay for books online, then pick them up on a cart they set outside each morning. It was especially helpful for customers who had difficulty managing the shop's stairs. Word was spreading quickly and most days they had a few orders to fill.

"My offer stands—I've got money set back and wouldn't mind helping you over the hump."

She offered a grateful smile. "That's very thoughtful of you, Logan. I appreciate the offer, but I'd like to do this on my own. I can hardly believe Thanksgiving is in two days—and then Black Friday." She'd have almost every bookseller on hand that day for the big sale they were running.

"I'm looking forward to spending the holiday together."

About that . . . She'd planned to wait until they'd finished eating, but he was almost done with his meal. It was time to admit this relationship wasn't working out. The persistent thoughts of Gray were enough to prove it. Not that she had a future with Gray—that would never happen.

The familiar memory surfaced, Gray's arms wrapping her up in the hull of the boat. She'd felt safe and cared for. At home. The memory and the feelings it evoked had come to mind too often in the week since it happened.

She pushed the memory away, her gaze skating over to Logan as he took a sip of his drink. Her feelings for Logan were tepid. Even their disagreements had been tepid. She'd been settling—no doubt afraid to engage her heart again after being hurt so badly by Gray. Maybe she'd been doing it since long before Logan.

But what kind of life would she have without true love? She needed a man she felt strongly about. A man she actually thought about when he wasn't around. And Logan deserved that too.

Shelby set her fork down and wiped her mouth with the cloth napkin.

"Hi, Shelby! Hi!" Daryl lumbered toward their table, beaming. His mother, Jill (essays and short stories), an attractive, slim brunette in her mid-forties, followed in his footsteps. She was a staple at a local insurance company and had worked her way to manager over the years.

"Hi, Daryl. It's good to see you. Hi, Jill. Do you guys know Logan Shackleford?"

"I don't think so," Jill said. "Nice to meet you."

"Likewise."

"Hi!" Daryl said. "Do you play basketball like me and Gray? I like to shoot hoops in the park. I'm not very good, but it's fun anyway."

Logan's eyes flitted to Shelby's and back. "I'm not much of a sports guy really."

Shelby searched for a change of subject. "Logan works at the bank, Daryl. The one across from the Dairy Bar."

His blue eyes lit up. "I like the bank. They give me suckers, but sometimes I have to ask. Do you have any work for me, Shelby? I need ice cream money."

Jill chuckled. "Daryl, that was a little pushy."

"I was just asking."

"That's okay," Shelby said. "I don't have any sticker work for you, but the leaves sure are coming down. How'd you like to do some raking for me?"

"Yes! I'll do it. I'll come tonight after we eat."

Jill patted his arm. "I think tomorrow would be soon enough. Does that work for you, Shelby?"

"That would be great. I'll have all the tools ready for you."

"We'll let you get on with your date."

"Nice to see you both," Shelby said. "I'll see you tomorrow, Daryl."

"Bye, Shelby! Bye, Logan!"

They said their good-byes and Shelby smiled as she watched him go.

Logan took her hand. "Not everyone would take the time to befriend someone with special needs. I admire that about you. You're a kind person."

Her heart sank. "Daryl's a delight. It's impossible to be blue when he's around."

"I can see that." He squeezed her hand, his steady gaze fixed on her. "You bring out the best in me too."

Ugh. She braced herself for what was coming. Worked that leading sentence around in her mind as she propped her lips up with a smile. "Listen, Logan, I was hoping maybe we could talk about us tonight."

His expression shifted as a glimmer of concern flashed in his eyes. "Okay . . . that sounds a bit foreboding."

She turned her hand over in his and squeezed. *Now or never.* "I so enjoy our time together, Logan. We've become very close over the past few months, and you're every bit the kind and bright man I've always thought you were."

His expression changed, a sign flipping from Open to Closed.

"I really like you as a person. You have so much to offer a woman in a romantic relationship."

He pulled his hand away. "Just not you?"

She winced. Cleared her throat. "I feel like we're at the point in our relationship where, if it's working, the feelings progress to the next level . . . but that just isn't happening for me."

He smirked. "Yeah. Ever since Gray Briggs came back to town."

She shook her head. "It's not Gray." At least not in the way he meant. "He's not even an option I'd consider—for multiple reasons. I'd really hoped something would come of this, Logan. You're such a great guy and you have so much going for—"

"Don't patronize me, Shelby. I don't need you building me up. I know who I am and what I have to offer. Don't worry, I won't go home and weep into my pillow."

The sharpness of his tone gave away his true feelings. He was hurt and putting up a front. No one liked getting broken up with.

"I'm not. All those things are true. I had hoped my feelings might develop into more and they just—"

"It's hard to develop feelings for someone you're holding at arm's length."

What? "I don't hold you at arm's length."

He gave a wry laugh. "You're kidding, right? You have a ten-foot wall around your heart."

Shelby blinked. That wasn't true. What did she have to protect herself from? He was just being defensive. Although he did seem pretty adamant. "I didn't know you felt that way."

"I guess it's beside the point now." He tossed his napkin on his plate.

She was glad they'd met at the restaurant. A tense ride home would be excruciating for both of them. "I'm sorry, Logan. I didn't mean to disappoint you."

He removed his wallet and fished out some bills.

She grabbed her purse. "I've got it."

He spared her a look as he set the bills on the table. "Say what you want, but I'm not stupid. This has everything to do with Gray."

"Give me some credit. Gray already left me once, and he'll be leaving again in a month. I wouldn't let myself get wrapped up with him again."

He pocketed his wallet. "Well, I guess we'll see if he can scale those high walls of yours, won't we?" He stood.

"Logan, please. Don't leave angry. Can't we talk a little more?"

"I don't see the point." He offered a mirthless smile. "See you around, Shelby."

Chapter 32

"Happy reading, Miss Clementine!" Shelby called as the seventy-something widow limped down the stairs with a bagful of thriller and suspense novels.

"See you next month."

The retired schoolteacher had arthritis that nearly debilitated her, and she passed the time by reading. Shelby wished the woman would let her assist her with the stairs, but she was stubborn and independent.

A minute later the bell tinkled at her exit and Shelby approached her bookseller.

Janet (contemporary romance) was arranging books on the Christmas Fiction table. She was in her fifties and had let her beautiful hair go gray. Her face was so youthful she hardly looked old enough for gray hair—or the readers perched on her head. "I told Miss Clementine about the to-go cart since it's so hard for her to get around these days."

"She likes to browse in person even though walking is painful."

"Can't blame her. The sight of new book covers, the smell of books . . . It's hard to beat the in-person experience."

"I'm betting our future on that conviction." Shelby took in Janet's sage-green wrap shirt, chic jeans, suede belt, and trendy boots. "You always look so put together. How do you keep up with the latest styles?"

"TikTok, honey. And Patsy's Boutique. That woman has excellent taste. I'd moonlight over there just for the employee discount if I didn't love books so much."

"Don't you dare leave me."

Janet gave Shelby a sideways hug. "Oh, not to worry. Style is an interest, but books are my addiction. You should see my to-be-read pile—and still I buy more."

"I'll happily remain your enabler *and* your dealer."

"Can't say no to that."

The phone rang and Shelby glanced toward the back where Haley wandered around the store. "Haley, can you get that, please?"

"Okay." The phone rang two more times before the girl picked it up on the back extension.

Janet offered a smile. "I've talked to her about answering the phones and helping customers. It just goes in one ear and out the other."

"I don't think she's cut out for this." Understatement of the century. The girl did what she was asked to do, but Shelby didn't want to micromanage her booksellers. Then again, her mom had been so grateful when Shelby ran into her at Publix. Maybe just a bit more coaching. She'd have a little review with the girl and explain her responsibilities more explicitly.

Shelby resumed setting up the Black Friday signs Gray had designed. The big sale was only two days away. They were counting on a profitable season, and Black Friday would kick it off. All their fiction was discounted, and they'd added sideline items such as gift bags and cards to make it a one-stop shop for holiday presents.

With all the work she'd been putting into the Christmas season, it was easy to forget about Thanksgiving. She'd texted her family about her change in plans without admitting to her breakup with Logan. Shelby committed to making a pecan pie and sweet potato casserole for their family dinner.

She was relieved to escape Thanksgiving with Logan's family. His parents were best friends with the Remingtons and hadn't been thrilled when he began dating her. After all, she'd once dated the Briggs boy, whom their best friends detested. And they hadn't exactly been happy about her recent partnership with Gray.

Small towns. Shelby shook her head.

"You take the good with the bad." Gram's voice rang in her head.

Gray was downstairs unboxing today's shipment of books. Since that night on the boat she'd been careful to keep their relationship strictly business. And she was trying hard to vanquish the memory of being in his arms. Why was it so darn hard?

"Because you liked it, that's why."

Shelby aimed a scowl at the ceiling.

"What are your plans for Thanksgiving?" Janet asked.

"Dad's having Caleb, Liddy, Ollie, and me over for dinner. He's handling the turkey and the rest of us are pitching in. How about you?"

"Charlie's family is coming in from Greensboro."

"Is that a good thing?"

"Mama Lucille loves to cook, so it's a wonderful thing. All I have to do is set the table and buy some pretty flowers."

"Sounds like a good deal." What was Gray doing for Thanksgiving? He hadn't mentioned any plans. Was that because he didn't have any? The thought put a pinch in her chest.

The shop was closed for the holiday, of course. Other than his dad, he had no family. Gray might've been invited to dinner by his boss or one of his coworkers. Three hours wasn't too long a drive, but she couldn't see Gray going all that way.

She couldn't stand the thought of him sitting home alone, heating a can of soup or something. Maybe he could actually cook, but even so, no one should have to eat Thanksgiving dinner alone.

She'd inquire about his plans just to make sure. If he wasn't going anywhere, she'd invite him to join her family. That wouldn't go over well with Dad or Caleb. But surely they wouldn't be all right with anyone—even Gray Briggs—spending Thanksgiving alone.

Sounds in the Mystery section alerted her that Haley was off the phone and back to rearranging books. Shelby sighed. "Haley, how are you with chalk? We have a standing sidewalk easel for Black Friday, but I haven't done the wording yet."

The girl pushed back a strand of brown hair that had escaped her messy bun. "I'm good with lettering."

"Perfect. The easel and chalk pens are down in the office, and Gray has the flyer with all the info. Why don't you take it out back and work on it?"

"Okay."

Shelby hoped the girl didn't make a mess of it. But at least she'd be doing something productive.

"I sure do like all the changes I'm seeing around here." Janet had moved on to the locally made necklaces. "Your gram would be so proud of you."

"I'm not so sure. She wasn't fond of change."

"Businesses have to adapt." She winked. "And that's exactly what you're doing. Ooh, this one's pretty." Janet held up a layered necklace with silver and rose gold chains, then set it aside. "I do believe it's going home with me. I admit I had my doubts about Gray at first. I didn't know him when he lived here before, but I knew of his reputation. Honestly, he's nothing like I expected him to be."

"He's a good guy—and very smart when it comes to running a business."

"Well, so are you, honey. In fact, I think the two of you make a great team." A teasing gleam lit the woman's brown eyes.

Shelby leveled her with a rueful look. "It's not like that."

"What? I didn't say a word."

"You didn't have to. I prefer men who live right here in town." And men who didn't up and leave her without notice.

Janet threw her hands up, palms out. "I'm just a woman happily married for thirty-four years. What do I know?"

"You're married to a prince. Charlie would keep you in all the books and stylish clothing you wanted even if you chose not to work."

"Well, that's true enough. But I'm too much of a people person to hang around the house all day. And don't think I didn't notice what you just did there."

Shelby blinked. "Whatever do you mean?"

"Change the subject all you want, Shelby Thatcher, but I know chemistry when I see it, and, girl—"

The phone pealed.

Shelby gave her a big grin. "Oh, shoot. I have to get that."

* * *

Gray carried the easel out back for Haley. It was about half the girl's size, and it seemed as if her twiglike arms might snap under its weight.

"Thanks, Mr. Briggs."

Mr. Briggs. Man, he was getting old. "Welcome."

He returned to the office. No one had even called his dad Mr. Briggs. It was just *Ferris*, or more often *Briggs*. He'd emailed his dad yesterday but hadn't yet gotten a response. Dad usually only wrote once a week. Gray had no idea what life inside was like for him. He didn't talk much about prison life. He shared what he was reading—he had access to a prison library. He wanted to know all about Gray's life in Riverbend Gap. Sometimes, not very often, Dad asked for a little money on his account or for a book, which Gray sent through an online retailer.

For the first time in Gray's memory, he had access, though limited, to a sober father. He liked this version better. Gray was used to visiting him once a month, but the drive was too far from Grandville unless he made a whole weekend of it. And he hadn't been able to take that much time away yet.

Dad had been up for parole twice but had been denied both times. Gray had mixed feelings on that. His dad planned to move to Riverbend Gap when he was released. But Gray feared he might go right back to the bottle. If that was the case, he'd be better off staying right where he was. But maybe he'd learned a thing or two while he'd been locked up. It was hard to say.

Gray always visited his dad on Thanksgiving and Christmas. It would be weird being away for the holidays. In recent years one of his bosses or coworkers invited him to their homes. He always accepted—it was the gracious thing to do. But also, who wanted to be alone for the holidays?

A knock sounded on the doorframe and Shelby peeked in, looking pretty in a red scoop-neck shirt and denim trousers. "How's it going down here?"

"Almost finished scanning in the new inventory. The store seemed pretty busy this afternoon."

"It has been. Did you find the chalk for Haley?"

"Yeah, she's out back working on the sign."

"Good." She shifted in the doorway. Tucked her hair behind her ear, her gaze drifting around the office.

She had something on her mind. He settled back in the chair and regarded her. "What's up?"

"Nothing. I was just thinking about the upcoming holidays. Thanksgiving. You know, turkey, stuffing, all that."

"Yes, I've heard of it."

She chuckled awkwardly. "Hard to believe it's tomorrow, huh?"

"Hard to believe."

"Dad's having us over for dinner around one o'clock. Then football, of course. You know, the usual. What about you? What are your plans?"

Ah, she was worried about him. No way would Shelby Thatcher be all right with anyone being alone on Thanksgiving. And if push came to shove, she'd invite him to join her family—even if it was bound to start World War III.

"Patrick invited me over for supper." It was true, sort of.

And well worth the fib when Shelby practically sagged with relief. "*Patrick*. That's great. That'll be fun. I hear he's a great cook—Melanie Phillips used to date him and she raved about his skills in the kitchen. Do you cook much?"

That was the most words she'd said since the boating fiasco. "I'm good for the basics, but that's about it."

"Well, you'll be in great hands with Patrick." The bell out front tinkled. She glanced over her shoulder, then back, offering him a smile. "I should get back upstairs."

As she slipped away, a lonely feeling swept over Gray. He hadn't been able to find a restaurant open for the holiday, so he planned on a turkey sandwich, semi-fresh from the deli, and a generous slice of the pumpkin pie he'd already bought from the bakery. Close enough.

Chapter 33

Eleven years ago

As Gray drove to work on Saturday, a fog of despair enclosed him, obscuring everything outside himself. He had finished high school under a cloud of scrutiny, and though his final grades placed him as salutatorian, he was stripped of even that honor because of his so-called cheating record.

His grandma went to the school and "gave them what for." She insisted they offer him a different test. But her demands went unheard. The decision had been made. There would be no Warner Scholarship. No free ride to college. And his reputation, such as it was, sank to an all-new level.

Shelby tried to comfort him. Tried to encourage him. But his future seemed so bleak that her words just deflected off him. Worse yet, he could tell Mr. Thatcher doubted his innocence. In recent weeks the man had begun warming up, chatting sports and college courses with Gray when he was over at the house. Now there was a marked coolness to his demeanor.

But Gray couldn't focus on that. He needed to reevaluate, make new plans. If he wanted a degree it would mean night school or online courses while he worked at the hardware store. He would have to mooch off his grandma another eight years or so and save every dime he made for school.

That would mean staying in Grandville long term. And he'd thought things were bad before the cheating incident. News spread far and wide. He was cast as desperate and greedy, trying to steal from Brendan Remington, the worthy athlete and scholar, what was rightfully his.

Graduation was yesterday but Gray hadn't gone. He never wanted to see those people—students or faculty—again. His grandma and Shelby tried to convince him to go, hold his head high. He'd done nothing wrong. But what good would that do?

And as it turned out, he didn't have to worry about working at the hardware store anymore. When he got to work, Mr. Lang shoved a copy of the *Grandville Gazette* in his face.

Gray zeroed in on the article's headline: "Grandville Student Stripped of Warner Scholarship After Caught Cheating."

Gray's face filled with heat as Mr. Lang berated him. He didn't need some low-life cheater working for him. Gray could steal product or rip off the customers when he wasn't looking—probably already had. Best he find someplace else to work, and good luck with that.

As Gray stormed from the building, anger clawed him from the inside out. It was all so unfair. Why did bad things always happen to him? He should've known better than to think he could have it all. When would he ever learn?

He got into his sweltering truck and punched the steering wheel with the palm of his hand. An idea had been whirling in his head since he'd left the principal's office that last day of school.

Just an errant thought.

An impulsive reaction.

But the notion lingered in the back of his mind this past week as he believed himself at rock bottom. But now he'd lost his only source of income. Who else would hire him when the whole town believed he was some kind of cheater? A chip off the old block. A bad seed. He had to get out of this town—and he wouldn't wait years to do it.

Gray pointed the truck toward Huntersville and accelerated.

* * *

Shelby checked her phone. She'd texted Gray a couple hours ago about the newspaper article, but he was at work now and she likely wouldn't hear from him until afterward. Since he was eighteen the article had included his name. He must be devastated.

The past week had been so awful. She'd kept a smile on her face through the graduation ceremony yesterday. Through the open house her dad had planned for her. She mingled and hugged and chatted her way through it all, somehow pretending everything was normal.

But deep inside she was so sad for Gray. So *angry* for him. Unbeknownst to him, she'd gone to the school this week and caught Mr. Donovan in his office. He'd always been friendly and supportive. All the faculty were.

But it was clear within minutes he'd made up his mind about Gray. He patronized her with false sympathy, but she could tell he thought she was stupid to believe in Gray. It was maddening.

On Thursday she'd gone to Brendan's house—something Gray had been threatening to do all week, but Shelby talked him out of it. A fight would surely ensue and that would only make things worse for him.

But Brendan or one of his friends was the likely culprit. Brendan was the one with something to gain from this false accusation. When her ex-boyfriend came to the door, she asked if he knew anything about the advanced test they'd found in Gray's locker. But either he was an excellent liar or he was innocent—she couldn't tell which. Either way, he wasn't about to incriminate himself or his friends with all that scholarship money on the line.

It was all so unfair. So hopeless. Gray seemed like a different person. He was sad and moody and reclusive. She couldn't blame him. And now this article! She just wished there were something she could do. Some way she could find out who'd put that test in his locker. She would confront Devon and Drew later. But for now, she had to be at the bookshop in twenty minutes.

When the store closed at six, Shelby still hadn't heard from Gray. She called but it went to voicemail. Worried, she called his grandmother and learned he hadn't come home after work. "I'm sure he's just blowing off a little steam, honey. He's had a rough week."

Shelby called a few more times, leaving messages, then went to all his favorite spots. The fishing bank at Seaver's Creek, Ramsey Park, Davey's BBQ. Finally she went home and waited to hear from him. But she went to bed that night without a word from him.

She hardly slept. This was so unlike Gray. It was barely six when she got up and got dressed. She headed to his house. Maybe he'd come home last night and just hadn't called her. But Gray's truck wasn't in the driveway. His grandma was an early riser, so Shelby knocked on the door.

The woman looked as if she'd had a rough night too. Her gray hair was tousled and her eyes were bloodshot. "Come in, honey."

Something was unsettling in the tone of her voice. "He didn't come home?"

"No. I went through his room late last night and some things were missing."

Shelby frowned. "Maybe he just needed to get away for a couple days. I couldn't blame him for it."

"But why wouldn't he have told us?"

Shelby's phone vibrated with a call. She snatched it from her pocket and the name on the screen spiked her pulse. "It's Gray!" She answered. "Gray, where are you? We've been worried sick."

"I'm sorry. I didn't mean to worry anybody."

"I'm at your grandma's house. Are you okay?"

"I'm fine. I'm in Columbia."

Only an hour and a half away. "It's so good to hear your voice. Why did you take off like that? I could've gone with you. I can come today. I'll let Gram know you need me and she'll be fine without me for a—"

"You can't come, Shelby." A brief pause. "I'm at Fort Jackson."

Fort Jackson? That was an Army base. What was he—? "*Gray.* Don't do something rash. I know you're frustrated. All your plans have fallen through, and that article must've been a terrible blow."

"I had to get out of town, Shelby. I can't take it anymore. And Mr. Lang fired me over that stupid article."

"Oh, Gray. I'm so sorry. But we'll get through this. We'll figure it out."

"I've already figured it out."

His resolute tone invoked a sense of doom. "The *Army*? No, Gray. You've never even mentioned enlisting before."

"That's because I thought I had a way to pay for college. But that's gone now, and I know it might seem extreme, but it's the only solution I can think of. They'll pay for my college."

"In exchange for what? Your *life?*" She couldn't believe he was considering this! What if he never came home? The thought sent panic racing through her. She clutched her chest.

"It's only three years, Shelby."

"Three years is forever!" And who was to say he'd ever return to her at all? "Come back. You'll get another job. You can still go to GU and we can still be together. I know it's not what you wanted, what you deserved, but it'll be okay. You'll see."

His grandma slipped quietly into the kitchen.

On the phone an unsettling quiet met her impassioned plea. A band tightened around her heart. A feeling of dread swept through her like poison, spreading to every organ, every nerve, every cell.

"Shelby . . ." he said finally. "It's too late."

The finality in his voice had her shaking her head. "No, it's not." Her words trembled with uncertainty. *Please, say it's not true.* He didn't enlist without even talking to her about it. He didn't just sign up for years in the Army after she'd turned down her scholarship at Belmont this week in order to stay here with him!

"I've already enlisted. Basic training starts tomorrow."

Everything inside went blank. Went numb, like after a blow when you knew the pain was coming but the nerves hadn't yet informed the brain. Then the blessed reprieve ended and the pain hit all at once. "*Tomorrow?* You just left without a word and basic training starts *tomorrow?*"

"It happened fast and I was afraid you'd try to talk me out of it. I'm sorry."

A snort of laughter escaped as a sob. "Oh, you're *sorry*! Well, okay then. Everything's fine."

"Please understand, Shelby. I can't stay in a town where I'm hated and looked down on. Where everyone only sees me as a murderer's son and now the guy who tried to steal from the town paragon."

"It's only been a week, Gray! People forget. People move on. If you'd just waited, some other juicy story would soon have all the tongues wagging. But now you're enlisted in the Army and *you left me!*"

"I didn't leave *you*. I left Grandville."

"Really? Because it feels like you left *me*, Gray!" She could almost feel steam shooting out the top of her head. "We're supposed to be a *couple*! And you made this colossal decision that affects both of us. You'll be gone for three years, Gray! Three years! And sometimes people die in the Army—did you think of that? Did you think of me at all before you abandoned me—?" *Just like my mom.* Her throat swelled at the thought. She couldn't believe this was happening to her again.

She'd trusted him, just as she'd trusted her mom—and look how that worked out. She should've known better than to go falling in love. Giving someone the ability to hurt her. To leave her. Just like Gray was doing.

"I really am sorry. I didn't . . . I should've—"

"That's right, you should've. But you didn't." Her heart was a jackhammer in her chest. She boiled with anger—and yet a lump the size of Texas swelled in her throat. Her eyes burned with tears that threatened to burst like a geyser. She didn't want to cry right now!

She'd never wanted to scream at anyone so badly in her life. She actually wished she could hit him! But what would that fix? There was nothing she could do or say to change this. Nothing. He'd left her. And now she just had to live with it.

Like she'd done with her mother.

She envisioned those stupid postcards she'd tacked to her pegboard with hopeful little hands. She'd waited and waited for Mom to come home. Waited for her to realize Shelby needed her. But all the hoping and wishing had been for naught. The postcards were all she'd ever gotten.

And Gray knew all this. He knew how badly her mom's abandonment had hurt her—she'd cried in his arms the night she told him the full story. And now he was doing the same thing to her!

Her next words came out as cold as ice, as solid as steel. "I don't want to talk anymore."

"Okay." His voice softened. "I understand. I know this is a shock. I'll call you later today. We'll talk about it some more and you'll see that—"

"*No.* I don't want you to call me later. I don't want you to call me at all." Her heart gave a loud, hard crack as she punched the Off button.

Chapter 34

Present day

Shelby cradled a sleeping Ollie in her arms as the rest of her family transferred the steaming food from the kitchen to the dining room. Drunk on love, she gazed down at her nephew. Those little lashes. That tiny nose. At three months his cheeks were beginning to fill out and he was nearly out of his newborn clothes. He could hold his head up, smile, and coo. He was growing so fast.

She'd been so glad when Caleb and Liddy announced an hour ago that they were extending their stay yet again—this time till the end of the year. Shelby could sure get used to having them around. But that was also when Gray would be leaving. How would it feel to have all of them leave at once? Not good, she was certain.

When the food was on the dining room table, they found their seats.

"Want me to put him down?" Liddy asked.

"I got him."

Dad had carved the turkey in the kitchen, and the savory aroma made Shelby's mouth water. In a world where there was so much pain and suffering, they were blessed to have this delicious feast and loved ones around the table with whom to enjoy it.

Although not all their loved ones.

Shelby's gaze drifted to the seat across from her. She felt Gram's absence like a physical ache. She usually did most of the baking. In recent years Dad cooked the turkey because of its weight. But it wasn't Gram's recipes they missed. It was her fun-loving presence. Her sometimes too-bluntly-worded statements. Her sarcasm. As beautiful as the table was and as divine as the food smelled, her grandmother's absence was the most noticeable thing in the room. She reached for her grandma's wedding rings and held tight.

I sure do miss you, Gram. It's just not the same without you.

"We all miss her." Liddy squeezed Shelby's arm.

Dad's eyes teared up. "She sure would've approved of this spread. Liddy, thank you for making her stuffing. It wouldn't seem like Thanksgiving without it." Dad put his hands, palms up, on the table. They linked together while he said a prayer thanking God for food and family with a special callout for Oliver, who was a new blessing to them this year.

"And, God, if You see my mom, can You tell her we love her?" His words wobbled to a halt. "Amen." He cleared his throat and grabbed the serving fork. "All right, now who wants a drumstick?"

"Something's wrong with the potatoes," Caleb said a minute later as he scooped them from the serving dish. It was the one dish he'd been responsible for.

"I'm sure they're fine."

His gaze zeroed in on the pile he plopped on his plate. "The texture's kind of weird."

"He used the mixer," Liddy told Shelby. "A lot."

Shelby's lips twitched. "Oh, Caleb. Not the mixer."

"I didn't know."

"What's wrong with using a mixer?" Dad said.

Liddy took a scoop of sweet potatoes. "Nothing—in moderation. I'm sure they're fine."

"Where's Louie?" Shelby hadn't seen Dad's bulldog since she'd been there. He was usually table side, begging for scraps.

Dad gestured down the hall. "I put him in the bedroom. I have a treat for him after supper."

"Why are they so runny?" Caleb dropped a forkful back onto his plate.

Liddy patted his arm. "They're fine, honey. And the sweet potatoes are delicious, Shelby. It tastes like dessert."

"Thanks. The yeast rolls are yummy. Did you make them from scratch?"

"Got the recipe off the Pioneer Woman website—I love that woman."

"Everything's delicious," Dad said. "I plan to eat my weight in starchy food. Honey, how's the bookstore doing? Things getting busier as you gear up for Christmas?"

"Very much so. Tomorrow will be crazy, I'm sure, with the sale we have going. Just about every bookseller will be working."

"What are you supposed to use if not a mixer?" Caleb wondered aloud through a bite of mashed potatoes.

"Is the clothing on sale?" Liddy asked. "There's a T-shirt I've been wanting."

"Which one? I'll bring it home to you."

"That's exactly why I didn't say anything."

"Fine. All apparel is 10 percent off."

Liddy beamed. "Sold!"

They enjoyed their meal with a steady flow of conversation. But Caleb was barely engaging with Shelby. She needed to get things back on track with him. Not that she owed him anything, but it was Thanksgiving after all. And she didn't want his opinions about Gray coming between them.

Feeling stuffed after two servings of almost everything, she pushed back her plate. "Caleb, how's your painting going? Everything on track for your show in December?"

He exchanged a glance with Liddy.

Had Shelby hit upon a sore subject?

"It's actually been pushed back a bit," Caleb said. "But I've been finding time to dabble with the paints in between clearing out Gram's house."

"Glad to hear it."

Dad lowered his fork. "You didn't mention the show being delayed."

"It's not a big deal. Just a scheduling issue."

"Not a big deal? Why do you have to head back to New York at the end of the year if you don't have an impending show?"

Caleb's jaw went tight. "Because, Dad. That's where we live."

"I'm just saying you have a perfectly nice house now right here in your hometown where your family lives. Why not take some time and enjoy it for a while?"

"That's what we're doing."

Shelby smiled through the tension. "The house is really coming along too. Have you been over there recently, Dad? Liddy's planning to redo the wood floors and put some fresh paint on the walls."

Liddy chimed in. "Now that most of the furniture is gone, you can see all the wear and tear. Caleb and I will do most of it together. It'll be a fun project."

Dad glanced at Caleb. "That's a lot to take on in such a short period of time."

"I'll help where I can," Shelby said. "I can paint a wall as well as the next person."

"We might have to hire out some of it," Liddy said. "I know you'll be super busy through the holidays."

"Yeah, Shelby." Caleb lifted his glass in a mock toast. "You and Gray will be super busy."

Shelby sent her brother a scathing look.

Dad's eyes toggled between the siblings. "What's going on between you and Gray?"

"Nothing's going on. Caleb is deluded."

Caleb snorted. Then jumped, his attention darting to Liddy—who'd obviously kicked him under the table.

"Sure didn't look like nothing when I fished you two from the lake at midnight last week."

Liddy frowned at him. *"Caleb."*

"The lake?" Dad pushed back his empty plate. "What's this all about, Shelby?"

"It's *nothing*. We went to Miss Phoebe's on Eagle Island to talk about business."

"And on the way home they ran out of gas," Caleb said. "The castaways called me to come rescue them."

And she was really starting to regret that. Her face warmed even as her blood pressure shot up. "We did run out of gas. Do you think I wanted to freeze out on the lake all night? Did I not call you the very second I had a signal? Now can we all please just move on to another topic? It's Thanksgiving."

As if sensing her tension, Ollie squirmed in her arms. She relaxed her shoulders. Popped his pacifier back in. He stilled in his sleep.

"Please tell me you're not falling under his spell again, honey."

She gritted her teeth. "Dad, it was an accident. There's nothing going on between Gray and me."

"I just can't help but remember how hard you fell for him in high school. If you're not careful, it'll happen again. You can't trust him."

Shelby rolled her eyes. "He's not the awful person you're making him out to be. He never was."

"Here we go . . ." Caleb scowled. "He's obviously getting under your skin again."

Dad's gaze zeroed in on her. "I'm not saying he's a bad person. But I won't forget the way he took off the second he graduated high school. Left you without a backward glance. He'll do it again."

"You need to send him packing," Caleb said. "Before you end up heartbroken again."

Liddy gave an awkward laugh. "Come on, you guys. Let's give her some credit here. She's not a teenager anymore. Anyway, she already has a boyfriend, remember?"

Shelby eyed the food on her plate as if it might tell her what to say next. Because she didn't have a boyfriend anymore. It wasn't really relevant except now that Liddy had brought it up, she kind of had to come clean. They were bound to find out soon through the grapevine anyway.

When she glanced up they were all staring at her. "Actually . . . I broke up with Logan."

"What?" Dad said. "When did this happen?"

Caleb tossed his napkin on his plate. "I knew it."

Liddy stared at her with confusion in her eyes. "You didn't tell me."

Shelby sent Liddy an apologetic look. "It just happened Tuesday. I didn't have a chance to tell you." But the real hurt probably stemmed from the fact that Shelby hadn't even given Liddy a clue that the relationship wasn't working out.

"Are you okay?" Liddy asked.

"I'm fine."

"I'm glad to hear it." Liddy's expression was stoic as she pushed her chair back and stood. "I'll start clearing the table. The Giants game will be starting soon."

Chapter 35

Shelby handed Ollie to Caleb, glowering as she did so. Then she grabbed their empty plates and followed Liddy into the kitchen.

Her friend was rinsing dishes and loading them into the dishwasher.

Shelby set the plates in the sink. "I'm sorry I didn't tell you what was happening."

Liddy's gaze roamed over her face. "Are you really okay?"

"Yes. It just hit me kind of suddenly that the relationship wasn't going anywhere, and prolonging it would've only been cruel to Logan. I don't know why I didn't talk it over with you. I guess I just felt bad about it. He didn't do anything wrong. And I was afraid everyone would think it was because of Gray."

"I'm not 'everyone.'"

Shelby winced. "No, you're not. I should've told you how I was feeling."

"Hard to develop feelings for someone you're holding at arm's length."

Liddy dried her hands on a towel and faced Shelby, her eyes full of empathy. "How are you feeling?"

"Confused. Logan accused me of holding him at arm's length. Like I held back a part of myself or something."

"Did you?"

"I didn't think so. But now I wonder if he's right. He said I had high walls."

Liddy seemed to consider this. "Well, your first experience with love ended in disaster. Most people would be a little guarded after a heartbreak like that."

Was that what she'd been doing? Guarding her heart?

"What was the defining moment? What made you realize you wanted to break up with him?"

"Honestly? When I was out on that boat with Gray last week, I remembered a lot of things. I remembered the way I felt back when we were together. I remembered the way his touch made me feel. Like I'd just die without it, you know? I loved him so much. I thought about him all the time. I wanted to be with him constantly. And he . . . *saw* me. He saw who I was and he didn't just love me—he adored me."

Liddy brushed Shelby's hair back, her blue eyes soft and warm.

"No one has made me feel anything like that before or since—certainly not Logan. I kept waiting to feel more for him. I mean, I like him. I respect him. On paper he's perfect for me."

"Except he's not."

Shelby shook her head. "I wish he were. It would be so much easier."

"The heart wants what the heart wants."

"My heart does *not* want Gray. He's a dead end. Grandville will never be his home. He made that clear even back then, and I can't even blame him for feeling that way. I was an idiot for ever thinking we could work out."

"Do you still have feelings for him?"

Shelby opened her mouth. Closed it again. Being with him again, she could see that young man who'd had everything stacked against him. The guy who was determined to make something of himself. The one who saw all the way down deep inside her and loved her anyway.

But she also saw the man he'd become. The one who'd risen from nothing. Who'd achieved his goals. He was steady and confident and comfortable with who he was. She was proud of him.

And every now and then he gazed at her as if he remembered what they'd had. Like he missed it too.

Liddy squeezed her arm. "We're being honest, remember?"

Shelby released a sigh. "I think a part of me will always care about Gray. People say you never forget your first love. That first time you fall is such an incredible experience. The spark, the passion, the way it completely consumes you. Maybe that's why I can't seem to move on. Why I can't seem to find anything that even comes close."

"You should hold out for that, Shel. Don't settle. You deserve to feel that way about someone. Deserve to be loved that way in return."

"But how will I ever get there if I'm afraid of heartbreak?" Did she have the courage to let herself fall so deeply again?

"Is it fear of heartbreak or fear of abandonment?"

"They seem to be one and the same for me. How did Caleb survive unscathed? Mom left him too."

"Oh, he didn't. That particular issue has reared its ugly head a time or two. We're working through it though. What we have, the love we have, is worth it. You remember what it feels like to be so deeply in love."

She studied Liddy, who'd been married to Caleb for five years. "But doesn't it . . . It can't burn like that forever, can it? Doesn't the thrill fade over time?"

Liddy smiled softly. "Well, it does change. New love is kind of like a sapling tree that pushes to the surface, fresh and beautiful and vibrant. But it's also vulnerable because it's young and fragile. Then over time its roots sink down deep so it can hold through the tough times—storms and droughts—because they're inevitable. Mature love grows deeper, stronger, with a beauty all its own. That's what Caleb and I have together. And it's worth waiting for. It's worth making yourself vulnerable in order to find it."

Shelby's eyes stung at the beautiful picture Liddy painted. Her heart clenched with yearning. "I want that." But she'd have to be willing to risk heartbreak to get it.

Liddy pulled her into a hug. "You'll find it. I know you will."

"Thanks." She gave Liddy a squeeze. She hoped she had the courage to open herself in that way. Having Gray in town, working with him, was bringing so many emotions to the surface. She wasn't sure yet if that was good or bad.

But one thing she didn't like was the way her brother and dad were responding to his presence. She pulled back from Liddy. "Maybe you can help me with Caleb. Why is he so stuck on this grudge against Gray?"

"Obviously he doesn't want to see you hurt again. But part of me also thinks he's fixating on it because . . . he's got other things going on. Things he doesn't necessarily want to dwell on."

A knot of concern tightened in Shelby's gut. "What's going on? Is he okay?"

"He's fine. He just . . ." Liddy paused as if weighing how much she should say. "He's having a bit of a dry spell with his work."

"What? Since when?"

"Quite a while now. Let's just say he was hoping the change in scenery would fix all his problems, and it hasn't really worked out that way."

Caleb entered with a stack of glasses. He took in the pair of them, then aimed a frown at his wife. "You told her."

Liddy crossed her arms. "There's too much secrecy going on around here. You guys are family. Act like it." Giving him a pointed look, she left the room.

Caleb approached the sink and set the glasses in, his expression slack, his eyes dull.

She hated that he'd been suffering silently. "She's right. You should've told us. What's going on with your art?"

"If I knew that, I would've fixed it by now." His flat tone broke her heart.

Shelby didn't know much about the creative process. Writers got writer's block. Did artists get painter's block? "Help me understand. What happens when you sit down to paint?"

He snorted. "Crap. That's what happens."

"Caleb. Maybe it's not as bad as you think. We're not always the best judges of our own work."

"Trust me, it's nothing I want framed and mounted in a gallery. I've had little blocks before but nothing like this. I've started dozens of pieces and they all end up in the garbage—right where they belong."

"Maybe you need to be near your subject." She hated the thought of them returning to the city, but she didn't like seeing her brother so miserable either.

"This whole thing started when we were in the city. This struggle's been going on for months. I hid it from Liddy and my gallerist." He turned weary eyes on her. Caleb's art meant everything to him. Enough that he'd left his home and family for it.

It obviously pained him greatly to be flailing. "Oh, Caleb. I'm sorry. I wish there was something I could do." She couldn't fix this. But she could pray for him.

His gaze sharpened on her, worry flickering in his eyes. "What if it doesn't come back, Shelby? What if I've lost it for good?"

She shook her head. "Not possible. You're an artist all the way down to your soul, brother. It'll find its way out again. You'll see. Does Dad know what's going on?"

"You kidding? He'd just use it as an argument for why I should move back to Grandville."

"You're probably right. Still, he wants the best for you. We all do."

Caleb forced a smile. "Sorry to be such a downer on Thanksgiving Day."

"I'm glad you told me what's going on. Well," she added when he shot her a look. "I'm glad *Liddy* told me what's going on when *you* should've. And hey, maybe the Giants will win and salvage our day."

He checked his watch. "It's about that time."

She smirked as she tossed the towel over his shoulder. "Too bad it's your turn to do the dishes."

Shelby leaned back against the sofa and groaned. "If I eat anything else within the next twenty-four hours, someone put me out of my misery." Her plate sat on the coffee table, not a crumb of the pecan pie or a smear of whipped cream left behind.

"I'm not eating for a week," Liddy said.

"I'm happy to keep all the leftovers." Dad was working on his second slice of pie, Louie lying at his feet, head resting on his paws.

The Giants had come through for the victory, but that couldn't eradicate Shelby's concern for Caleb. He didn't exactly have a plan B for his career. And Liddy had chosen to stay home with Ollie. He must feel so much pressure to produce, and Shelby couldn't imagine that would help his creativity.

"What's up with Louie?" Caleb asked. "He usually stares us down when we're eating."

"His appetite's been a little down," Dad said.

"Is he eating his food?" Liddy asked.

"Yeah, just not all of it. I'm sure he's fine, but I'll have to wait till Monday to figure out what's going on. I called Patrick Ballard's office yesterday to make an appointment, but Patrick's out of town for the holiday weekend."

Shelby had only been half listening to the conversation until she heard Patrick's name. Her mind played back her dad's words. Patrick was out of town? But Gray was having supper over there tonight.

"I can always take him to that vet in Cornelius. But Patrick knows his medical history, so I'd rather wait."

"What about that emergency clinic in Huntersville?" Caleb said.

Dad petted Louie, who perked up at the attention. "If he gets worse I'll give them a call. He seems fine otherwise."

Shelby leaned forward in her seat. "Did you say Patrick was out of town for the holiday weekend?"

"Yeah, why?"

Was it possible she'd misunderstood? That Gray had gone out of town with his friend? But didn't Patrick's family live in Asheville? That was two hours away. Seemed kind of too far to drive when he had to be at the store bright and early for the big sale.

Her dad was waiting for her reply. "No reason."

Shelby gathered the pie plates, took them to the kitchen, and set them in the dishwater. Either Gray was out of town or he'd lied about his plans. Whichever it was, she was determined to find out.

Chapter 36

Gray disassembled the deli sandwich and placed the turkey in the microwave. As the machine hummed and the plate spun, he tossed the single-serving bag of barbecue chips onto the table. This might be the most pathetic Thanksgiving dinner he'd ever had. Even back when Dad had spent the holiday drunk, his grandma made sure Gray was well fed.

A pang of loss hit him hard. Granny had been his rock. So proud of him when he'd gotten a college degree. So happy for him when he settled at a good company where he was appreciated and respected. He'd felt a bit unmoored since her passing. Though being back here in her home brought a sliver of comfort.

How had he found himself in his late twenties with no close friends? Didn't most men have a guy friend or two from college he could count on? His grandma had always said he pushed people away. He used to scoff at that. But maybe she was right.

His gaze caught on Shadow, who sat at his feet, aiming a pair of hope-filled eyes his way. Gray had even pushed the dog away. Tried anyway. That didn't seem to be working out so well. The little mutt was worming his way into Gray's heart. He'd gotten used to his paws clicking behind him on the wood floors. To his wet nose waking him every morning.

It was probably time for Gray to start taking a chance on people. Animals. Whatever.

He wasn't going to find someone to take the mutt. Wasn't even going to try. He peered down at the dog, something like affection warming him through. "I guess you're stuck with me. How do you feel about that?"

Shadow's gaze darted to the open-faced sandwich and back to Gray.

"Really? That's your response? That's *my* food. Here's yours." He nudged the bowl with his foot. It was filled with the expensive dog food the pet store employee had talked him into. Probably had as much real meat as the sandwich Gray was about to eat.

He turned his attention to the darkened window over the sink. The moonlight cut a shimmering path across the lake. The sight brought back the memory of Shelby and him on that boat almost two weeks ago. Brought back all those feelings that had swamped him as she lay shivering in his arms. He could no longer deny the attraction was still there.

Attraction? Really, pal?

He gave a wry huff. Who was he kidding? The feelings were still there, vibrating with life. Maybe they'd gone dormant while he'd been away. But being with her again had resurrected them. And just like that he was head over heels with a woman who belonged to someone else.

Déjà vu.

Maybe that had worked out for him back then, but everything was different this time. He lived hours away and Shelby had built a full life here without him. Maybe she'd forgiven him for leaving without a word—and that felt really good. Downright amazing really. But it was a far cry from trusting him again. That much was clear from the professional distance she'd put in place after that night on the water.

The microwave dinged. He withdrew the plate and stacked the steaming turkey on the wilted bed of lettuce. He pivoted to the table, Shadow underfoot, and sat down to his dinner in a spot that offered him a view of the game playing on TV.

After a brief prayer he opened his eyes to find Shadow gawking at him. The dog licked his chops and emitted a pitiful whimper.

Oh, what was one little bite? It was Thanksgiving after all. He pulled a piece of turkey from the sandwich and held it out. "Just this one piece—then you go over there and eat the doggy cuisine I practically took out a loan for."

As Shadow gulped down the meat, lights cut across the living room. The hum of a motor grew louder. Must be company for the neighbors.

But no. Sounded like the car was right outside in his driveway. He pushed from the chair and strode to the foyer, where he peered out the sidelight.

Shelby.

He drew back with a frown. He was supposed to be at Patrick's right now. But there was no hiding the fact he was home. His car was in the drive. His lights were on. He'd been caught. Caught having no real friends or family to take pity on him. Why did it have to be Shelby of all people?

The engine went silent. A car door closed.

No escaping this. Bracing himself, he ran his fingers through his hair. Wished he wore something nicer than the sweats and T-shirt in which he'd been lounging in front of ESPN all day.

The doorbell pealed. He waited a few seconds, then opened the door. "Shelby. What are you doing here?"

"What am *I* doing here? What are *you* doing here?"

He shrugged. "Change of plans."

Her eyes narrowed on him. "Save it. I know Patrick's out of town for the holiday." She pushed past him and into the house.

He closed the door behind her. "Come on in," he muttered to himself, then followed her into the kitchen.

He stopped behind her near where Shadow crouched, head hanging low. He knew that look. Gray's gaze darted to the table where the paper plate sat, bearing only a few forgotten crumbs.

He scowled at the dog. *You little thief.*

"Why'd you tell me you had plans if you didn't?"

Oh, maybe so he didn't seem quite so pathetic?

Shelby set a brown bag on the table and crossed her arms, waiting.

"I don't know."

"I would've invited you over."

"I'm sure your dad and brother would've loved that. Not to mention Logan."

"It's Thanksgiving, Gray. If my family can't welcome a guest into their home for a holiday meal, they're not the people I think they are."

Maybe so, but he wouldn't come between them again. Not when he was leaving in a month.

She began unpacking the bag—stacks of food containers.

"You don't have to do this. I don't need your pity."

She gave him a mock scowl. Then, ignoring the paper plate on the table, she helped herself to his grandma's china and began dishing out portions of all the traditional fixings.

"I had a perfectly nice meal planned until someone"—he gave Shadow a withering look—"stole it."

"Well, good thing for you we had plenty of leftovers."

* * *

You don't have to eat the mashed potatoes." They were the last thing remaining on Gray's plate. "You should save room for pie anyway. Pumpkin or pecan? Full disclosure, I made the pecan, and it turned out pretty good if I do say so."

"It sounds great, but I'm going to let things settle a bit." Gray stood and took his plate to the sink.

Cheering sounded as the Cowboys scored another touchdown. Though the game had been on the whole meal, their conversation had taken precedence.

He stowed the pie slices in the fridge. "Stay and watch the rest of the game?"

She glanced at her watch. Tomorrow was a big day, but it was early yet. He'd been alone all day. And besides, she was enjoying his company too much to turn him down. "Sure."

In the living room Gray stacked logs in the fireplace and nursed the flame until it caught. Once it was ablaze he settled on the sofa, a safe distance away.

Though neither had a stake in the game, they complained loudly and often about the missed catches, poor throws, and officials' calls.

At halftime he made coffee. It was a noisy affair with the loud grinding of beans and low hiss of steaming cream. He returned with two warm mugs of coffee topped with froth.

"Thanks." The complex aroma invited her to take a sip. The flavor hit her tongue, vibrant and well balanced. Delicious. She shot him a surprised look. "What sort of magic coffee machine is this?"

"No magic. Just a good machine, quality beans, and a little expertise."

She took another appreciative sip. "If I had coffee like this every morning, I'd never be in a bad mood again."

Her cup was empty when halftime ended and they got caught up in the close game. During commercials they chatted about the shop, his job back home, and his decision to adopt Shadow, who now lay on a rug by the hearth, eyes drifting shut. For some reason, that decision made Shelby happier than she could say.

During the third quarter when the game returned from commercial, they forgot to stop talking. At some point Gray lowered the volume.

"I really missed Gram tonight," Shelby said when the quiet stretched between them. "It wasn't the same without her."

"I'm sorry. I know just how you feel. Everything in this house reminds me of my grandma. But it's so quiet here without her."

"The two of you were close. I remember her always having a crossword puzzle in her lap."

Gray's smile was nostalgic. "She loved those things."

"And those red glasses always perched on her nose."

"She couldn't see a thing without them."

Dorothy had been the only family who'd stuck by him, but she was gone. Who did he have in his corner now? It didn't sound as if he was particularly close to anyone back in Riverbend Gap. He always had pushed people away.

Maybe they had something in common.

Their gazes connected across the space, which seemed to have closed somehow in the past hour. His thigh now touched hers. Their arms brushed. The moment lengthened as warmth crept into her limbs. As prickles flared beneath her skin. Want stirred low in her belly. Pushing him away was the last thing she wanted right now.

"I'm sorry I lied about having plans tonight."

The low timbre of his voice transported her back to the old days. To the lonely boy he'd been. An outcast who put up barriers, always expecting rejection. Old habits died hard. In many ways Gray had grown and changed, but he was still that lonely boy who guarded his heart. An ache spread through her at the thought. "It's okay."

"Thank you for this."

The food? The company? Both? "You're welcome."

The fire crackled and sizzled. A log shifted. And still they consumed each other with their eyes. He was so handsome in the firelight she couldn't look away. The fire's golden glow kissed his cheekbones and danced in his eyes. The scruff on his jaw gave him a roguish look.

What would his unshaven skin feel like against her palm? She reached for the answer. The soft flesh of her fingers tingled against the bristly landscape of his jawline. His familiar scent wove around her. She drank him in while a herd of wild horses trampled her chest.

Then she met his gaze again as awareness crackled between them.

"You have any idea how much I want to kiss you right now?"

She brushed her thumb along his jaw. "What's stopping you?"

His blink was slow and tortured. "I'd like to think I've grown up a little in the years we've been apart. I don't go around kissing unavailable women these days."

The memory of their first kiss washed over her like a warm wave. Would it still be like that? She was desperate to find out. "That's good . . . because I'm not unavailable anymore."

A question flared in his eyes, quickly replaced by desire. As if needing no further explanation, he leaned close. His lips brushed hers as soft as a breath.

As charged as a live wire.

His fingers threaded into her hair, holding her steady.

But she wasn't steady. Wasn't anything close. Steady was overrated. It was just as it had been before. Just as it had always been. They were combustible, sparking and sizzling at a mere touch. A fire out of control. Molten lava.

He palmed her face. His hands slipped down to her shoulders, around her waist, pulling her close. They mapped out every inch of her back.

She remembered now. How had she forgotten what passion was? How had she let herself settle for such a poor imitation when *this* was out there?

Because he broke your heart.

She tried to pluck the errant thought. But the pernicious weed was already growing roots. Strong ones that wouldn't give way no matter how hard she tugged.

As if sensing her hesitation, Gray began retreating in degrees. His hands returned to her face, softening. The kiss slowed. An inch of space edged between them, then two.

Then his forehead was against hers, their ragged breaths mingling between them.

"Man, I've missed that," he said.

Missed didn't begin to cover it. But that weed stretched and twined, strangling every good thought and feeling his kiss had planted in her heart.

He drew back. "Shelby?"

"Give me a minute." She was breathless. Mindless. His kiss, his touch, had scrambled her thoughts.

"You do the same to me. Rattle me. All these years I've let myself believe what we had must've been a fluke. Youth, hormones, whatever."

"Um, nope."

He chuckled. His eyes sparkled in the firelight.

The exchange lightened her mood. They'd always had passion, yes. But they used to have fun together too. He could be funny when he let down his guard. She used to wish he'd let others see that lighter side of himself.

And she'd forgotten about this bolder side of herself. He'd always brought that out in her. She'd been the best version of herself when she was with him, and she'd missed that. Hadn't realized how much until now.

"What happened between you and Logan?"

"I broke up with him on Tuesday. It just wasn't working. He didn't . . . We were always a dead end, I think." And what about Gray and her? Weren't they a dead end too—for completely different reasons?

"I almost feel sorry for the guy."

Their gazes met and clung as her thoughts spun. His life was hours away from Grandville and he wasn't welcome here. Just being back in this town must bring back such awful memories for him. "What are we going to do?"

His thumb swept across her cheek, his eyes growing intense. "I want to be with you, Shelby."

Her heart did a slow roll. "But how will that work?"

"We'll figure it out."

That was too vague. She'd gone into this the first time thinking they'd figure it out, and look what happened. She drew back. "That's not a plan."

"I know we have some obstacles—"

"Putting it mildly."

He acknowledged that with a nod. "All right. Fair. We live in separate towns."

"And you've wanted out of Grandville since forever—not that I can blame you. That's just the beginning."

"You'd never leave your grandmother's shop, and your family hates me with a passion." His eyes gleamed. "That about cover it?"

Everything except the biggest obstacle. Might as well put that on the table too. "Then there's the past. You up and left me, Gray. You left me just like my mom did."

The gleam faded. His expression turned stricken. Either it was a trick of the firelight or his eyes glazed with a sheen of tears.

He hadn't realized. Hadn't made the connection till now.

"Shelby . . . I'm so sorry. The last thing I ever meant to do was hurt you. What an idiot I was."

"I'm not trying to rub your nose in it. I've forgiven you—but I'm not a slow learner."

"Neither am I. I've paid for my stupidity a hundred times over by losing the best thing I ever had. I'll never stop being sorry for leaving you the way I did or for the pain I caused you—especially now that I understand it better." He pinned her with an unswerving look. "But, Shelby . . . I will never up and leave you again. You have my word on that."

She wanted to believe him. She could see he meant what he said.

But they had other problems and no foreseeable solutions. It all seemed rather hopeless.

"Relationships always have obstacles. And we're not kids this time. I know I have to rebuild trust with you. I'm willing to put in the effort. We can figure all this out one step at a time."

The trust thing was daunting enough on its own. As for the rest, she didn't see any easy answers. But she also couldn't see giving up what they had together now that they'd found it again.

I still love him.

The thought hit her like a punch to the heart. How could that be true? She wasn't sure, but it was. She felt it down to her soul. And she'd spent too many years trying to find this special something with other men not to appreciate its rarity.

"This is worth fighting for, Shel. I believe it with everything in me." He gave her a little space, held eye contact for a long moment. "But the ball's in your court. If you can't go there with me again . . . I understand. I'd hate it, but I'd understand. If that's the case, I'll do whatever you want—stay and help you through the holiday or . . . pack my things and leave."

The very thought made her want to hide his suitcase. She wouldn't send him packing. But her heart, though bursting with love for him, was wary. She had to keep her senses about her somehow until they found reasonable solutions to their problems. Maybe that was a lost cause, but she had to try. "We'd need to take it slow."

Relief flared in his eyes as a grin tipped his lips. "You're calling the shots here, Sunshine."

The old nickname warmed her through. But she was too busy thinking of their obstacles to dwell on it. Like her family and their feelings toward Gray. "No sneaking around like last time."

"I think we both learned our lesson on that one."

Were they really going to do this? A thrill of pleasure shot through her. He stroked the back of her hand, the touch resurfacing that runaway kiss they'd just shared. If she was going to keep her head, they'd have to dial it way back. "And we need to take those kisses down about ten notches."

"Whatever you say."

She gave him a stern frown. "I mean it."

He lifted both hands, palms out. "You're the boss."

Hmm. All this power was starting to agree with her. She should use it to her best advantage. "All right then, Grayson Briggs. Get over here and kiss me again. But mind you keep that tongue in your mouth, mister."

His grin split wide open. "Yes, ma'am."

Chapter 37

The next morning Shelby blinked at the standing easel Haley had left by the register. The store specials were spelled out in a curly artistic font. There were chalk-drawn illustrations: a stack of books, Christmas ornaments, a garland draping across the top. It was whimsical and beautiful!

She carried the sign over to where Gray and the other booksellers stood, including Haley. "Haley, this sign . . ."

The girl peered up at her. "Is it okay? Did I forget to add something?"

"It's wonderful! I didn't know you were so artistic."

Her cheeks tinged with pink. "I like to draw in my free time."

"Well, you're officially in charge of the signs from now on."

Haley beamed. "Really?"

"I want this easel out front every day. You can switch up the messages."

"Maybe we could use quotes from books sometimes."

"I love that idea." Who knew the girl had such talent behind that quiet facade?

Shelby checked her watch. "All right, everyone. Let's do this!" She carried the easel down the stairs and out the door. After propping it at the entrance, she flipped the sign to Open. *Let the games begin.*

Black Friday was passing in a blur. It seemed everyone Shelby knew came into the store and made purchases. For once, Haley's favorite task, straightening the merchandise, was actually full-time work. Gray stayed mostly in the background, but even so Shelby was supremely aware of his whereabouts at all times.

Caleb and Liddy stopped by with Ollie. Shelby had all of two minutes to admire the baby's chubby cheeks and adorable grin. Her dad came in the afternoon and purchased a newly released biography despite the fact that she'd always given books to her family for free.

She'd have to tell them soon that she and Gray were together again. But she couldn't think about that right now. She stopped in the middle of the Fiction section and glanced around the shop. Theresa, Brenda, and Wanda assisted customers. Adele and Zuri handled checkouts. Happy readers perused the shelves, pulling books, devouring cover copy. In the Children's section, kids sat in cozy chairs reading or played with toys on the fluffy rug while parents checked out the merchandise.

They'd always been busy on Black Friday, but not like this. Gray's advertising had worked wonders. A bubble of hope swelled inside. She soaked in the moment.

Do you see this, Gram? All these people? All these readers gathered together for the love of books? You did this. I hope you can see it. It sure is a beautiful sight.

She caught Gray's eye across the room, watched his handsome face light with a smile. And just like that, everything was right in the world.

Shelby was on cloud nine after the successful day. And the next day was also a busy one at the shop. On top of their fabulous in-store sales, the preorders for Phoebe's upcoming release were flooding in. November was shaping up to be their best month of the year. The success brought a modicum of relief. A feeling that maybe, just maybe, they could turn this shop around.

But as she pulled up to Dad's house late in the afternoon, she had a feeling she was about to come crashing back down to planet Earth. She had to tell her family about Gray and her. They'd agreed not to sneak around, and she didn't want her loved ones finding out from someone else. Gray had wanted to tell them together, but it would go down easier this way. She hoped. Also, she wanted to spare Gray from any darts they might sling his way.

Dad and Caleb had been very protective of her back when Gray left. They'd seen her at her lowest. When someone devastated the person you loved, it was difficult to forgive the perpetrator. She got it. But there were extenuating circumstances, and hopefully they'd see that. Surely they'd give him another chance when they realized how much she cared for him.

She didn't need their permission; she was a grown adult. But she was close with her family and wanted to keep it that way. She wanted Gray to have their acceptance. Wanted him to have the sense of belonging he deserved. Maybe that was a pipe dream, but that was what she hoped would happen—eventually.

As she exited her car she spotted Caleb in the backyard and headed that way. He was hunched over an easel, which depicted the landscape in front of him. The painting was done in an impressionist style, swaths of color hinting at the image of a sunset glimmering on the lake's surface.

It was so unlike his modern city paintings, which were beautiful in their own right. But this one evoked a sense of peace and also a feeling of playfulness. "Whoa. That's stunning, Caleb."

He didn't even lift his brush. "Thanks."

"Seriously. It's amazing. You've clearly got your mojo back."

"Yesterday Liddy suggested I go back to my roots—back to when I first loved painting. Remember all those landscapes I did in high school? I can feel that fire inside again. I've been working on this for two days and I don't want to stop."

"I can see why. You know I love your cityscapes. But this is . . . Wow.

You have to put this in a local gallery. It'll go for a pretty price. Or better yet, can I afford it?"

"I don't even care about the price right now." He added a splash of periwinkle to the sky. "It just feels so good to be inspired again."

Shelby studied the painting, watched him work a minute. How did he do that? Just add splashes of color, seemingly so random, and yet it all came together in such a wonderful way?

"I was afraid I'd lost my passion for good. I'm so relieved to feel unblocked again."

"I'll bet." Would he remain unfettered after this piece? When he tried his hand at another cityscape? She didn't vocalize the thought. No reason to steal the joy he'd finally recaptured.

"My work has sold so well in the city. I can hardly complain when I've been able to make a living as a painter—so many artists would give anything to be in my shoes. But, Shelby . . . God's honest truth? I'm sick to death of painting cement and glass. I'd rather paint a poker-playing dog on a velvet canvas than eke out one more cityscape."

She chuckled. "Maybe you won't have to sink quite that low. Seems like you've found another direction."

"Sure feels like it."

A minute later he stepped back, studied the canvas. He did his paintings in stages. He'd work awhile, then take a break. Come back to it with a fresh eye. He put down his brush and began packing up.

"Done for the day?"

"I'm losing light."

True enough. Once he had his paints and the wet canvas in hand, she grabbed the easel and they headed inside.

Shelby got invited for supper, which Dad and Liddy cooked while Shelby reveled in the pure sweetness that was her nephew. Caleb seemed more his old self now that his painting was back on track. Shelby got it. Her worries over the bookstore had been all-consuming. She felt a similar relief after these past two extraordinary days.

But art was surely even more precarious. It wasn't a spreadsheet with numbers to add and subtract. Creativity was fickle. You couldn't quantify inspiration. You couldn't manufacture it—and you sure couldn't buy it.

She was glad Caleb seemed to have it sorted out—at least for the time being. And selfishly, she hoped his good mood would make her announcement more palatable.

After supper they settled in front of the TV for the last college football game of the regular season between Notre Dame and USC. Dad was a fan of Notre Dame, but no one else cared who won so the rest of them chatted quietly throughout the game.

Ollie was down for the night and it was getting late. Shelby would tell them at halftime, then go home. The two busy days at work had worn her out.

When the game clock wound down and the station went to commercial, Shelby braced herself and dove right in. "There's something I need to tell you guys."

Dad, who'd been just about to retrieve another Coke, sank back into the recliner, his dark brows pulling together. "What's wrong?"

"Nothing's wrong at all. I just—" She glanced at Liddy, who offered an encouraging smile.

Caleb's eyes flickered knowingly. "You and Gray are together. Shocker." His voice was accusatory, though it held less rancor than she'd expected.

"Caleb's right. Spending all this time together, I've been reminded of who he is and all the things I love about him. I know he let me down before, and that was hard. But we've both grown up and learned a lot. I'm giving him another chance—and I hope you will too." Her gaze shifted between Caleb and her dad.

Dad set his glass back on the end table, obviously stalling for time.

Caleb stared back at her wearing an enigmatic expression.

Liddy grabbed Shelby's hand. "If you're happy, I'm happy. I don't know Gray very well, but what I do know I like."

"It's not really that simple," Caleb said. "He's obviously not welcome in this town."

"And you'd never leave Grandville." Dad's statement held a hint of a question. A trickle of fear.

"I can't see myself ever leaving Gram's bookshop. And speaking of that—Gray did give me back ownership of the store without so much as a fight. And he dropped his whole life to come and help me with the store. I don't know if I could've turned things around without him. And he did it for nothing. Hopefully you can see his kindness in that. And as for Grandville, it really isn't the whole town who's against Gray. Mostly just the Remingtons and their friends. And their blaming Gray for what his dad did is wholly unjustified." Even Caleb and Dad had to give her that.

Her brother weighed in. "He got a reputation of his own though—the fighting, the test scandal."

Shelby gritted her teeth. "That was years ago—and he didn't deserve any of that!"

"I think we all realize he was something of a scapegoat, honey," Dad said. "We never really believed he cheated on that exam. And though all this may have happened a long time ago, the Remingtons have very long memories."

"And a lot of friends," Caleb said. "They're not the sort of people you want as enemies."

"I don't care what they think. Doesn't the truth matter at all? Once people give Gray a chance, they'll come to see he's not what they've made him out to be." She turned to her dad. "You saw what kind of person he was, Dad. You came to respect him; I know you did."

"I don't deny that, honey. I don't buy into every rumor that flies around town. I go by a person's character, and he showed me he had some—until he left you the way he did. You've never been a parent, so maybe you can't understand how hard it was to see him break your heart like that."

Realization hit Shelby—she wasn't the only one who'd been triggered by Gray's abandonment. Dad had been abandoned by his wife. It must've been traumatic to see the same thing happen to his daughter.

And maybe Caleb's leaving for New York had had the same effect on him. She flagged the thought for later.

"Watching me go through that had to be difficult for you, Dad. Gray knows leaving the way he did was a mistake." Her eyes softened on her father as she weighed her words carefully. "But he didn't run off to Hollywood to become a star, Dad. He went into the military because the situation here was untenable. And he did try reaching out to me several times. I was the one who shut him down. I was the one who ended things."

Dad's eyes teared up. "I guess that's a fair point."

She'd just tromped across sacred ground. But it had to be said. Her mother's abandonment was still affecting their father, still affecting all of them. "Gray and I have talked it through. I've forgiven him and we're going forward from here."

"And what will that look like exactly?" Caleb said. "He must hate it here. How could he not?"

Liddy leaned forward. "I think what Shelby's saying is, this is happening, and we all need to get on board. She deserves our support."

Shelby shot her a grateful look, then turned back to her dad and brother. "I know you feel protective of me, but I'm an adult and you'll just have to trust that I can handle this."

"It's not you I'm worried about," Caleb grumbled.

Liddy scowled at him.

Dad's brows relaxed as a small smile curved his lips. "I won't say this doesn't worry me. But if you're willing to give him another chance, I guess I'll have to do the same."

Gray had won him over once before. She had no doubt he could do the same again. "Thanks, Dad. I appreciate it." She drilled her brother with a look. "And what about you? Are you going to behave when I bring him around? Because I am going to bring him around."

Caleb glanced at his wife. Shelby didn't even have to glance Liddy's way to know she was pinning her husband with a fierce look. "Fine. I'll give him a chance."

A while later after Shelby said her good-byes, Dad followed her to the door.

"Are you upset about my announcement, Dad?"

"More than anything I just want you to be happy. I'm worried about how this might play out, but you're a grown-up. I trust you can handle whatever happens." He gazed at her, his expression growing intense. "How did you get to be so smart?"

Ah. The reference she'd made about her mom. About his being triggered by Gray's sudden departure all those years ago. Her heart squeezed tight. Maybe Dad still had an issue or two. But he'd raised Caleb and her single-handedly. She'd always felt loved and cared for. Safe. He wasn't perfect, but she admired him just the same. "I guess I'm just a chip off the old block."

He gave a wry grin. "If that's the case, then why am I just now figuring out why I've been so frustrated with your brother all these years?"

She gave his cheek a soft pat. "Better late than never, Dad."

Chapter 38

Hard to believe it was already December. In four weeks Gray would return to Riverbend Gap and his job, putting three hours between him and Shelby. Where would they go from there?

He pushed the thought from his head and hunched over the laptop at his dining room table. He was recording the construction company's incoming and outgoing finances. Gavin and Wes's business was doing well. Their profits were up 38 percent over last year.

Gray sat up straight, stretching his neck. He'd been at this for almost two hours, but he was nearly finished. His phone buzzed with an incoming call and he grabbed it, hoping Shelby was reaching out. He couldn't seem to get enough of her and planned to squeeze in every moment while he could.

But it was Gavin's name on the screen. He accepted the call. "Hey there. I was just finishing up the books."

"How's it looking?"

"Good as usual. I guess you know you're having another great year."

"Sure feels like it. We've been busy enough."

"I hope you guys aren't too overwhelmed with me gone."

"We're managing. But we'll be happy to have you back. In fact, that's why I'm calling. Wes and I have been talking . . . We'd like to extend that offer of co-ownership we mentioned before. We were hoping you might like to buy into the business over the next few years. We'd love to have you on our team long term."

Gray fell back in his seat. Well, this was sudden and unexpected. Yeah, they'd mentioned it in passing before, but not this directly. Maybe Gray's leave of absence had them squirming a bit. "I don't know what to say. I'm honored you'd want to bring me into the business. You and Wes have worked really hard to build it."

"You've been a big part of that, Gray. We'd love to ensure you remain a part of it. I just wanted to put that out there so you can give it some thought. If you're interested we can discuss terms and such when you return."

Over the next few minutes Gavin caught him up on the open jobs, then Gray asked about the family. Gavin and his wife had two kids, and Wes and his wife, Avery, were expecting their first. The Robinson family seemed to be bursting at the seams.

When Gray finally ended the call, he sat there speechless. He truly was flattered they'd offered him a piece of their family business. Owning a company was something he'd been gunning for ever since high school, but would a partnership work for him? Would it give him the autonomy he craved? Part of his desire also stemmed from his inability to trust others. But he'd been healing in that area. He'd grown to respect and trust Gavin and Wes.

But ownership in Robinson Construction would also root him in Riverbend Gap. It was yet another layer of complication between Shelby and him.

The next evening Gray's eyes drifted around the restaurant. Lit garlands draped from the nearby fireplace mantel, and two wreaths hung on the stone walls. Christmas music played lightly in the background, and the buzz of quiet conversation carried throughout the spacious room.

Gray gazed across the table at his beautiful date. Shelby's light brown hair tumbled over her slim shoulders in waves, and her brown eyes gleamed in the candlelight, rivaling the sparkle of her grandma's diamond earrings. Somehow Shelby had gotten even more gorgeous in the years he'd been away. She'd always been strong and smart and giving. But there was even more to admire about her now. He felt so proud as he watched her run the shop. She'd grown into the position with such confidence.

They were dining at The Grille at Bayside Marina tonight, Grandville's most prestigious restaurant. When he'd made the reservation the other night just before closing, Shelby protested. She was worried about putting their relationship on such a big stage so quickly. "Can't we ease into it? Walk the trails at Ramsey Park or grab supper at Davey's BBQ? There's a certain faction that won't be pleased we're dating, you know."

He poked her in the side. "Like Brendan Remington?"

Her ex-boyfriend was recently divorced, but he hadn't so much as glanced her way when she last spotted him at Publix. "If he's still holding a grudge over a high school breakup, he needs to grow up. I just don't want anything else happening to you."

"Relax. We are easing into it. Our reservation is for Wednesday night. There'll hardly be anyone there." He wrapped his arms around her, loving the feel of her. "Besides, I used to dream of taking you to The Grille—and now I can finally afford to."

Her expression softened. "I never cared where we went. I only wanted to be with you. But that's very sweet."

He pulled her closer. "Sweet enough I can have my way?"

Her eyes twinkled mischievously. "Fine, The Grille it is. But only if you let me have *my* way." And then she'd kissed his socks right off.

"Hello? You in there?" Shelby wore an amused expression.

"Sorry. What'd you say?"

"I said you look very handsome tonight. That shirt matches your eyes. And how is it you still have a summer tan in December?"

"How is it you're the prettiest woman in every room you enter?"

She chuckled. "Oh, you've turned into quite the charmer, Briggs."

"Just calling it like I see it."

The server came to refill their water glasses.

The past week together had been like a dream. He didn't realize how much he'd missed her all these years until she was back in his life. The forgiveness she'd granted him had been such a lavish gift. One that left him grateful and relieved. It felt as if a weight had slipped from his shoulders. With Shelby he was at peace. At home. He could let down his guard because he trusted her—and that was more than he could say for most people.

This week he'd thought a lot about Thanksgiving night. Most of his ruminations brought a smile to his face. But there was one thing she'd said that hit him like a bucket of cold water.

"You up and left me. You left me just like my mom."

The words had eviscerated him. Not once in his harried departure, or in all the years since, had he considered that he'd done to her exactly what her mom had done. He pictured her mother's postcards on that bulletin board. Shelby's hopeful expectation of her return. The ultimate rejection she felt when the woman never materialized. Those postcards had ended up in the garbage right alongside all her hopes.

He made himself think about this now. Because he hadn't then. He'd only been thinking of himself and his desperation to escape Grandville. He'd already apologized. He wouldn't dwell on his failure, but he would make sure she knew he appreciated the second chance she was giving him.

Speaking of which . . . "There's something I've been meaning to tell you."

"Uh-oh."

"It's nothing bad. Well, I guess that depends on how you look at it. Gavin called last night to check in." He paused a beat. "He and Wes want to offer me co-ownership in their business."

Something flickered in her eyes. "Wow. That's big. They're brothers-in-law, right?"

"Yes. We haven't discussed details, but I'm sure I'd be a minor player in the equation."

"It says a lot about what they think of you—that they'd offer ownership to someone outside the family. That's quite an honor. And this has always been your dream."

"Yes, but it's also my dream to be with you."

Some of the tension fell away from her expression. "What are you thinking then?"

"I don't know. Let's just put it on the back burner for now. I don't want to complicate things any more than they are. But I have a lot of trust to build back with you, and that starts with transparency . . . so I wanted you to know."

She gifted him with a smile. "I appreciate that. Thank you for telling me."

After their server returned with refills, Gray was glad when Shelby changed the subject. "Did you hear Patsy asked Haley to make a sign for her boutique? I told Haley she could easily have a side gig if she wanted one."

"She's got talent. I'll bet other stores in town would love her help."

"She'd do a great job with those handwritten chalkboard menus, too, like the ones at the coffee shop and deli. I'll have to mention it to her."

"You're such a caring person. Most people would've fired her weeks ago—I was in that camp if you'll recall." He took her hand and swept his thumb across her knuckles.

At the sign of affection her gaze darted self-consciously around the dining room.

The restaurant had filled since they'd arrived. There were Bill and Trudy Jennings, and way across the room, the Shacklefords—Logan's parents. Hopefully Shelby wouldn't spot them—*awkward*. Dave and Janine Pullman were looking their way. Weren't they friends of the Remingtons? Oh well.

Shelby wasn't the only one who needed to stop worrying about what other people thought. He had no control over that. Feeling sorry for himself was a waste of time. He wouldn't let anyone make a victim of him ever again.

He squeezed Shelby's hand and offered a confident smile. "Hey, where'd that smile go?"

"I can't help it. Everything's just perfect and I don't want anything to spoil it."

Her words warmed him through. But he also had to fight the natural inclination to worry about that other shoe—the one that always seemed to drop on him.

But no, that was his past talking. He wasn't a teenager anymore, at everyone else's mercy. He was worthy of a good life. Of success. Of love. "Everything *is* perfect. Let's just enjoy it."

The server arrived at their table, presenting a circular tray laden with sizzling steaks and expertly garnished vegetables.

The aromas made Gray's mouth water. He gave Shelby's hand a final squeeze. Yes, that was exactly what they would do. Just enjoy each other.

That thought flew from his mind a few hours later after he dropped off Shelby. He pulled into his driveway and his headlights swept the front of his house. Frowning, he exited his SUV and approached the porch. He hadn't left a light on, so he unlocked the door, stuck his hand inside, and swept it over the switch. The porch illuminated—and so did the large black words spray-painted on the white siding.

Go home, loser!

Chapter 39

The Christmas Shop and Stroll had finally arrived. But not so much at the bookshop. Shelby finished shelving Liane Moriarty's recent release and glanced around the quiet store. Zuri restocked the shirts on the apparel rack and Janet had slipped off to the restroom.

No hurry since there were only two customers in the store. Shelby went downstairs and propped open the front door, hoping the warmth and smell of books would draw customers inside.

She frowned as she recalled the act of vandalism perpetrated on Gray's house two nights ago. One of the Remingtons, she assumed. Probably Mason's doing since, naturally, he'd been the first cop on the scene. It was obvious he felt above the law. He was quick to suggest it was likely a teenage prank, and the childish act certainly reinforced that theory. But Mason could've committed the crime with the intention of throwing suspicion elsewhere. It seemed he'd be a thorn in the side until Gray left town.

Gray went through the motions of filing a report, but neither of them held out any hope the police would actually do anything about it. Yesterday they'd talked about the situation as the two of them spent hours scrubbing off the paint.

"We should go to the station and tell the chief what's been going on." Shelby was infuriated that the harassment he'd experienced as a teenager was recurring. "You're being bullied again and we're not kids anymore. We have to do something."

"If there was anything I learned about being bullied, it's that telling only makes things worse. I have to leave at the end of the month, and I don't want the blowback coming on you after I'm gone."

"I can take care of myself. Gray, we're in this together. And I know you're leaving soon, but you should be able to visit me here without being harassed."

He'd looked at her for a long moment, scrub brush still. "All right. But let's get through the Christmas Stroll first. I'll go to the police station Monday morning."

A wave of relief washed over her. "I'll go with you."

Shelby's thoughts scurried from her mind as Janet returned from the restroom. Her gray hair was caught up in a youthful ponytail, and her red readers swung from a chain around her neck. "This is strange. We're usually so busy during the Stroll."

"I was thinking the same thing." It was after eleven and they'd only had a dozen or so customers. Fridays, especially in December, were usually busy. And the Shop and Stroll was the second busiest holiday weekend.

"Maybe everyone did their book buying on Black Friday."

"But the sidewalks are teeming with shoppers." A feeling of dread swept through her. "I might as well send someone home if we're going to be this slow."

"Zuri has finals coming up. She'd probably be grateful for the extra study time." She winked at Shelby. "Plus I haven't had a chance to get the scoop on your date the other night."

Shelby appreciated her efforts to lighten the mood. "Now, Janet, I'm not one to kiss and tell."

She snorted. "Since when? Throw an old girl a bone. Who can I live vicariously through if not you?"

"Isn't that what romance novels are for?"

"Well, sure, but seeing it play out in real life is even better." Her gaze darted toward the stairs. "He's such a hunk."

Shelby's lips twitched. "Hey, eyes off my—" Boyfriend? Was Gray officially her boyfriend?

"Go ahead and say it, honey. Anyone can see he's head over heels for you." She sighed dramatically. "I remember when Charlie used to gaze at me that way."

"He adores you. You guys are great together."

"We are. But there's old-shoe comfortable love and brand-new sizzling love." She waggled her eyebrows.

Shelby chuckled. "On that note . . ." She headed toward the front of the store to let Zuri know she could head home.

"You're just gonna leave me hanging?" Janet called. "I thought we were friends."

When noon came around the next day and they'd only had a dozen customers, that dread turned to terror. She sent Theresa and Janet both home and checked the sign to make sure it was turned to Open. Then she peeked out the front door for the third time. The town was overrun with shoppers, flowing in and out of galleries and boutiques. People were spending money—just not at the bookshop.

Francine Walsh (literary fiction) passed by on the sidewalk with a large shopping bag in one hand and her goldendoodle's leash in the other.

Shelby beamed at the woman. "Hi, Francine! Beautiful day, isn't it?"

The woman glanced her way. "Shelby." She didn't even offer a smile as she swept past.

Strange. Worry gnawed as Shelby went back inside. She found Gray in the office scanning titles into the system. He'd been shut up in here all day so he probably didn't realize today was just as slow as yesterday. Which was even worse because today was the Saturday of the Stroll—there were only two more Saturdays before Christmas!

He looked up at her entry, and his warm smile wilted as he read her expression. "Still slow?"

"Worse than yesterday. We've only had a dozen customers all morning. We always keep three or four booksellers busy on the floor throughout December, and even more during the Stroll."

Gray leaned back in his chair. "What do you think is going on?"

"I don't know. This has never happened before. We have slow days like this in January or February, but not in December. And this is the second day in a row. I have a bad feeling about this, Gray." Especially coming on the heels of that vandalism.

"Maybe it's just a fluke. It's been nice and sunny, unseasonably warm. People could be out enjoying the weather."

"They're out enjoying all the other stores! The town is swamped with shoppers."

Frown lines crouched between his brows just as the bell over the door tinkled.

"Finally, a customer." Shelby offered him a half-hearted smile, then turned to go sell some books. But it was Liddy who'd entered the store. Shelby stopped her before she went upstairs, noting her somber expression. "What's wrong? Is Ollie okay?"

"He's fine. Everyone's fine. I just came from The Big Tease. Glenda Something was doing my hair . . . ?"

"Glenda Ellsworth."

"Right. Well, shortly before I came in she had RaeAnne Something in her chair, and in the chair next to her was . . . Imogene Mae?"

"Ida Mae. She and RaeAnne are in the Garden Club together."

"Okay, well, they were talking, and Glenda overheard everything they said. Long story short—the Remingtons are hatching some plot to drive Gray out of town. They've been using all their influential friends to spread the word. They were careful about what they said, so she only got the gist of it, not the specifics."

The news sank like an anchor in Shelby's stomach. "Oh, I think I have the specifics. We were unusually slow around here yesterday, but today has been absolutely dead. They've talked all their friends into boycotting my store."

"Surely not. Why would they want to hurt you?"

"Now that I'm with Gray, I'm consorting with the enemy, I guess. And they're afraid Gray will move back to town."

"Well, so what? It's a free country."

"You don't understand these people. They hold a grudge against Gray's family because of what his dad did. And then there was that cheating scandal in high school."

"That was eons ago!"

"The Remingtons don't want Gray around and are pretty used to having their way." They'd done things like this before—manipulating and scheming. Nothing outside the law. But they knew how to use their money and influence to gain the upper hand.

"But you didn't do anything wrong! This is not okay."

"They think if they hit my bottom line I'll bow to their pressure. But boy do they have another thing coming." That was the anger talking. The more rational side of her sang a different tune. She needed sales now more than ever. She was on the verge of losing the store!

"Atta girl. You need to stand up to these bullies. Anyway, they can't have the whole town in their back pocket."

Maybe not quite all. Her family had their own set of friends. But, yes, the Remingtons were pretty influential. Recently they'd put up the cash for the new museum. "The patriarch of the family, Richard, is part of the chamber of commerce that has brought a lot of businesses to the area over the past twenty years. He's been a big part of the town's growth. His wife, Renee, serves on city council and has her own influential circle of friends."

"They're the parents of the man Gray's dad killed?"

"Troy, yes. And of course their grandson Mason is a police officer." It all felt pretty overwhelming.

"The one who pulled Gray over without cause."

"And possibly vandalized his house."

Liddy set a hand on her arm. "It'll be okay. You have a loyal clientele, and readers need their books!"

They did have loyal buyers. But there were plenty of other places to purchase books. And this store—all stores—depended on holiday sales to get through the year. Twenty-four percent of their annual sales happened during the Christmas season. They depended on the last three months of the year to keep the doors open through the slower months—and they were digging out of a deep hole.

"I just can't believe the town would treat you this way, especially now when you need the sales so badly."

"They don't know how dire things are. They just think if they turn up the heat for a while, I'll cave and then everything will return to normal."

Liddy scowled. "Well, we can't let that happen."

"What can we do?"

"Let's get our heads together and figure something out."

It would need to be ASAP. Each day they went without business, they were digging themselves deeper. "Tonight?"

"Your dad has some big meeting at the college. How about tomorrow?"

Her brother and Dad might very well think Gray's leaving town would be best for everyone. But that wasn't on the table. "Gray was talking the other night about having the family over. Let's meet at his place for supper tomorrow night, and we'll come up with something."

"Sounds like a plan. We can't let these people push you around, Shelby. We will come up with something."

Shelby hoped she was right. Because the Remingtons' actions were jeopardizing everything she held dear.

Chapter 40

They were halfway through the meal before Gray's nerves began to settle enough to enjoy the Luigi's pizza Shelby had brought. Upon entering his house, Stanley and Caleb had offered reserved smiles and handshakes. *We're only here for Shelby's sake*, their demeanors screamed. *We'll tolerate you.*

They'd decided to strategize after eating. So as the meal lengthened, the conversation in his dining room was casual: Caleb's artwork, the upcoming town hall meeting, Ollie's first laugh, instigated by Stanley, who was very proud of this accomplishment.

Shadow sat between Shelby and Gray, gaze flickering between them, hoping for a scrap. Periodically the dog checked the darkened living room where the baby lay in his car seat—he'd fallen asleep on the way over. The little guy had apparently been teething and sleep was sporadic. You'd never know it by Liddy, who brought a certain energy to the gathering. She'd apparently come prepared to bridge the gap between Gray and the family. He was glad Shelby had such a good friend and ally.

When the conversation turned to Ollie's birth story, Gray excused himself to retrieve more drinks. The meal was winding down and they'd soon move on to strategizing. Gray had been able to think of little else since yesterday when he realized what they were up against. He felt so responsible for this.

His ideas focused primarily on direct contact with Shelby's loyal customer base—her email database and their online presence. If they shifted their marketing efforts that direction, maybe they could lessen the boycott's impact. But it wouldn't reverse the damage.

Shelby entered the kitchen as he opened the fridge. She wrapped her arms around his middle and laid her head on his back. "Doing all right?"

"I'm fine. I'm eager to hear any ideas your family might have." He pulled out a couple cans of Coke and placed them on the counter, then gave Shelby his full attention. She gazed up at him adoringly, and he went soft inside at her warm expression.

"Thanks for hanging in there with them. They'll come around."

"Hope you're right." It wasn't lost on him that the simplest way to stop the boycott was to give the Remingtons what they wanted. At least Caleb and her dad hadn't thrown that in his face—not yet anyway.

"I am." She stretched up on her toes and pressed a quick kiss to his lips.

But he tightened his arms, holding her there. "When they leave, I want more of that mouth."

A sexy sparkle entered her eyes. "That can be arranged."

Might as well get a head start. Just a little one. He brushed her lips with his, the touch kindling a fire inside. Her hands crept up his arms and snaked their way around his shoulders. He found the curve of her waist, the arch of her back, giving himself fully to the moment.

Laughter erupted from the dining room. They weren't alone—yet.

As if coming to the same realization, Shelby eased away. "How is it when I'm in your arms I forget everything else?"

"Same."

She gave him a final kiss. "I think we're about done with the pizza and ready to talk business."

"I'll grab my notes."

"And I'll grab the drinks." Casting a grin his way, she swiped the cans and headed back to the dining room.

He'd left his notes in the living room so he moved that way, his mind turning to strategy. Though the room was dark the porch light shone through the windows, illuminating the white paper on the end table. He skirted the baby carrier in front of the TV and grabbed his notebook. Shelby's family knew more people in town, so maybe they'd have some ideas about how to—

A loud *pop* sounded.

A *crunch*. The window.

Gunfire.

"Get down!" *Ollie!* Gray dove over the baby carrier just as another shot rang out. "Get down, get down!"

Shadow barked.

"Ollie!" Liddy screamed.

"I've got him!" Gray called.

"Stay down!" Caleb ordered as he tore into the living room, hunched low.

Tires squealed outside.

Beneath Gray, Ollie squalled. Had the baby been hit? Gray leaned back as Caleb charged forward.

Gray came to his feet and flipped on the light.

Caleb fumbled with the car seat restraints. The gunman had gotten off a shot before Gray had covered the infant. Had the child been hit?

Please, God, no.

Caleb lifted the wailing baby from the carrier, searching for injuries. "I think he's okay," he called after a torturous moment. "He's all right!"

Stanley rushed to the door and peered through the sidelight. "They're gone." He reached for his phone.

Liddy and Shelby rushed in, Shadow on their heels and barking.

Liddy took the baby as Shelby flung herself into Gray's arms. "Oh my gosh. Are you okay?"

"I'm fine. Did you see anything?" he asked Stanley over Shelby's shoulder.

He shook his head. "I'd like to report a drive-by shooting at 2318 Juniper Drive."

"Are you sure the baby's all right?" Gray said.

"Yeah." Liddy comforted the infant, pressed a kiss to his head. "He's fine. He was just startled."

Shelby eased away from Gray, her eyes widening on her hand. "You're bleeding." She turned him around. "Gray, you're bleeding!"

"I'm fine." Wasn't he? Had he been shot? Why didn't he feel any—? The very thought seemed to trigger pain in his shoulder. Not terrible pain. He glanced down to search his chest for an exit wound. Nothing.

"We're going to need an ambulance," Stanley said into the phone.

"I think it's just a graze," Shelby called over the baby's cries.

Caleb stepped away from Liddy and Ollie to take a look. "I don't see an entry wound. Yeah, I think it's just a graze."

"Sit down," Shelby told Gray.

"Let's move into the other room," Caleb said.

Once they were all in the dining room, Gray sank onto a chair, feeling shakier than he'd like to admit.

Shelby took off her sweater and pressed it to his shoulder. "It's bleeding a lot." Her tone conveyed her worry.

"I'm fine, honey."

Shadow brushed against his leg, whimpering. Gray offered him some comfort.

"They'll be here in a few minutes." Stanley approached, frowning at Gray's shoulder. "You all right?"

"It's just a scratch." Gray's gaze drifted around the room. "Everyone's all right. Thank God. It could've been so much worse."

Silence pervaded as shock settled in. Someone had shot at his home.

Ollie could've been killed. Gray could've been killed. What kind of hatred was this that someone would do such an awful thing?

"He covered Ollie." Caleb's voice was loud in the sudden silence. All heads swung his way. But Caleb was staring at Gray, eyes wet. "You protected my son from that bullet."

A shiver passed over Gray. That thought hadn't occurred yet. It had all happened so fast. There hadn't been time to think.

Tears trickled down Liddy's face. "Thank you, Gray. I can't even tell you—" Emotion prevented her from finishing the sentence.

Shelby squeezed his shoulder.

"I just did what anyone would've."

"Thank you, Briggs." Caleb blinked. "I won't forget this."

A siren wailed in the distance. They all stayed put until it was silenced. Red and blue flashed outside the home. Stanley went to the door and opened it. A moment later the cop appeared in the doorway, his gaze falling on Gray. He had the nerve to smirk.

Gray scowled at the sight of Mason Remington. "Are you the only cop in this godforsaken town?"

Chapter 41

Shelby didn't want Gray to leave. It was after midnight and they were saying good night on her stoop. He'd insisted on following her home and refused to stay, fearing his presence would endanger her.

The paramedics had treated his wound at his house. The bullet took a nice chunk from his shoulder, but his arm was working okay. She couldn't believe how close she'd come to losing him.

While the paramedics cleaned his wound, her dad and brother boarded up his windows with some plywood from his garage. She'd convinced him his home wasn't safe so he was headed for the Lakeside Inn, which had clean, cozy rooms and interior entryways. But the nightmare they'd been through tonight made it hard to part ways with him.

Especially since Mason Remington was on the case. He'd feigned concern and acted determined to find the perpetrator. But she and Gray knew better. Surely the cop hadn't been behind this crime. But then, he was just smug enough to believe he could get away with it.

Who would believe them though?

"Hey." Gray smoothed a hand over her hair. "Stop worrying. Everyone's fine."

"For now. Someone's going to great lengths to chase you out of town, Gray. Someone could've been killed tonight."

"I don't think that was the intention though. They were just trying to scare me off."

"They shot at your house! You could've died."

He took her chin in his hands. "It's just a scratch. I'm fine."

For now. But things were escalating, and whoever had done this wouldn't give up. Gray wasn't safe here. "What are we going to do?"

"I'll start by going to the police station first thing in the morning just as I'd planned. I'll have a word with the chief. If I don't, I'm afraid tonight will be the beginning and the end of the investigation."

The idea buoyed her spirit. "What time? I'll meet you there."

"*No.* Not after someone shot at my house. You're already too involved in this. I can handle it myself."

"But Chief Jameson knows my family. My presence might make a difference."

"I'll be casting aspersions on one of his officers—serious ones. I'm more likely to make an enemy of him, and I don't want you getting caught in the cross fire."

Maybe he was right, but she still wanted to go. However, he had that stubborn look on his face that told her she wouldn't get her way on this one. She felt so helpless. Tears threatened. "I don't like this at all."

His expression softened as he took her in. "It's late, honey. We're both exhausted and need some sleep. Things'll seem better in the morning."

But would they? Nothing would change overnight. The Remingtons would still want Gray gone. The town would still be boycotting her store. How could a relationship between Gray and her ever work? And how would she give him up when she loved him so much? The thoughts stole her breath away.

As if sensing her despair, he pulled her into his arms and held her tight. "I love you, Shel."

Her heart squeezed tight. Her throat constricted. "I love you too." But would that be enough?

"Lock up behind me."

"I will. Be careful."

She tightened her arms around him, buried her face in the cradle of his neck. She never wanted to let him go. But in her heart of hearts, she feared she might have to do just that.

Chapter 42

Gray held back a yawn as he drove toward the police station with Shadow the next morning. Since he'd gotten up so early he went home and measured the broken windows. Put an order in with Gavin without divulging why they needed to be replaced ASAP. Gray also had an interesting chat with his neighbor Mrs. Lyons.

The whole event last night tormented him. He'd hardly slept. Kept reliving the shooting over and over. So many things could've gone wrong. What if Shelby had been in the living room when the bullets came flying through the windows? What if he hadn't covered Oliver in time?

Guilt weighed on him like a lead cape. His presence had put Shelby and her family in the direct line of fire last night—literally. One of them could've died. And for what? So he could cling stubbornly to his right to be here? So he could be with the woman he loved?

What kind of love risked the lives of his woman and her family? Risked the beloved business she'd inherited from her grandmother? She'd be better off without him.

A hollow spot opened inside him at the thought of leaving her. He didn't want to. He just didn't see any other option. If he went away, all her problems would end: The boycott would stop and she would be safe. Those were the things that mattered.

As the police station came into view, he braked. This visit to the chief was a Hail Mary at best. It would probably only paint a bigger target on his back, but he had to try.

He pulled into the station at the stroke of eight o'clock. He could only hope that since Officer Remington had worked late last night he wouldn't be at the station this early. Once in a parking space Gray shut off the engine and exited the vehicle. "Be right back, boy."

He shut the door and locked the SUV. As he rounded the front, two shadows closed in on him. He blinked in surprise at the sight of Caleb and Stanley. His steps faltered.

"Shelby told us you'd be here this morning," Caleb said.

"We won't let you do this alone." Stanley's chin hitched in the same way Shelby's did when she dug in. "I've known Terrence Jameson for years. He'll at least hear us out."

Their presence lifted the weight from Gray's shoulders. Warmed a place inside him that had been cold a long time. "Thank you."

As they made their way toward the building, hope surged inside Gray, but he gave it a solid downward push. Inside the precinct phones pealed and staff shuffled papers. The office was already a hive of activity. He glanced around the station, searching for Remington. No sign of him.

Gray approached the front desk and asked the fortysomething brunette if he could speak with Chief Jameson.

"Do you have an appointment?" she said with a benign expression.

"No, but this concerns a crime that happened on my property last night."

"Oh. Well, let me set you up with Officer Stokes. He's in charge of—"

"Morning, Kim." Stanley stepped forward, offering a friendly smile. "How are you?"

The woman's face lit up. "Oh, hi, Professor Thatcher. Niki and I were just talking about you yesterday. She's really enjoying your English class."

"Glad to hear it. She's a bright young lady. A pleasure to have in class."

Kim beamed with pride. "She's always been an excellent student—she must get that from Greg."

"I'm entirely sure that's not true. Listen, I know Chief Jameson is a busy man, but we have a matter of some import we'd like to discuss with him. Do you think you could get us a few minutes with him?"

"Oh, I think I can manage that. Have a seat in the lobby and I'll see what I can do."

"Thank you, Kim. We sure do appreciate it."

"Of course." She headed back toward the offices and the men took seats in the waiting area.

Good thing Stanley was here. Gray wouldn't have stepped foot past the chief's doorway. As it happened, less than three minutes later Kim ushered the men into Jameson's office.

The fiftysomething man rose from his seat. He was at least a few inches over six feet. The fluorescent light gleamed off his rich-brown dome. His uniform stretched over a barrel chest and muscular arms. If the guy spent most of his time behind a desk, he must make good use of a gym membership.

The chief greeted Stanley and Caleb like old friends, and Stanley formally introduced Gray, though the man undoubtedly knew him by reputation.

"Please, have a seat. I heard what happened last night, Gray. I'm glad no one was hurt."

"We were lucky. But I *was* grazed by a bullet, sir. A bullet that could've hit Caleb's son."

The chief's keen brown eyes sharpened on Caleb. "I wasn't aware."

"Gray threw himself over Oliver after the first shot was fired. He may very well have saved my baby's life."

"Well, thank God for that. I haven't had a chance to read the report yet." His gaze returned to Gray. "Why don't you tell me exactly what happened."

Gray told him the full story, from the first shot to the discovery that he'd been nicked by a bullet. The man took notes on a pad of paper, listening without interruption. His expression gave away nothing.

When Gray finished, Jameson leaned his elbows on his desk. "The front room was dark? And two windows were shot?"

"Yes."

"It sounds like this might've been meant as some kind of warning."

"I don't think the gunman necessarily meant to kill anyone, but that doesn't negate the fact that he could've."

"Fair enough. Do you have any enemies in town, Mr. Briggs? Anyone who might be holding a grudge?"

"Come on, Terrence," Stanley said. "You know who wants Gray out of town."

"I've heard the rumors, sure. But I don't give much credence to gossip."

Of course not. "You must know about the vandalism incident at my house last week—I filed a report. And back in November one of your officers pulled me over without cause."

"Which officer was that?"

"Officer Remington stopped me for driving while intoxicated—even though I don't drink alcohol at all and wasn't swerving or breaking any traffic laws."

He made a note. "Were you given a Breathalyzer test?"

"Yes. After he put me in handcuffs and brought me in. I was held for five hours. My test came back clean."

"I'll look into that."

Stanley leaned forward. "We appreciate it, Terrence. It may be a rumor that the Remingtons want to chase Gray from town, but you might find it interesting that ever since my daughter and Gray officially began dating last week, her business has suffered terribly. Even through the Stroll she had very few customers. Believe me when I say it was unprecedented—and no coincidence."

Caleb spoke up. "When my wife, Liddy, was at The Big Tease last week, Glenda Ellsworth told her she overheard RaeAnne and Ida Mae talking about the Remingtons' scheme to chase Gray out of town."

He jotted more notes. "No one saw the shooter last night? The car, anything?"

"We took cover right away," Gray said. "But I talked to one of my neighbors this morning. She saw a white truck race away immediately after the gunshots."

"Name?" Jameson asked.

"Ellen Lyons."

"Anything else I should know?" His tone was moderated, his face unreadable.

"I think that about covers it," Gray said.

"We take the safety of our citizens seriously around here. As I said, I'll check into this." When the chief stood, the men followed suit. "Thanks for coming by."

Stanley extended his hand. "We appreciate your efforts, Terrence. Thank you."

Once they reached the parking lot, Gray thanked the men for showing up today, then they parted ways. Their presence meant a lot to him. More than they would probably ever realize.

But Gray wasn't a fool. The chief might have the best of intentions, but going up against the powerful Remington family? Turning on one of his officers? Seemed pretty unlikely.

But he'd done all he could do. If it wasn't enough . . . well, that was the story of his life.

The bookstore was closed today, but he headed there anyway. He'd put out a newsletter to Shelby's customer base, featuring their new releases and advertising their December sales. He'd line up a few weeks of social media posts that would carry her through Christmas. But first he had to stop by his house.

Gray might not be able to expose the Remingtons' scheme, but he could and would save Shelby's store—if it was the very last thing he did.

Chapter 43

Oh, if someone could just bottle this scent. Shelby breathed in the smell of Ollie's sweet head, letting the baby's fragrance calm her. Liddy had arrived a few minutes ago and the infant was perched on Shelby's shoulder, checking out the coffee shop's atmosphere. "He's becoming so alert."

Liddy lowered her mug. "He loves sitting up and looking around. The sad thing is, I hardly get to cradle him anymore. And he's officially out of newborn size."

"Say it isn't so."

"I know. So sad they have to grow up." A sparkle entered Liddy's eyes. "But I have some news you are gonna like—it's been killing me to keep it under wraps. You ready?"

"Oh my gosh, yes. I could use some good news."

"Caleb and I"—Liddy beamed expectantly—"are moving to Grandville!"

"*What?* Are you serious?"

"We've been talking about it for a few weeks. Then these local landscapes he's been doing—did you know he's completed eight paintings in one week? He said he feels 'set free.' He wants to come home, and he's been speaking confidentially with the gallery owners around town. Do you know Ben and Sara Freemont?"

"Wait. I'm still in shock over here." Shelby gave her head a shake. "The Freemonts own Muse and Masterpiece."

"Right. Well, unsurprisingly, Caleb had multiple offers, but he decided to sign with them."

Shelby's breath escaped. "He signed? It's a done deal?"

"It's a done deal."

Shelby grabbed Liddy's hand and squeezed. "My brother and bestie are moving to town!" She pressed a kiss on Ollie's cheek, her eyes stinging with tears. "Oh, Liddy, I can't tell you how happy this makes me."

"This is the right move for all of us. I can feel it in my bones. And it's so great to see Caleb inspired again. He was struggling a bit even before he got blocked. I haven't seen him so happy in years."

"Does my dad know?"

"Caleb told him first thing this morning. He actually cried. Things have been better between them for the past week or so—ever since they realized your dad was dealing with abandonment issues. Thank you for that, by the way."

"I'm just glad they've sorted things out. It'll be so wonderful having the family together again."

"Just think . . . We can have girl time anytime we want."

Shelby couldn't stop the smile that split her face. "And you have a babysitter at your disposal. *Two* babysitters."

Liddy's eyes twinkled. "That definitely weighed in."

Shelby's phone buzzed with an incoming call. The screen lit up with Gray's picture. All previous thoughts washed away at the sight. "Sorry, I have to get this. It's Gray."

"Go ahead."

Shelby accepted the call. "Hey."

"Is everything okay?" Gray asked. "I swung by your house and you weren't there."

"I'm fine. You don't have to worry about me. I'm at Latte Da with Liddy. How'd it go at the station?"

"About as well as can be expected, I guess. Thank you for giving your dad and brother a heads-up. I'm not sure I would've gotten an audience with Jameson without them."

"I was afraid you'd be mad about that."

"Exactly the opposite. It was nice to have people who . . ."

"Have your back?"

"Yeah, that."

Her insides clenched. How sad that it was such a rare occurrence for Gray. She'd love to change that. "Do you feel like he'll do anything with the information you gave him?"

A pause ensued. "I don't know," he said finally. "He said he'd check into it."

"But . . ."

"But . . . he's up against a brick wall. The Remingtons are a force in this town and I'm sure Chief Jameson likes his job."

And who was Gray Briggs but an ill-reputed loser who didn't even live here anymore? Shelby's stomach dropped. "I hope he has more integrity than you're giving him credit for."

"I hope so too. Is that Ollie I hear?"

Shelby pressed a kiss to the baby's head. "He says hello."

"Give him a kiss for me. I'll let you get back to the snuggles. I'm at the store. Thought I'd work on a newsletter, try to get people back into the store."

"That's a great idea. I'll swing by when I'm finished." They said goodbye, then she ended the call.

"That didn't sound particularly hopeful," Liddy said.

"Maybe Dad and Caleb will have a different take. Gray's not exactly used to things going his way around here."

"True." Liddy checked her phone, her expression falling. "It's Caleb. He says the chief promised to investigate it but didn't seem all that inspired by the facts presented."

Shelby's heart plummeted. "I wish just for once something would work in Gray's favor."

An hour later Shelby unlocked the bookshop and slipped inside. The lights were off but sunlight flooded through the plate-glass window, illuminating the path to the office. Boxes of books were stacked along the hallway. Gray had texted that Phoebe's upcoming release had arrived—and boy had it. At least fifteen boxes lined the hallway leading to the back door.

Chaucer crept out from behind a box, emitting a loud meow as Shadow approached. Their noses met, twitching as they sniffed. Shadow's tail wagged exuberantly and Shelby waited for Chaucer's hiss. But it never came. The cat simply slunk away as Shadow turned his affection on Shelby.

"That's a good boy. It's great to see you two getting along. Where's your daddy, huh?" She found him in the office. Gray glanced up from the computer, his expression softening at the sight of her. Something like relief flared in his eyes.

Gray was worried about her when he should be worried about himself. Someone wanted to chase him out of town badly enough to bring a gun into the picture. She extended the Americano she'd brought from Latte Da.

"Thanks. I could use some caffeine. Almost as much as I could use a little taste of you. Come here."

She eased onto Gray's lap, careful of his coffee, and pressed a kiss to his lips. "How's that?"

"Ah, much better. I don't like you being out of my sight right now."

"You're the one with a target on your back."

"But whoever it is knows I care about you. That puts you in danger too, Shel."

"Do you think whoever did it meant you physical harm? Or were they just trying to scare you off?"

"The chief seems to think it's the latter. That might be true, but we really have no way of knowing—and I'd just as soon err on the side of caution."

She didn't want to talk about this right now. The implications of their situation stirred up a cauldron of dread. "Guess what—Caleb and Liddy are moving to Grandville."

"Hey, that's great. I know you were wishing they would."

She filled him in on Caleb's representation at the gallery.

"How were Liddy and Ollie doing? I feel like last night must've traumatized everyone."

"They're fine. How's your shoulder?"

"I can hardly feel a thing."

He was probably downplaying the injury. She stroked the planes of his face, her fingers meeting uncharacteristic stubble at his jawline.

"Forgot my razor at the house."

"Are you staying at the hotel again tonight?"

Something flickered in his eyes before he averted his gaze. "Uh, no. Did you get hold of Phoebe?"

"Yeah, she's actually in town today so she's going to pop over and sign the books for us. That way we can start packaging them."

He lifted a brow. "For the record, I'm not here."

Upon Phoebe's arrival Gray slipped from the office to greet the woman (whose face lit up like a Christmas tree at the sight of him). The flush that crept up his neck tickled Shelby to no end.

But he handled the older woman's flirtation well, even teasing her about getting hand cramps from the autographs.

By the time Shelby locked up behind the author, it was suppertime and her spirits were higher. The presale orders would go a long way toward alleviating the loss of revenue from the apparent boycott. As long as it didn't go on much longer.

Please, God.

She headed down to the office, Shadow on her heels. As she approached the door she caught sight of Gray hunched over the keyboard, brows pulled low over his beautiful eyes. He'd been working so hard for her. For this store. He'd put aside his job and his life to be here for her.

"Have I told you how grateful I am for your help?"

His attention turned to her, his eyes turning to a liquid blue pool. "You would've been just fine without me. You've got everything you need to turn this store around, Shel." His words bolstered her, but something in his expression begged for a change in subject.

"Thanks. You must be hungry. Wanna come over for supper? I have a pizza in the freezer with your name on it."

He pushed his chair back from the desk, his eyes piercing hers. "Come here, honey."

A nervous chuckle escaped. "Tired of pizza? I can grab takeout. The Savory Spoon's still open."

He held out his arms. "Come here."

His somber tone and knowing eyes made her want to run the other way. "I don't like that look." But she approached anyway. Sank onto his lap and curled into him.

He grasped her, holding eye contact for a long, torturous moment. "We have to talk about this. My presence is putting you at risk, putting your business at risk. This can't go on. It's not safe."

"It's not fair. You didn't do anything wrong."

"That doesn't matter at this point. All that matters to me is you. Last night proved it's not safe for anyone to be around me. Your nephew could've died. Any of us could've died—and the simplest solution is for me to—"

"Don't say it." She tightened her arms and buried her face in his neck. "Don't say it." She wanted to just hide here until this was all over. But how would it ever be over? If the police let this go as Gray feared, what hope was there? The violence could escalate. Something terrible could happen to Gray. Something far worse than his leaving town. Tears stung her eyes. She didn't want it to be true, but it was.

His hands roved over her back in slow, comforting strokes. His breath fell on her neck, where he placed a tender kiss.

Darn him for making her face the thing she'd avoided since last night. If this person was serious enough to fire a gun, Gray's life was in danger and staying here would be foolhardy.

She made a decision. Pulled back, making eye contact. "If you're leaving, I'm going too."

"Shelby . . ."

"I mean it. If this town won't have you, I won't have it."

He thumbed away a tear. "You can't leave your grandma's store, honey."

"I *can*."

He regarded her silently as memories of Gram washed over her. Memories of her pulling herself up after her husband's death and opening this shop. Her second story. She hadn't wanted another man. No one could replace her husband of forty-six years. She just wanted to pull the community together and use her passion for books to accomplish it. And she'd done just that.

Until Richard Remington had interfered.

Selling the store would be impossible given their current financial situation. If Shelby left now, she'd have to close it. She'd have to empty these beloved shelves, sell off what was left, and turn the sign to Closed for the last time. Her heart gave a loud, sharp crack at the thought.

She buried her face in his neck again. Breathed in that familiar smell of him. Threaded her fingers into the dark hair at his nape. Tasted the salt of her own tears. "I don't want you to leave."

"And I don't want to leave you. But I would've been going in a few weeks anyway." He gave her a squeeze. "You always believed in me, Shel. You'll never know how much that means to me."

"Stop it. This is not good-bye." She clung to him as if she could hold him there. But he was right. He wasn't safe here. That was the important thing. "When are you leaving?"

"Now."

She jerked back. *"Now?"*

A sheen of tears covered those beautiful eyes. "I already packed up my things."

This was hard for him. Nothing about his whole life had been easy. She wasn't going to make this hard for him too. She pressed a kiss to his lips. "I love you."

"I love you too."

Chapter 44

Gray tried to put on a brave face as Shelby walked him to the door. But the boulder in his throat and grit in his eyes made it almost impossible to pretend this parting wasn't wrenching him in half.

He tightened his hand on hers as if he could keep her at his side. But drawing this out would only make it harder on both of them. She seemed to think they could make things work, even from a distance. But he wasn't so naive. He couldn't live here, and she couldn't leave Grandville and her gram's shop. Where did that leave them?

When they reached the door she fell into his arms. And what could he do but wrap her up tight? Memorize the sweet scent of her hair? The slight press of her body? These impressions would have to last him a lifetime. Because Shelby was it for him. There was no one else.

He couldn't believe he'd found her only to lose her again. Why did things always have to end in ruin for him? And just when he was starting to think he might be worthy of good things.

"This isn't the end," she said. "I'll get the store back on solid ground again and then I'll be able to sell it."

"I don't want you to give up this place, Shel. You were meant for this store."

"Then I'll hire someone to run it and move to Riverbend Gap."

He closed his eyes as he slid his fingers into her hair. He knew better than to get his hopes up. They were in a fight they couldn't win. He should know—he'd been in it most of his life.

"I'm not giving up hope."

"That's one of the things I love most about you." He found the willpower to pull back. Cradled her face in his hands and gave her a long look. "Focus on saving the shop, okay? It'll make me smile thinking of you here in your gram's store. She'd be so proud of you."

"Will you accept Gavin's offer of ownership?"

He hadn't even thought that far ahead. "I don't know. We'll see."

"Call me when you get home." Another tear spilled over.

She was killing him. He swept the tear away. "Honey . . . maybe it would be best if we just . . ." He couldn't even finish the sentence.

"*No.*"

Want tugged so hard it took all his willpower to resist the tide. "So . . . what? We keep seeing each other now and again? Talk on the phone? FaceTime? And then what? It'll always come back to where we are right now. An untenable situation. It's already ripping me in half to leave you."

"Not if I'm able to move there. Don't give up on us. Promise me."

She had him heart and soul. He could deny her nothing. "Okay. I promise."

Shadow nudged them apart.

Shelby's lips wobbled and she reached down to pet him. "I'll miss you too, Shadow. Be good for your daddy."

The dog, clueless, wagged his rear end from side to side.

Shelby turned her attention back to Gray and their gazes tangled for a long, pain-filled moment. Her eyes said everything that was in her heart.

Gray framed her face and brushed her lips with one last lingering kiss. When he drew away, he dredged up a smile. "I'll call you." Then he opened the door and slipped outside with Shadow before he could change his mind.

A minute later Gray pulled from the curb, offering Shelby a forlorn wave. As he drove away a million emotions rose like malicious vines, entangling him. But he couldn't give way to them yet—because he had one last stop to make before leaving Grandville.

Chapter 45

The meeting was well under way by the time Gray entered the town hall. The place was packed as they were supposed to discuss the controversial installation of a stoplight at Main and Third.

That very subject was the topic of conversation as Gray slipped into a seat at the back of the room. He'd left Shadow in his vehicle with the windows cracked. With any luck, the meeting would soon advance to the next portion and he wouldn't be delayed long.

As citizens shared opinions from the podium in the center aisle, Gray's gaze drifted around the room. Many familiar faces, some friendly, some not. He didn't see a single Remington, but it wouldn't have mattered anyway. He needed word to spread quickly that he was leaving—for Shelby's safety and for the sake of her business.

He shifted in his seat as one person after another had their say. Finally the panel had answered all the questions and heard all the opinions.

"Are there any other matters anyone wishes to bring to the board's attention?"

Before anyone else could stir, Gray stood and made his way up the aisle. The whole room hushed at the sight of him. Then quiet murmurs spread throughout the room. He could imagine what they were saying. He wasn't even a member of the community anymore. But he had something these people needed to hear.

He arrived at the stand and adjusted the microphone. It gave a loud squawk.

He cleared his throat and stared at the three board members. "For those of you who don't know who I am, I'm Gray Briggs. I used to live here, and I returned a couple months ago to help Shelby Thatcher with her bookshop after her grandmother passed.

"That endeavor was going pretty well until recently. When a certain family in town wanted me gone so badly they convinced many of you to boycott the bookshop. Since then the store has taken a devastating financial hit.

"I'm sure I don't have to tell you what a wonderful human being Shelby is. I'm sure I don't have to remind you that she's always there to lend a hand. She's there when you need free books for charities and fundraisers, never mind the bottom line. She does it because she believes in this community. And yet in her time of greatest need, this town has abandoned her."

He gritted his teeth, shifting his gaze from the panel to the audience. "Y'all should be ashamed of yourselves. I came in today to tell you I'm leaving town—right now. SUV's all packed and ready to go. You got your way. Now I hope you'll do the right thing and end this boycott aimed at one of your own. Shelby deserves your support now more than ever."

He gripped the edges of the podium until the blood drained from his knuckles. "And while I'm here, I have something else to say. Years ago my dad did a terrible thing. He was put in prison for it and rightly so. But I was just a boy when that happened. All of a sudden I was living with my grandmother and spurned by half the town. There was a lot of gossip going around that wasn't even true. And I'm sure I'm wasting my breath here, but I have to say it anyway—I did not cheat to win that scholarship. Someone planted that test in my locker, and because of all the rumors about me, I was presumed guilty. I didn't deserve that. I didn't deserve any of that, and y'all ought to have a little care about how you treat people around here. That's all I've got to say."

He turned from the stand—and nearly ran right into Stanley.

Shelby's dad put a hand on Gray's shoulder as he stepped up to the mike. "Well, *I've* got more to say. I've lived every year of my life in this town, and I've never been so ashamed of this community. Not only have you turned on my daughter, but you apparently advocate violence. Some of you might've seen the notice in today's paper about the drive-by shooting at Gray's house last night." He gave a wry laugh. "But most of you probably didn't—because it was buried on page 16 and took about three lines of copy. But I'm sure you heard about it.

"Well, here's what you might not have heard. At the time of the shooting, my grandbaby was in Gray's front room sleeping. And this man"—he squeezed Gray's shoulder—"this man, who's been the target of some pretty nasty darts recently, threw himself over that child, took a flesh wound for him. This town has been beating him up for one thing or another most of his life, and—"

"For good reason!" someone called.

"Nothing but trouble!"

"We don't need the likes of—"

"Order!" a woman on the panel called. "We'll have order, please. If you have something to say, get in line. Go ahead, Stanley."

Shuffling sounded behind him as people got in line. "Hey," Gray whispered to Stanley, "this isn't necessary."

"Yes, it is." Stanley held Gray in place as he turned back to the mike. "This has gone far enough. You can't judge a man for something his father did—can we just start right there? What is wrong with y'all? Someone wants him gone badly enough to fire a gun and endanger lives. Does anyone care about that?"

Someone edged up to the mike. Daryl. Gray had never seen the guy's face flushed with emotion. Stanley stepped aside and let him speak.

"I care about that. Gray's my friend. He plays basketball with me and he's always nice to me. Miss Shelby lets me work at her bookstore and gives me ice cream money. Why are you being mean to them? That's not nice."

Eyes full of tears, Daryl threw himself at Gray.

He embraced the man in a big hug, his own eyes stinging. "Thank you, Daryl. You're a good man."

Daryl patted him on the back. A moment later he drew back, wiping his eyes. Then returned to his seat.

Gray wished he could follow, but Stanley had a tight grip on his arm.

"Gray's leaving town because this community rejected him on account of what his father did. Because of a bunch of gossip."

"He's lying about that scholarship."

"He cheated Brendan Remington! That's not gossip!"

"Eloise, Howard," a panelist said. "Please wait your turn."

"Since you brought it up, let's talk about that so-called cheating scandal," Stanley said. "Anyone could've put that test in Gray's locker. The faculty chose to believe he was guilty based on his reputation—a reputation he didn't even earn. I got to know this young man back then and he gained my trust. He's managed to earn it again. As far as I'm concerned, that says it all."

Caleb stepped up behind them and Stanley gave him access to the microphone. "I admit I was skeptical about Gray. I'm ashamed to admit I believed the rumors—the very same rumors that drove him from Grandville the first time around. But I can see now they're undeserved. A man who's willing to sacrifice his own safety for someone else—that's the kind of man we want around here, isn't it?"

Someone else pushed through. Gray's gaze connected with Shelby's.

His heart skipped a beat at the sight of her.

She offered a steady smile as she stepped up to the mike, then her expression turned all business. "You all know me. I was born and raised here. Do you think I'd give my heart to someone who isn't worthy of it—twice over?"

Shelby met Gray's gaze, holding him mesmerized. A glassy sheen covered her eyes. "He is such a good man. When my gram left him half ownership of the bookshop, he signed it back over to me. And then he dropped his whole life to come here and help me run the store. To come here and face all the bad memories he left behind here. And for all his generosity, what did he get in return? Vandalism. Police harassment. Gunshots fired at his home! He doesn't deserve any of that, and he shouldn't have to leave town just to stay safe."

Some of the crowd seemed remorseful. A few nodded their heads. A red-haired woman nearby nudged the man beside her. They whispered back and forth, then the man got up and approached the mike. Though he wore a neatly trimmed beard now, Gray recognized him as Drew Lennox—one of Brendan's two minions from high school.

Great.

Shelby took his hand and led him down the aisle to two empty seats when Gray would've preferred to keep right on going. Once seated she pulled his hand into her lap. Their gazes caught and held for a long second. He squeezed her hand. He had no idea what would happen from here, but having Shelby at his side meant everything to him.

"Go ahead, Drew," the panelist said.

As the man started talking, Gray's gaze drifted over the familiar faces in the queue that had formed. Liddy was second in line, followed by Janet, Zuri, and Haley from the bookshop. Miss Phoebe came next, then his friend Patrick. And a handful of their loyal customers rounded out the line, which now stretched to the back of the room. A strange buoyant feeling swelled inside.

"Most of you know I'm a journalist for the *Grandville Gazette*," Drew said. "I was good friends with Brendan Remington in high school. We haven't been as close in recent years. Let's just say my wife's been a good influence on me. I'm embarrassed to say that Brendan and I used to bully Gray. I didn't think of it as bullying back then, but that's what it was.

"And I'd like to set the record straight about that cheating scandal . . . That test was put in Gray's locker. It was a setup. I had the locker a couple down from Gray, and Brendan asked me to get his combination." He paused. "Brendan put that test in his locker. Gray rightfully deserved that scholarship, and it was Brendan who did the stealing—not the other way around."

Gray's head jerked back. His skin tingled with realization.

The room filled with murmuring as Shelby clutched his arm, tears in her eyes.

He'd always suspected Brendan had done it. But he'd never dreamed the truth would come out after all these years. Much less that it would happen in such a public way.

"I'm sorry I didn't stand up for Gray back then," Drew said. "I guess I didn't have the courage. But when I heard about last night's shooting, I knew I couldn't keep quiet anymore. Brendan always worried his father would find out what he'd done and cut him out of his business. And that's pretty much the only thing Brendan cared about. I should've come forward when I heard about the vandalism, because Brendan certainly had motivation to drive Gray out of town. But after last night's shooting I couldn't keep quiet anymore. This morning I went to the station and told Chief Jameson about what Brendan did all those years ago."

Gray blinked. That buoyant feeling was making his head float.

"I guess they looked into it, because the newspaper received notification late this afternoon that Brendan Remington was arrested for that drive-by shooting."

Gray reared back.

Shelby gasped.

Brendan had been the one shooting at his house? He'd been arrested?

The police had arrested a Remington? It was almost too much to fathom. Too much to hope for.

The murmuring in the town hall had reached an uproar, and the board members were trying to regain control.

He turned to Shelby, his thoughts as chaotic as the room.

She was smiling at him from ear to ear, her eyes sparkling with tears. "It's over, Gray. It's finally over."

Chapter 46

Forty-five minutes later Gray's head was still spinning as he walked Shelby outside. The air was brisk and the night was quiet. White Christmas lights danced in the trees lining Main Street, and a breeze sent brittle leaves scuttling across the nearly empty parking lot. The meeting had ended a while ago, but so many people wanted to talk to him, many of them apologizing for their part in making him a town pariah.

He gave his head a hard shake. Had all that really just happened?

When Shelby shivered he set the jacket he carried around her shoulders.

"Thanks. When I got Caleb's text I dashed out of the store without my coat."

"I'm so glad you were there. That was . . ." He chuckled. "I don't even know what that was." All those people saying all those nice things about him. Publicly. It was amazing. Embarrassing. Humbling.

She curled an arm around his waist. "It was all true. And long past time the people of this town defended you. Did you see Dede Myers? She was in tears."

The woman had worked in their high school office. "I always suspected she had a soft spot for me."

"And Phoebe! She was so eloquent." As they reached the side of his

SUV, Shelby drew him into an embrace. "And she didn't even once mention your studly biceps."

He chuckled. The release felt good. Everything inside him felt good—and he couldn't even remember the last time that was true.

The biggest surprise of the night was Brendan Remington's arrest. Gray couldn't believe the man had been so desperate to cover that long-ago misdeed that he'd fired a gun at Gray's house. "I guess we know now why the Remingtons weren't present at tonight's town hall."

"Seems they had a few other things on their minds. I can't believe Brendan was arrested. They must have enough evidence to convict him—and now that he's been exposed, you're safe."

"And so are you. I thought for sure it was Mason."

"Brendan used to be so desperate for his dad's approval. With Barry fixing to retire, Brendan was set to take over the investment firm. Then when you came back to town, I guess he must've feared you could reveal what he'd done."

"I suppose when you run an investment firm your reputation is everything," Gray said. "If people can't trust your character, they sure won't trust you with their money."

"No matter what happens to Brendan from a legal standpoint, he's out of the business for sure."

"I'm struggling to find any sympathy right now."

"Oh, he deserves everything coming his way. And so do you, Gray—all of it good."

He leaned back enough to get his eyes on her. To cup her chin and gaze at her beautiful face. Streetlights cast a golden glow across her features, highlighting the curves of her cheeks, the soft swell of her lips. "You anchor me, Shel, in the best of ways. You believe in me. You always have."

"I'm so proud of you. You've persevered in the face of so many challenges. You deserve to be accepted, Gray."

He took in the words. Let them settle. "You make me believe that." He leaned down and brushed her lips with his. Went back for seconds . . . and thirds.

Moments later her low moan had him deepening the kiss, pulling her closer, hands mapping the planes of her back. He couldn't believe she was back in his arms—for good this time. He never wanted to be away from her again.

A long time later, with the discipline of a saint, he pulled back, set his forehead against hers. Love for her swept over him, engulfing him in the best possible way. "It's always been you, Shel. No one else will do."

"I tried to find what we had in someone else. It doesn't exist. I love you so much."

"And I love you." He brushed her soft cheek, marveling at her words. "I guess it goes without saying I'm moving back home."

"I was kinda hoping." She gazed up at him, a gleam in her eyes. "How do you feel about a full-time job in a floundering bookshop?"

His lips twitched. "Depends. What kind of benefits can I expect?"

She leaned back, aiming those smoldering eyes at him. "What kind were you hoping for?"

"Kisses in the middle of the workday."

Her low chuckle had him buzzing like a neon sign. "That was quick."

"I've got a whole list."

"I'm confident we can come to a mutual agreement."

A bark startled them both. Shadow's shiny nose protruded through the window's gap.

"Poor guy. You've been very patient." Gray unlocked the door and the dog leaped out. He collected attention from them, his tail wagging boldly.

Shelby glanced into his back seat, which was packed to the ceiling. "Looks like we've got some unpacking to do."

"And at least a couple truckloads from my apartment up north."

Shelby's expression sobered. "How do you think Gavin and Wes will take the news? They were hoping you'd be their partner."

He seemed to consider this. "They'll probably be disappointed. But they're family men through and through, so I think they'll be happy for me too."

"Will you hate leaving the job behind? The community you've been a part of?"

That buoyant feeling overwhelmed him again. *Hope* filling him to the brim. It was a new feeling. A new start. He put his arms around her once more, pulling her to his chest, and set a kiss on top of her head. "How could I regret anything when I've finally found my home?"

Epilogue

Shelby whipped out the tablecloth and let it drop over the picnic table. The July heat was made bearable by a gentle breeze—which also carried the savory scent of grilling burgers. Her stomach gave a hearty rumble. "How's it going over there?"

Her husband had his hands full with the meat and with Shadow, who danced around his feet, whining pitifully. "Another fifteen minutes or so. Your family on their way?"

"They'll arrive any minute now." Smoke rose from the grill, dissipating into the air.

She focused on the man behind the grill. He wore the *Caution: Extremely Hot* apron she'd given him on Valentine's Day. The same night he'd surprised her with a heartfelt proposal and a brilliant solitaire diamond. The memory washed over her along with all the love it conjured. She went to him and wrapped her arms around his middle. Pressed her cheek against his back.

He set down the spatula and set his arms over hers. "Well, this is nice."

"It was the apron."

"It reminded you I'm hot?"

She chuckled. "It reminded me of your proposal." That February day had dawned sunny and unseasonably warm. He'd taken her on a picnic to the park where they'd met so many times as teenagers. Shelby could've fainted dead away when he dropped to one knee in the big white gazebo.

Three months later they married in a small church wedding. They'd already waited years to be together and didn't see the point of wasting any more time. It was an intimate ceremony, just family and close friends. Gray's dad sent a very nice note of congratulations.

Gray still made the trip once a month to see him, and sometimes Shelby went along too. He was up for parole again next spring and Gray hoped he'd be released—though they all agreed it would be wise for him to settle near his cousins in Chattanooga.

Gray turned from the grill and cradled her face, gazing down at her. There had been something new and fresh about his appearance since that town hall meeting. He was at peace. It was a great look on him. In the town where Gray was once rejected, he'd found acceptance and community. She was proud of her town for recognizing their prejudice and proud of Gray for his spirit of forgiveness.

"No regrets about the simple wedding?" he asked.

"It was a perfect day. I just wanted to be married to you. And here we are." So content with their new life together. So happy.

After the wedding they'd spent two nights in downtown Charlotte. They were planning to take a longer honeymoon on their first anniversary—Shelby hadn't felt comfortable leaving the bookshop just yet. It was a topic they'd dreamed about over the winter though.

"Jamaica?" he said as if reading her mind.

"Hmm. Too tropical."

"Tropical sounded pretty great in February."

"But now it's July and tropical sounds miserable."

"Alaska?"

"Too cold."

"Anybody home?" Dad came around the side of the house, Ollie in his arms.

Gray greeted his father-in-law as Shelby eased from his arms.

"Hi, Dad." She offered him a hug, then stole Ollie away. Their sweet baby nephew would turn one next month. He was already a crawling machine. "Where are Caleb and Liddy?"

"They're in the kitchen warming something up."

Dad joined Gray at the grill while Shelby carried Ollie down to the shoreline so he could see the ducks. A few minutes later Caleb and Liddy joined them, and they all exchanged hugs on the patio.

It did Shelby's heart good to see the way Caleb and her dad's relationship had thrived since he'd moved home. They'd worked on Gram's old house together over the winter: replacing the furnace and adding a half bath. Gray had pitched in when he could.

And Dad had bought that lakeview painting Caleb had created in his backyard—it was his very first gallery sale at Muse and Masterpiece. The work of art hung right over Dad's fireplace.

Shelby set Ollie down and he immediately crawled toward the grass. "Good thing you put him in pants," she said to Liddy.

"Now if we can just keep him off the pier."

Shadow trotted over to the baby and stopped short, sniffing Ollie's face.

The boy erupted in laughter, then grabbed Shadow's ear. The canine easily extricated himself and licked Ollie's feet, provoking a belly laugh.

"That dog is so gentle with him," Liddy said.

Caleb joined them. "Told you we need a dog, babe. A nice black Lab or golden retriever. A lake dog."

"Or a rescue dog . . ." The debate had been going on for weeks.

Caleb's gaze caught on the lakefront. Without another word he headed down the gentle slope of the lawn, pulled his phone from his pocket, and began framing shots.

"Uh-oh," Liddy said. "Looks like he found more inspiration."

Shelby took in the view. The sun was setting at their backs, bathing the homes around the bay in a buttery glow. The sunlight glimmered like gold on the water. "I can see why."

These days Caleb continually found inspiration in the beauty surrounding their hometown. His paintings were selling like crazy at Muse and Masterpiece.

A minute later Caleb joined them again. "Did you see the lighting on those houses?"

"Your next masterpiece," Liddy said.

"I don't know about that, but I can't wait to paint it."

"How's Haley doing at the gallery?" Shelby asked. In May her former bookseller had taken a position at Muse and Masterpiece.

"She seems to be doing great. She's a budding artist. Showed me some of her work. It's fresh and interesting."

"Caleb's thinking about asking her if she wants an apprenticeship with him."

"Oh wow." Shelby was so glad the girl had found her passion. "I'll bet she'd love that. She could learn a lot from you."

"How's business been this week?" he asked.

"Very busy with all the tourists in town for the holiday. It's nice to have a Saturday off." She thought back to the night when everything had shifted—the town hall meeting. The next morning the store had a line out front, and the shop was crazy busy all through December. Between in-store sales and Phoebe's preorders, they'd easily paid the back rent due in January.

They'd even remained busy during their slower winter months, allowing them to put back a little cash. *"I knew you could do it."* Gram's voice echoed in her head. *"My Sweet Girl has a head for business."*

Shelby glanced out over the water, feeling her grandmother's presence like the breeze on her skin. Sometimes she missed her so much it was a physical ache. But she also knew Gram would be proud of her. And proud of Gray—she'd always believed in him.

And so did Shelby. In April she'd drawn up papers, offering Gray the 49 percent ownership that Gram had bequeathed to him.

He'd offered her a warm smile, a soft kiss. "This is your store, honey. We're partners in life and business. I don't need papers to prove that."

"Maybe not, but Gram wanted you to have it, and so do I. You've earned it, Gray. It's yours if you want it—if being a partner is enough for you."

His eyes softened on her. "Being your partner in business and life is a dream come true."

In May Brendan's case had finally gone to trial. Because there was an eyewitness to the shooting—one of Gray's neighbors—he'd taken a plea deal for a lesser offense. But he was still sentenced to three years. He'd probably be out in half that, but Shelby and Gray weren't bitter. He'd lost the respect of the community and his position at his father's investment firm.

Later that same month, Richard Remington had shocked them both when he'd come into the store and handed Gray a check. It was enough to cover the scholarship his grandson had stolen from Gray.

"I'm not sure I'll ever forgive your father for what he did to our son," Richard said. "But my wife and I realize you bear no fault in Troy's death. This money is rightfully yours."

"I appreciate what you're saying. But I can't accept this check. You didn't take that scholarship from me."

"I cultivated an environment that framed you as a bad person. Both my sons adopted my attitude and did you wrong. I was culpable. Please take it. My wife and I want you to have it."

The money still sat in their bank account. Last month they'd decided to offer a partial scholarship each year to a disadvantaged Grandville graduate. Gray felt good about giving back a little, and Shelby was so proud of his generous heart.

They both felt a little sorry for Richard and Renee. Their grandson was now in jail, and shortly after the town hall meeting, Mason was suspended from the police force without pay, pending an investigation. He was eventually found guilty of misconduct for pulling Gray over without cause. In May he'd been reinstated on a probationary basis.

"Put that down, Ollie," Liddy called.

The baby sat on his rump with a twig in his hand. He gave his mama a toothy grin.

"Don't you put that in your—"

Ollie stuck the twig in his mouth.

Liddy rushed over as an expression of distaste came over his face. "We have actual food coming, silly goose."

"Speaking of which," Gray called from the grill, "come and get it!"

The firework's *boom* vibrated inside Shelby, then red bloomed across the sky. Its reflection sparkled on the lake below. The family gathered on a hodgepodge of blankets in their backyard. Shelby rested between Gray's legs, nestled into his chest.

"Look at Ollie," Liddy said between fireworks.

The baby sat in Caleb's lap, staring up at the sky wide-eyed.

"I was afraid the noise would scare him."

"Not this boy," Caleb said. "The noisier the better."

Another firework shot into the sky and shattered into a dazzling green display. The sparks fizzled in a cascading waterfall of light.

Gray whispered in Shelby's ear, "Our first fireworks as husband and wife . . ."

She smiled at the thought, her mind immediately going back to another Independence Day. "Remember our first Fourth of July? Our first kiss?"

"How could I forget? You ruined me for all other women that night."

She turned her head to meet his gaze as a white explosion lit up his face. "I'll keep right on ruining you, if you like."

"By all means."

She obliged, pressing a quick kiss to his lips. Except the quick kiss led to another . . . and another. She curled her hand around his neck. His pulse thudded against the flesh of her palm. This man still lit her up like the night sky.

"Aww . . ." Liddy said. "You guys are so cute."

"You're making me look bad, dude," Caleb muttered.

Shelby drew away, falling into Gray's love-drunk eyes. His face glowed green as another firework exploded. Just as suddenly, an idea burst into her mind. "Ireland."

He blinked. A smile split his face. "Ireland."

She was smiling as she turned and settled back against him. *We're going to Ireland, Gram.* She folded her arms over Gray's, feeling the kind of contentment she'd only dreamed of.

When Gram had passed it seemed like Shelby would never be truly happy again—especially after the reading of that will. But what seemed like a curse had turned to a blessing, and now she couldn't imagine her life without Gray.

The fireworks intensified as the show entered its grand finale. They were so big and loud Shelby wondered if Gram could see and hear the display from heaven. If she could see her family, happily gathered on the lawn. See Gray and her, finally in each other's arms where they belonged.

Shortly after their engagement had been announced, Mr. Greenwood from the law firm appeared at the bookstore. After greeting Shelby, he turned to the business matter that had brought him there. "All the stipulations of your grandmother's will have been carried out to the letter—except for one last thing." He extended an envelope that bore her name—in her grandmother's handwriting. She couldn't imagine what it was. But having one last message from Gram was the most special kind of gift. She pressed the envelope to her chest.

Once Mr. Greenwood left, she took the letter down to the office, which was quiet as Gray had recently left to meet Patrick for lunch. Her hands worked greedily to open the envelope. Then she pulled out the lined sheet of stationery and read.

My Sweet Girl,

If you're reading this letter, then it means I was right—and you know how I like being right. I'm sure you'll forgive me for my postmortem interference in your love life. I never could mind my own business, especially where you and Gray were concerned. I always knew the two of you were meant to be. There were simply too many obstacles for your young love to survive. Your grandma decided you needed a helping hand.

And now I can rest in peace knowing the love between you still burns so brightly. I got to spend my life with my special soulmate, and nothing makes me happier than knowing you'll get to do the same. Love each other well. You both deserve your second story.

All my love,
Gram

Acknowledgments

Bringing a book to market takes a lot of effort from many different people. I'm so incredibly blessed to partner with the fabulous team at HarperCollins Christian Fiction, led by publisher Amanda Bostic: Savannah Breedlove, Kimberly Carlton, Caitlin Halstead, Margaret Kercher, Becky Monds, Kerri Potts, Nekasha Pratt, Taylor Ward, and Laura Wheeler.

Not to mention all the wonderful sales reps and amazing people in the Rights Department—special shout-out to Robert Downs!

Thanks especially to my editor, Kimberly Carlton. Your incredible insight and inspiration help me take the story deeper, and for that I am so grateful! Thanks also to my line editor, Julee Schwarzburg, whose attention to detail makes me look like a better writer than I really am.

Writing a book about a bookshop was a true pleasure. I could almost smell the books each time Shelby entered the Second Story Bookshop! And although I've frequented my share of such stores, I wanted to get the details of ownership right. Enter manager Jessica Nock of the delightful Main Street Books in Davidson, North Carolina (the town that inspired Grandville). She was so kind to sit down with me and answer all my questions. I couldn't have written this story without her detailed expertise. If you're ever in Davidson, be sure to swing by this lovely bookshop. Any mistake that made its way into the book is mine alone.

Acknowledgments

Author Colleen Coble is my first reader and sister of my heart. Thank you, friend! This writing journey has been ever so much more fun because of you.

I'm grateful for my agent of nineteen years, Karen Solem. After a long and brave struggle with her health, Karen passed away recently. I will forever be indebted to her for her wonderful wisdom and supportive direction. Rest in peace, friend.

To my husband, Kevin, who has supported my dreams in every way possible—I'm so grateful! To all our kiddos: Justin, Chad and Taylor, Trevor and Babette, and our four beautiful grandchildren. Every stage of parenthood and grandparenthood has been an adventure, and I look forward to all the wonderful memories we have yet to make!

A hearty thank-you to all the booksellers who make room on their shelves for my books—I'm deeply indebted! And to all the book bloggers and reviewers whose passion for fiction is contagious—thank you!

Lastly, thank you, friends, for letting me share this story with you. I wouldn't be doing this without you. Your notes, posts, and reviews keep me going on the days when writing doesn't flow so easily. I appreciate your support more than you know.

I enjoy connecting with friends on my Facebook page: www.facebook.com/authordenisehunter. Please pop over and say hello. Visit my website at www.DeniseHunterBooks.com or just drop me a note at Deniseahunter@comcast.net. I'd love to hear from you!

Discussion Questions

1. Who was your favorite character and why?

2. Because the Second Story Bookshop was her grandmother's beloved store, Shelby always felt a deep connection to it—and all the more after Gram's passing. What was your favorite thing about the bookstore? Is there a place to which you have a special connection or feeling of belonging?

3. Discuss why Gray's reappearance in Shelby's life shook her so deeply. Did fear play a part?

4. Was Gram right or wrong for meddling in her granddaughter's life posthumously?

5. Shelby's family experienced her mother's abandonment in different ways. Discuss how it impacted the entire family. How did it affect her relationship with Gray? Have you ever been abandoned? What was its impact on your life? How have you begun to heal from it?

6. As a teen Gray was treated unfairly by townspeople and bullied by

Discussion Questions

peers. How did that make you feel? What advice would you give young Gray? Have you or a loved one ever been targeted or bullied? Was anything done to rectify the situation?

7. Gray experienced shame as a result of that treatment. Discuss what shame is and how it might be overcome.

8. How was Shadow symbolic of Gray himself? How did the dog help Gray in his growth?

9. How did you feel as Gray was again targeted in the present-day story? Did you feel there was more he could do?

10. How did you feel during the town hall scene as people spoke on Gray's behalf? Tell about a situation when others have stood up for you—or when you stood up for others.

About the Author

Photo by Salve Ragonton

Denise Hunter is the internationally published, bestselling author of more than forty books, three of which have been adapted into original Hallmark Channel movies. She has won the Holt Medallion Award, the Reader's Choice Award, the Carol Award, and the Foreword Book of the Year Award and is also a RITA finalist. When Denise isn't orchestrating love lives on the written page, she enjoys traveling with her family, drinking chai lattes, and playing drums. Denise makes her home in Indiana, where she and her husband raised three boys and are now enjoying an empty nest and four beautiful grandchildren.

* * *

DeniseHunterBooks.com
Facebook: @AuthorDeniseHunter
X: @DeniseAHunter
Instagram: @deniseahunter

LOOKING FOR MORE GREAT READS? LOOK NO FURTHER!

Thomas Nelson
Since 1798

Visit us online to learn more:
tnzfiction.com

Or scan the below code and sign up to receive email updates on new releases, giveaways, book deals, and more:

@tnzfiction

"Readers in the mood for a sweet second-chance romance with a twist will be delighted."

—*Publishers Weekly*

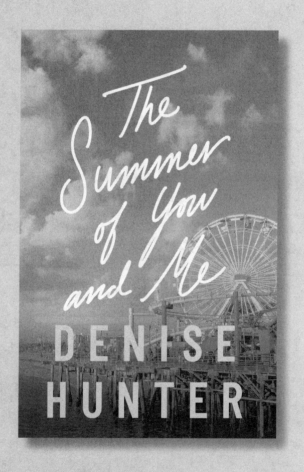

AVAILABLE IN PRINT, E-BOOK, AND DOWNLOADABLE AUDIO

The Riverbend Romance Novels

Don't miss the Riverbend Gap romance series from Denise Hunter!

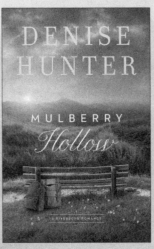

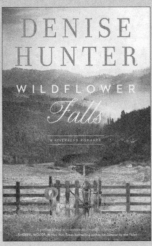

Available in print, e-book, and audio